W9-AHE-146

IMPROVING
COLLEGE
WRITING

IMPROVING COLLEGE WRITING

A Book of Exercises

James A. Reinking

Jane E. Hart

Andrew W. Hart

ST. MARTIN'S PRESS
NEW YORK

Copyright © 1981 by St. Martin's Press, Inc.

All Rights Reserved.

321
mlkg

For information, write St. Martin's Press, Inc.,
175 Fifth Avenue, New York, N.Y. 10010

ISBN: 0-312-41060-3

Contents

Preface

Improving College Writing is the result of our experience over a good many years with students of widely varying backgrounds and abilities. We have found that through a sensible, step-by-step program of exercises that train the eye and the ear, students can develop an intuitive grasp of the essentials of good sentence writing. Practice is the key, but the practice must be systematic, controlled, focused on basics. It must also be progressive and finally creative—moving, that is, in clearly discernible steps from explanations to simple recognition exercises to more demanding exercises that require students to generate sentences of their own. Further, students should have some means of confirming their own progress as they go along, so that they need not be wholly dependent on the instructor.

Improving College Writing consists of thirty-six separate units grouped in four sections: "Looking into the Sentence," "Sharpening Your Usage Skills," "Learning to Punctuate Properly," and "Becoming a Proficient Speller." The units in the first three sections all follow the same carefully patterned approach. Explanations of individual points are followed immediately by recognition exercises that ask the student to identify instances of what has just been discussed—a particular grammatical element, a correct usage, or the like. Following these explanations and exercises is a unit self-test that allows students to check their grasp of all the material presented so far (using answers provided in the back of the book) before proceeding further. The unit concludes with two unit review exercises, designated A and B, the first a recognition exercise and the second an exercise requiring that students do some original (but guided) writing in which they must apply what has been learned. Each of the two unit review exercises is printed on pages that contain no other material and so may be torn out and handed in, if the instructor wishes it, without reducing the usefulness of the rest of the book for reference later on.

The strategy in every unit is to allow the student to deal with the material in small, easily managed segments and to enable the instructor to monitor students' progress as closely as may be desired. We have provided more exercises than most instructors are likely to assign to any given group of students, but it has seemed desirable to provide a choice in any case. Instructors will know best how to use the book with their own students, but we do strongly recommend that if possible some of the exercises that require student writing be assigned, even though these are more time-consuming than the other exercises. Only by generating examples of their own can students really achieve the mastery of basic principles that will enable them to produce satisfactory written work in the future.

The units in the fourth section of the book, on spelling, differ in their organization from the units in the first three sections. The first spelling unit discusses the four most important spelling rules, offers some memorizing tips, and concludes with a unit self-test and a review exercise that provide practice in applying the rules. The next unit, unlike any other unit in the book, contains no exercises at all but consists simply of a list of 400 words frequently misspelled, presented in eight 50-word groups for easier study. The final unit includes four groups of homonyms, each followed by a review exercise covering all of the items in the group. Taken together, these three units provide an overview of spelling that goes well beyond the treatment found in most other texts.

Like all authors of textbooks, we are indebted to a great many people for help or inspiration. Our thanks, first of all, to our students, many of whom volunteered to supply sentences for the exercises. These students include Patricia Adams, Mary Allen, Tina Ballard, Kim Blodee, Jon Brecheison, Wendy Edick, Joseph Fifer, Paul Gabriel, Katherine Graham, Mary Kleinhans, Susan Koritz, Brian Martin, Teressa Mazzei, Robert McMahon, Ann Miller, Pamela Platka, Rebecca Reid, Catherine Ross, Joan Seiler, Katherine Simpson, Craig Van Sumerin, Katherine Thompson, James Trevillian, Bernardine Walker, William Wideman, Angela Winters, William Yang, and Lugene York. Special thanks are due Ms. Helen Hart and Professors Elliot L. Smith and Lucille Wright for the sentences they have furnished.

We are grateful to Tom Broadbent and Charles Thurlow of St. Martin's Press for their advice and assistance and we extend our thanks to the anonymous reviewers whose perceptive criticisms and suggestions have improved our manuscript immeasurably.

James A. Reinking
Jane E. Hart
Andrew W. Hart

IMPROVING
COLLEGE
WRITING

Looking into the Sentence

Learning what English sentences consist of and how they are put together will not make you a better writer, but it will give you the background you need to understand and avoid many of the writing problems you will deal with later. For example, before studying the agreement of subjects and verbs, you must know what these two elements are and how they are used. Once you know about subject and verb agreement, you will be aware of the disagreement errors that can occur. You'll then be unlikely to commit such errors, but if you do slip up, you'll know what's meant and what to do when your instructor points out the mistake.

This section will acquaint you with the essentials of the English sentence. The section first considers the simple sentence, then moves to the parts of speech, and ends by discussing clauses and phrases. When you have read the explanations and done the exercises, you'll be ready to turn your attention to usage, the next step to effective writing.

UNIT 1

The Simple Sentence

Writing can be viewed as a process of adding one idea to another in order to make a finished composition. This composition may be a letter, a report, a theme, or the like. Our opening section takes up the simple sentence—the basic unit for presenting complete ideas and one of the key building blocks you'll use when you write.

Subjects and Predicates

A simple sentence has two main parts, a *subject* and a *predicate*. The *subject* usually names something about which a statement is made or a question is asked. A *predicate* expresses what is said or asked about the subject.

| **Subject** | **Predicate** |
| The tall man | laughed loudly. |

Often, the subject can be thought of as the "doer" of the sentence or as the "actor" of an "action." At other times, the subject simply exists. The subject can also receive an action. A *simple* subject consists of one or more words that name one or more persons, places, things, actions, qualities, or ideas. A *complete* subject includes the simple subject plus certain other words that describe it. Here are five simple subjects and five complete subjects.

Simple Subjects	Complete Subjects
man	the tall man
trees	the slender, leafy trees
complaint	your complaint
baby	the baby
Mr. Davis	old Mr. Davis

The predicate tells what the subject does, or is, or has done to it, and completes the idea of the sentence. A *simple* predicate consists of one or more words, called *verbs,* that show action—what someone or something did, does, or will do—or existence—what someone or something was, is, or will be. Examples of action verbs are *haul, run, swim, shout, throw,* and *cook.* Each of these verbs "does" something. In contrast, the various forms of the verb *to be* (*is, are, was, were,* and so on) indicate a *state of being* (that is, of *existence*) and are called *linking verbs.* (See page 25 for additional information about linking verbs.) A *complete* predicate includes the simple predicate plus words that expand and modify its meaning.

Simple Predicates	Complete Predicates
laughed	laughed loudly
are swaying	are swaying in the wind
will be discussed	will be discussed next Wednesday
is	is in its crib
was	was the neighborhood grouch

Combinations like *are swaying* and *will be discussed* are called *verb phrases*—two or more *verbs* that function as a single unit.

Notice that none of our subjects and predicates can stand alone; they don't convey a complete idea by themselves. However, combining a subject with an appropriate predicate gives us a complete sentence and therefore a complete thought.

The tall man laughed loudly.
The slender, leafy trees are swaying in the wind.
Your complaint will be discussed next Wednesday.
The baby is in its crib.
Old Mr. Davis was the neighborhood grouch.

Notice that the first two sentences tell what the subject does, the third sentence tells about an action that the subject will receive, and the last two sentences tell about their subjects' states of being.

EXERCISE

Place a slash mark (/) between the complete subject and the complete predicate of each sentence.

1. Our new car / was damaged by vandals.

2. My favorite recreation / is golf.

3. My cousin Adelaide swam in the 1972 Olympics.

4. The money from the sale has been donated to the children's fund.

5. The whole family drove to the beach after work.

6. The new helper will finish the job soon.

7. An angry listener shouted insultingly at the speaker.

8. The old clock ticked away in the corner.

9. The crew of carpenters worked all day.

10. The north wind is blowing more strongly than ever.

Recognizing Subjects and Verbs

Let's begin by repeating two of the sentences from the last section, this time with their simple subjects underlined once and their verbs underlined twice.

The tall <u>man</u> <u>laughed</u> loudly.
The slender, leafy <u>trees</u> <u>are</u> <u>swaying</u> in the wind.

In each of these sentences, the main idea is expressed by the simple subject and verb—a fact that holds true for every other sentence as well. Learning to identify these elements, then, will help you to know what sentences are saying.

Picking out these key parts is not difficult. Simply locate the verb part of the sentence, and then ask yourself who or what controls the verb. Consider the following two sentences.

Elmer <u>gave</u> the old beggar a dollar.
The <u>car</u> <u>was</u> in the garage.

In the first instance, the answer to the question "Who or what gave?" is clearly *Elmer* rather than *the beggar*. Similarly, the answer to the question "Who or what was?" is *the car* rather than *the garage*. Thus, *Elmer* is the subject of the first sentence, and *car* is the subject of the second sentence.

When identifying subjects and verbs, you will find it helpful to keep a few pointers in mind. First, as already noted, the verb part of a sentence may be a verb phrase. In the following examples, the subject is underlined once and the verb twice.

> By tomorrow, I will have finished my report.
> Jane should arrive within the next hour.

Sometimes one or more words may interrupt the verb phrase or come between the subject and the verb.

> Joyce had completely forgotten her appointment with the dentist. (A word interrupts the verb phrase.)
> Marvin has certainly not shown any talent as a writer. (Two words interrupt the verb phrase.)
> The clock on the mantel once belonged to my grandfather. (Four words interrupt the subject and verb.)
> Do you believe that story? (A word interrupts the verb phrase.)

Note that in the last example the interrupting word is the subject of the sentence. This verb-subject-verb pattern occurs in many sentences that ask questions.

Some sentences have compound subjects (two or more simple subjects), compound verbs (two or more individual verbs), or both.

> The house and garage burned to the ground. (compound subject)
> He jogs and swims for exercise. (compound verb)
> The knight and the squire mounted their horses and rode off. (compound subject and compound verb)

In most sentences, the subject comes ahead of the verb. Sometimes, though, the verb comes first and may be preceded by one or more other words.

> Across the river stands a lone pine tree.
> Here is my house.
> There goes Jack.
> When is your theme due?
> Where are the keys to my car?
> How are you today?
> Why was he so angry?

If a sentence begins with *here* or *there* or a question begins with *when, where, how,* or *why,* the subject is likely to follow the verb.

In sentences expressing a command or a request, the subject, which is always "you," may be unstated but understood.

> (you) Come here right away!
> (you) Hand me that wrench, please.

EXERCISE

For each of these sentences, underline the simple subject once and the verb twice (remember that each element of a verb phrase is a verb). If the subject is unstated, supply it at the proper point.

1. The couple married and moved to another city.

2. In the pond swam a number of swans.

3. Rob and Jim went to the movies.

4. There are many rooms in my father's mansion.

5. When will she ever learn?

6. Go to the head of the class.

7. Your jacket and trousers are at the cleaners.

8. Will you let the dog out?

9. Several students in my graduating class have joined the army.

10. You have totally missed the point of the story.

11. One man and two women applied and were hired.

12. How goes the battle?

UNIT SELF-TEST

Place a slash mark (/) between the complete subject and the complete predicate of each sentence; then write the simple subject and the verb or verb phrase in the blanks to the left. Some sentences may have more than one subject and one verb. If the subject interrupts a verb phrase, set the subject off with a pair of slash marks. If the subject is unstated, put a slash mark at the beginning of the sentence.

Subject(s)   **Verb(s)**

mother   _is planning_   My mother/is planning the guest list for my wedding.

Subject(s)   **Verb(s)**

you   _will do_   What will/you/do after gradu-
                                  ation?

you   _put_   /Put the package on the table.

tractor   _Sat_   1. Behind the barn/ sat a rusty
                                 tractor.

dog   _Jumped_   2. The little dog/ jumped and/
               barked   barked at the door.

You   _are feeling_ 3. Are/ you/ feeling any better to-
                                 day?

They   _Waited_   4. With great impatience, they
                                 waited at the corner for the pa-
                                 rade.

You   _look_ You 5. Look over there by that big
                                 tree!

The answers are on page 441.

UNIT REVIEW EXERCISE 1A
The Simple Sentence

Place a slash mark (/) between the complete subject and the complete predicate of each sentence; then write the simple subject and the verb or verb phrase in the blanks to the left. Some sentences may have more than one subject and one verb. If the subject interrupts a verb phrase, set the subject off with a pair of slash marks. If the subject is unstated, put a slash mark at the beginning of the sentence.

Subject(s)	Verb(s)	
mother *father*	*are*	My mother and father/are in New York this week.
Matilda	*did buy*	Where did/Matilda/buy her dress?
you	*do*	/Do your homework now.
I	*do*	1. I/do not understand the directions for this test.
We	*are going*	2. Are/ we all going to the game?
hunter	*found*	3. The hunter/ found the campsite.
Bob + Jim	*went*	4. Bob and Jim/ went to the movies.
Protesters	*remained* *argued*	5. A few protesters/ remained behind and argued with the police.
wrist *Tommy's*	*was*	6. Tommy's wrist/ was severely sprained during the Little League game.
Miranda *family*	*drove*	7. Miranda and her family/drove to Chicago and visited the planetarium.

9

Subject(s)	**Verb(s)**
Janice	*will be learning*

8. As an apprentice, Janice will be learning the plumbing trade.

City	*lies*

9. Under this city lies an ancient ruin.

I	*will do*

10. This year I will do my Christmas shopping early.

TV list	*is*

11. Where is the TV listing for this week?

Titus Can	*goes*

12. There goes old Titus Canby on his weekly visit to his bank.

Children	*begged pleaded*

13. The children begged and pleaded for more candy.

You	*remember*

14. Remember us in your prayers.

You	*did hear*

15. When did you hear about the accident?

UNIT REVIEW EXERCISE 1B
The Simple Sentence

PART A

Supply a complete predicate of at least five words for each of the following complete subjects.

My father and his friend _have finished building the shed._

1. Some of the workers _ate their lunch befor they did their work._

2. The nervous English instructor _spoke very quietly behind the podium._

3. This new sports car _raced down the highway at high speed._

4. The tallest person in the group, _although only 5 feet, was is Stateboes._

5. Our most prominent citizen _was given an award for excellence_

PART B

Supply a complete subject of at least four words for each of the following complete predicates.

The Statue of Liberty
stands in New York's harbor.

1. _The watermelon crop in Ca._
is heavily polluted by chemicals.

2. _____
were exhausted by their difficult day.

3. The ferotious little Chiuauh
chased the boy and snapped at his heels.

4. wrinkly old mr. Jhonson
stood menacingly in the doorway.

5. Although enthusiastic, the Gerber Co.
has completely misrepresented my position on this matter.

UNIT 2

More About the Predicate

Now that you know the basic parts of the simple sentence, let's take a closer look at the predicate. As we have said, a predicate always includes one or more verbs. In addition, it may also have one or more *complements*—words or word groups that help complete the meaning of the sentence. There are four kinds of complements: *direct objects, indirect objects, subject complements,* and *object complements.*

Direct Objects

A direct object names the person, place, or thing that receives or is the product of the action of the verb.

> Henry struck *William*. (The direct object *William* receives the action of the verb *struck*.)
>
> Inez built a *fire*. (The direct object *fire* is the product of the action of the verb *built*.)
>
> Ingrid has bought a *painting* for her room. (The direct object *painting* receives the action of the verb *has bought*.)
>
> They took a *radio* and a *camera* to the game. (The direct objects *radio* and *camera* receive the action of the verb *took*.)

As the last example shows, verbs can take compound direct objects. Similarly, compound verbs can take single direct objects.

> She *wrote* and then *revised* her *theme*. (The compound verb *wrote* ... *revised* takes a single direct object, *theme*.)

13

EXERCISE

Underline the direct object or direct objects in each of the following sentences.

1. I understand the problem and its solution.

2. The baby spilled milk on the floor.

3. Sally made the statue on the mantel.

4. I don't understand the directions for this test.

5. The judge revoked the driver's license for six months.

6. My mother is baking pies right now.

Indirect Objects

An indirect object names one or more persons, places, or things for whom (or which) or to whom (or which) something is done. It always precedes a direct object in standard modern English.

> Ramona Chavez sold *me* her slide rule. (The indirect object *me* tells to whom the slide rule was sold. *Slide rule* is the direct object.)
>
> They built the *dog* a kennel. (The indirect object *dog* tells for whom the kennel was built. *Kennel* is the direct object.)
>
> Al has made *Mother* and *Father* a table and chair for their anniversary. (The indirect objects *Mother* and *Father* tell for whom the table and chair were made. *Table* and *chair* are compound direct objects.)
>
> He gave the *door* a kick. (The indirect object *door* tells the thing to which something was done. *Kick* is the direct object.

EXERCISE

Underline the indirect object or indirect objects in each of the following sentences.

1. They have offered Anita the job at least three times.

2. The dealer promised me a big discount on the used car.

3. Several tourists bought themselves new luggage and cameras for the trip.

4. Calvin and Grace gave their children bicycles for Christmas.

5. The bank has sent my wife and me someone else's canceled checks.

6. Please send me a copy when the books arrive.

Subject Complements

A subject complement follows a verb that shows what something is, was, or will be. It renames or describes the subject. (See explanation of linking verbs on pages 4 and 25.)

> Lucille is an *architect*. (The complement *architect* renames the subject *Lucille*.)
>
> The music was too *loud* and *disturbing* for me. (The complements *loud* and *disturbing* describe the subject *music*.)

EXERCISE

Underline the subject complement or complements in each of the following sentences.

1. David has been supervisor of the stock room for two months.

2. Autumn is a sad season for me.

3. Eunice was especially alert and eager that particular morning.

4. Synonyms are words with the same meaning.

5. I will be ready soon.

6. His jokes were offensive to his listeners.

Object Complements

An object complement follows a direct object and renames or describes it.

> The class elected Mary *president*. (The object complement *president* renames the direct object *Mary*.)
>
> They painted the room an ugly *green*. (The object complement *green* describes the direct object *room*.)

EXERCISE

Underline the object complement or complements in each of the following sentences.

1. The critic called Shepherd's fourth novel an interesting failure.

2. Bob considered Lulu especially beautiful and intelligent.

3. We thought his remarks witty.

4. This tranquilizer has made me sleepy.

5. I keep things very tidy in my house.

6. The king appointed Sir Nigel prime minister.

UNIT SELF-TEST

Each of the following sentences contains a complement printed in italics. In each case, identify the type of complement by writing the appropriate letters in the blank to the left.

DO = direct object   SC = subject complement
IO = indirect object   OC = object complement

__*OC*__   I consider that suggestion *foolish*.

_____ 1. Mona and Rose were very *angry* over their low test scores.

_____ 2. That movie on concentration camps has left me very *sad*.

_____ 3. The dog rejected the *plate* of table scraps.

_____ 4. Sam gave *Debbie* a new wristwatch for her birthday.

_____ 5. Herman has been telling the *children* stories for the last two hours.

The answers are on page 441.

UNIT REVIEW EXERCISE 2A
More About the Predicate

Each of the following sentences contains a complement printed in italics. In each case, identify the italicized complement(s) by writing the appropriate letters in the blank to the left.

DO = direct object   SC = subject complement
IO = indirect object   OC = object complement

_SC_   That statuette is an *heirloom*.

_____ 1. The superintendent of the building gave the *workers* a safety award.

_____ 2. We did not have enough *time* for the test.

_____ 3. The road was almost *impassable* because of the rain.

_____ 4. The crowd surrounded the speaker's *platform*.

_____ 5. Everyone called the movie *terrible*.

_____ 6. José and Juanita have made the *birds* a feeding station.

_____ 7. At night the abandoned house was quite *spooky*.

_____ 8. The local machine shop has donated a *lathe* to the school.

_____ 9. Last week my girlfriend knitted *me* a green muffler with purple tassels.

_____ 10. Mr. Samsonistes is the new *manager* of the Delilah Hair Styling Salon.

_____ 11. The millionaire donated *paintings* and *sculptures* to the museum.

_____ 12. These mosquitoes are making things *miserable* for us.

_____ 13. The meadow behind our house is the *home* of many rabbits.

_____ 14. I'll certainly give *him* a piece of my mind.

_____ 15. The students elected Mary *homecoming queen.*

UNIT REVIEW EXERCISE 2B
More About the Predicate

PART A

Supply a direct object for the sentence following the example, and then write three similar sentences containing direct objects.

Chester found a ____*glove*____ in the snow.

The police checked the ____*plane*____ for a bomb.

1. _____

   _____

2. _____

   _____

3. _____

   _____

PART B

Supply an indirect object for the sentence following the example, and then write three similar sentences containing indirect objects.

I can give ____*her*____ three minutes of my time.

They bought their ____*daughter*____ a new snowsuit.

1. _____

   _____

2. _____

   _____

3. _____

_____

PART C

Supply a subject complement for the sentence following the example, and then write three similar sentences containing subject complements.

Salvatore was a _sergeant_ during the Korean War.

They are _crazy_ for believing that wild tale.

1. _____

_____

2. _____

_____

3. _____

_____

PART D

Supply an object complement for the sentence following the example, and then write three similar sentences containing object complements.

His enemies call him _unprincipled_ .

Everyone in the class thought the instructor a _success_ .

1. _____

_____

2. _____

_____

3. _____

_____

UNIT 3

Nouns, Pronouns, and Verbs

Traditional English grammar classifies words into eight parts of speech. These parts are *nouns, pronouns, verbs, adjectives, adverbs, prepositions, conjunctions,* and *interjections.* This unit will tell you how nouns, pronouns, and verbs function in sentences; the next unit will do the same for other parts of speech. Later on, we will deal with these parts of speech in greater detail.

Nouns

Nouns name. The things named may be persons, places, things, qualities, ideas, events, or actions. In the following examples, the nouns are italicized.

> *Angelo* drove to *Colorado* in his *car.* (The first noun names a person, the second a place, and the third a thing.)
> He has never shown *compassion* for anyone. (The noun names a quality.)
> *Socialism* has never appealed to me. (The noun names an idea.)
> The *party* was very successful. (The noun names an event.)
> Her *departure* was abrupt. (The noun names an action.)

Some nouns name particular persons, places, things, or events. These nouns are always capitalized. Here are two sentences with nouns of this type. For a fuller discussion of such nouns and the rules for capitalizing them, see the unit on capitalization.

> *World War II* began when *Hitler* invaded *Poland.* (In the sentence are named one particular event, one particular person, and one particular country.)
> *Marie Jacobs,* head of *Peerless Drug Company,* addressed the graduating class at *Abell Technical Institute.* (In the sentence are named one particular person, one particular company, and one particular school.)

21

EXERCISE

Underline each noun in the following sentences.

1. The cowboys rounded up the herd for shipment to Chicago.

2. Sylvia Broom was born in Newark, Ohio.

3. Thoughtlessness has destroyed many good friendships.

4. The Acme Club rates loyalty above all other qualities.

5. Two members of the committee presented a report on the cost of the project.

6. Scientists believe that the surface of the planet Uranus is cold and barren.

7. In our town, the Acme Textile Company is the chief industry.

8. Raymond filled his tank with twenty gallons of gasoline.

9. A robbery in progress was reported by a passerby.

10. Most children love sweets, especially candy.

Pronouns

A pronoun takes the place of a noun or a word group functioning as a noun.

> Cats are nocturnal animals. *They* like to prowl at night. (The pronoun *they* in the second sentence takes the place of the noun *cats*.)

> Working as an airline stewardess may seem glamorous, but actually *it* can be quite boring. (The pronoun *it* takes the place of *working as an airline stewardess*.)

Pronouns serve several different purposes in sentences. One group of pronouns refers to specific persons and things. These pronouns are called *personal pronouns*. Personal pronouns include *I, you, he, she, it, we,* and *they; my, mine, your, yours, his, her, hers, its, our, ours, their,* and *theirs;* and *me, him, us,* and *them.*

> Anton bought the book *he* had been meaning to read. (The personal pronoun *he* refers to a specific individual, *Anton*.)
> The car is parked where *it* usually is. (The personal pronoun *it* refers to a specific car.)

Mary's hair is longer than *mine*. (The personal pronoun *mine* refers both to the general subject *hair* and to *the specific speaker of the sentence*.)

A second group of pronouns includes pronouns that do not refer to specific persons and things. These pronouns are called *indefinite pronouns*. Indefinite pronouns include *all, another, any, anybody, anyone, both, each, either, everybody, few, many, most, much, neither, nobody, none, several, some,* and *such.*

Neither of the students wrote a good exam. (The indefinite pronoun *neither* does not refer to a single, specific student.)

Something seems to be bothering Jake. (The indefinite pronoun *something* does not refer to a known, specific thing.)

Yet a third group of pronouns asks questions. These pronouns are called *interrogative pronouns* ("to interrogate" is "to question"). *Who, whose, whom, what,* and *which* are the most common interrogative pronouns.

What is the matter with the dishwasher? (The interrogative pronoun *what* begins the question.)

Who will be playing third base? (The interrogative pronoun *who* begins the question.)

A fourth group of pronouns relates *subordinate clauses* to the *main clauses* of their sentences. A *subordinate clause* is a group of words that contains a subject and a predicate but cannot stand alone as a sentence. Just as an army private is "subordinate" to a corporal, so is this type of clause subordinate to a *main clause,* which can stand alone and which expresses the sentence's controlling idea. (See pages 38–39 for further discussion of subordinate clauses.) The pronouns that perform this function are called *relative pronouns* (they "relate" the subordinate clause to the main clause). The relative pronouns are *who, whose, whom, which,* and *that.*

Harvey Wilson, *who* worked here for twenty years, is retiring. (The relative pronoun *who* relates the subordinate clause *who has worked here for twenty years* to *Harvey Wilson* in the main clause. Notice that this type of subordinate clause can interrupt the main clause.)

Please return the book *that* you borrowed. (The relative pronoun *that* relates the subordinate clause *that you borrowed* to *book* in the main clause.)

Other pronouns point out. These pronouns are called *demonstrative pronouns* (think of the verb "to demonstrate"). The four demonstrative pronouns are *this, that, these,* and *those.*

That is the movie to see. (The demonstrative pronoun *that* points ahead to the noun *movie*.)

Still other pronouns, called *reflexive pronouns,* turn actions back upon the doers of the actions (think of the verb "to reflect," as when a mirror reflects an image). Reflexive pronouns always end in *-self* or *-selves* and include *myself, yourself, himself, herself, itself, ourselves, yourselves,* and *themselves.*

> I cut *myself* while shaving. (The reflexive pronoun *myself* is the direct object of the verb *cut* and refers back to the subject *I.*)

Identical to reflexive pronouns in form are *intensive pronouns,* which "intensify" or give emphasis to a noun in the sentence.

> The manager *herself* handled the complaint. (The intensive pronoun *herself* gives emphasis to the noun *manager.*)

Finally, there are *reciprocal pronouns,* which indicate an exchange between two or more people or things ("to reciprocate" is "to give and take mutually"). The two reciprocal pronouns are *each other* and *one another.*

> Larry and Ellen always help *each other* with algebra problems. (The reciprocal pronoun *each other* shows an exchange between *Larry* and *Ellen.*)

EXERCISE

Underline each pronoun in the following sentences. In parentheses to the right of each sentence, identify the type(s) of pronoun(s) in the order in which they appear in the sentence.

1. He can afford to pay for it himself.

2. Help yourself to whatever you wish to eat.

3. Now, that is the right way to do it!

4. They themselves are to blame for the problem.

5. What is the matter with Evelyn?

6. To whom am I speaking?

7. Let us help one another, and then everyone will find the task easy.

8. Of the two themes, yours is written better than hers.

9. These are problems we can solve by ourselves.

10. Anyone who wants a second helping of pie can have it.

Verbs

A verb is a word that indicates action or existence and helps express the main idea of a sentence. Verbs may be classified as action verbs, linking verbs, and helping verbs.

As its name suggests, an action verb expresses an occurrence or activity.

> The mechanic *installed* the carburetor.
> Bill *works* in a large office.

A linking verb shows a state of being or existence and connects or links the subject of the sentence to a subject complement. The most common linking verbs are forms of the verb *be (is, are, am, was, were, being, been.)*

> Mr. Condorelli *is* the club's treasurer. (The linking verb *is* links the subject *Mr. Condorelli* to the subject complement *the club's treasurer.*)
> That movie *was* scary. (The linking verb *was* links the subject *movie* to the subject complement *scary.*)

A helping verb accompanies an action verb or a linking verb, allowing it to express shades of meaning, such as when an action takes place. Common helping verbs include *shall, will, should, would, must, can, could, may, might,* and the above-mentioned forms of the verb *be.*

The following sentences illustrate the function of helping verbs. In each case, the helping verb has been underlined once and the main verb twice.

> Peggy is changing the tire. (The verb phrase *is changing* expresses present action.)
> Bill should give to charity. (The verb phrase *should give* expresses obligation.)
> Mr. Condorelli will be our club's treasurer. (The verb phrase *will be* expresses a future situation.)
> Mr. Condorelli may be our club's treasurer. (The verb phrase *may be* expresses a present or future possibility.)
> Mr. Condorelli might have been our club's treasurer. (The verb phrase *might have been* expresses a past possibility.)

EXERCISE

Underline each verb in the following sentences. Then circle any verb phrases.

1. We have been waiting all day for news from the hospital.

2. Jeremy must be home by six o'clock.

3. I am taking a survey for the local school board.

4. If that tree could only talk, it could tell all sorts of interesting stories.

5. Please be careful when you pack the dishes.

6. Can you begin the new job right away?

7. I will have nearly finished this project by afternoon.

8. Harley is six feet tall, but his parents are both very short.

9. Do you remember Uncle Harry?

10. Dandelions and crabgrass have overrun my lawn.

UNIT SELF-TEST

    Each sentence contains two italicized words. Identify the part of speech of each word by writing the word with its correct abbreviation in the blanks to the left.

N = noun
P = pronoun
V = verb

_____N_____ _____P_____ *Edmond* worked for *her* several years ago.

_____ _____ 1. *She* is as pure as the driven *slush*.

_____ _____ 2. Professor La Fontaine *spent* his sabbatical leave in *France*.

_____ _____ 3. *Forget* your homework for now, but remember to do *it* after supper.

_____ _____ 4. A *herd* of cattle was *grazing* in the meadow.

_____ _____ 5. Lucy's *plan* pleased *nobody*.

The answers are on page 442.

UNIT REVIEW EXERCISE 3A
Nouns, Pronouns, and Verbs

Each sentence contains two italicized words. Identify the part of speech of each word by writing the word with its correct abbreviation in the blanks to the left.

N = noun
P = pronoun
V = verb

_____P_____ _____N_____ *He* has found an excellent Mexican *restaurant.*

_____ _____ 1. Morris looks like the *cat* that *swallowed* the canary.

_____ _____ 2. Tell *me* what *is* wrong with this stew.

_____ _____ 3. *Be* still and know that I am the *boss.*

_____ _____ 4. *Everybody* needs to conserve *energy.*

_____ _____ 5. *Love* makes the world go round, or so we're *told* anyhow.

_____ _____ 6. *They* invited *themselves* to go with us.

_____ _____ 7. The students *agreed* with *one another* that the test was too hard.

_____ _____ 8. *Fear* caused *him* to run faster and faster.

_____ _____ 9. *Neither* of us understood the *assignment.*

27

_____   _____   10. An old weather-beaten house *stood* at the *bottom* of the hill.

_____   _____   11. My grandmother *owns* a clock *that* is at least two centuries old.

_____   _____   12. Neville had convinced *himself* that he would never overcome his *shyness*.

_____   _____   13. I *myself* will *supervise* every phase of the project.

_____   _____   14. Can you *tell* me who those oddly dressed people *are?*

_____   _____   15. That book is *hers,* and this is *mine.*

UNIT REVIEW EXERCISE 3B
Nouns, Pronouns, and Verbs

PART A

Write four sentences, each including at least three nouns, one of which names a particular person, place, or thing.

That man has made a large contribution to the Salvation Army.

1. _____

_____

2. _____

_____

3. _____

_____

4. _____

_____

PART B

Write four sentences, each including at least two pronouns. In this exercise use at least one example of each type you have studied. In parentheses after each sentence, indicate the types of pronouns that you've used in the order in which they appear in the sentence.

This is a terrible mixup, and nobody seems to know who has caused it.
(Demonstrative, indefinite, relative, personal)

1. _____

_____

_____

2. _____

_____

_____

3. _____

_____

_____

4. _____

_____

_____

PART C

Write four sentences, one including an action verb, one including a linking verb, and two including a helping verb plus an action or linking verb. In parentheses after each sentence, indicate the type(s) that you've used.

You have mishandled this project from the very start. (helping verb plus an action verb)

1. _____

_____

_____

2. _____

_____

_____

3. _____

_____

_____

4. _____

_____

_____

_____

UNIT 4

Adjectives, Adverbs, Prepositions, Conjunctions, and Interjections

Adjectives and adverbs serve as modifers, prepositions and conjunctions join parts of sentences or whole sentences, and interjections express emotion or call for attention.

Adjectives

An adjective *modifies* a noun or pronoun by describing or limiting it or in some other way making its meaning more exact. Sometimes the adjective is positioned next to the word it modifies. At other times, one or more words may come between the two of them. Here are some examples.

> Mary is *beautiful*.
> *Grouchy* men irritate me.
> The *yellow* car belongs to Bob.
> He is *wrong*.
> *Three* people have applied so far.

You will notice from the last example that numbers, when used to limit nouns, are adjectives. The words *a, an,* and *the,* known as articles, are also considered adjectives. Unlike most adjectives, an article *must* precede the noun it modifies.

The girl brought *an* apple and *a* sandwich to *the* picnic.

Often, two or more adjectives modify the same word.

The tall, leafy tree has *gray* bark.

Adjectives add precision and variety to your writing. Without adjectives, you couldn't describe Mary, the men, or Bob's car; offer an opinion about the unnamed "he"; or let your reader know how many people have applied. Adjectives allow you to express whatever quality, characteristic, condition, or number you have in mind.

Mary is (beautiful, intelligent, sick, tired, angry).
(Grouchy, Smug, Overbearing, Cowardly, Macho) men irritate me.
He is (wrong, right, foolish, ignorant, clever).
The (yellow, battered, red, Plymouth, sports) car belongs to Bob.
(No, Three, Few, Some, One thousand) people have applied so far.

EXERCISE

Underline the adjectives in the following sentences.

1. We had three weeks' vacation.

2. A clean, tidy house will sell faster than a dirty one.

3. Because of the good pay, thirty people applied for the job.

4. A tall, thin man wearing a red ski mask held up the local bank yesterday.

5. The dishonest salesperson cheated me by selling me a defective car.

6. Skiing in damp, foggy weather, Doug caught a bad cold.

7. We shared an orange and a banana at lunch.

8. Few people live without some stress.

9. A soft breeze wafted through the window and promised a pleasant night.

10. Arnold was delighted when he won the lottery after buying many tickets.

Adverbs

An adverb is a word that modifies a verb, an adjective, another adverb, or a whole sentence. Adverbs generally answer the questions "How?" "When?" "Where?" "How often?" or "To what extent?"

The painter worked *rapidly*. (The adverb *rapidly* modifies the verb *worked* and answers the question "How?")

The package will arrive *tomorrow*. (The adverb *tomorrow* modifies the verb *arrive* and answers the question "When?")

Fred drove *home* after leaving the expressway. (The adverb *home* modifies the verb *drove* and answers the question "Where?")

I *sometimes* watch TV in the evening. (The adverb *sometimes* modifies the verb *watch* and answers the question "How often?")

Adverbs that modify other adverbs, adjectives, and whole sentences are common.

The painter worked *very* rapidly. (The adverb *very* modifies the adverb *rapidly* and answers the question "How rapidly?")

The painter's work was *very* rapid. (The adverb *very* modifies the adjective *rapid* and answers the question "How rapid?")

Perhaps the painter will work rapidly. (The adverb *perhaps* modifies the whole sentence, but does not answer any specific question.

Adverbs make it possible to answer questions in many ways. Consider, for instance, the following ways you might answer the questions "When will the package arrive?" and "Where did Fred drive after leaving the expressway?"

The package will arrive (early, late, soon, tomorrow).

Fred drove (downstate, uptown, west, home) after leaving the expressway.

Often, adverbs offer a way of expressing different shades of meaning.

I (always, frequently, never, sometimes) watch TV in the evening.

Selecting the right adverb, then, lets you express exactly what you have in mind, thus reducing the chances that your reader will mistake your meaning.

EXERCISE

Underline the adverbs in the following sentences.

1. The train moved slowly down the track.

2. I studied very hard for that history exam.

3. We went skiing yesterday, and I can barely walk today.

4. They finished the project more quickly than we had expected.

5. Actually, everyone made many mistakes.

6. The Blakes went north for their summer vacation.

7. Cassandra is usually too tired to watch the late, late movie.

8. Please divide the tasks equally and finish them quickly.

9. Pigs are considered very intelligent animals.

10. If this speech lasts much longer, I'll fall asleep.

Prepositions

A preposition links its object, which consists of a noun or noun substitute, to some other word in the sentence and shows a relation between the two. This relation is often one of space, time, possession, means, or reason or purpose. Following is a list of common prepositions, some of which consist of two or more words.

above	by reason of	of
after	contrary to	on
against	during	onto
along with	except	out of
among	for	over
at	from	since
because of	in	through
before	instead of	to
below	into	toward
beside	like	under
between	near	with
by	next to	without

To clarify the use of prepositions, let's consider a few possible spatial relations between you and your car. As you open its door, you are *next to* the car. While you are driving, you are *in* the car. If you change its oil, you may need to crawl *under* the car. And occasionally—for example, to see over a crowd—you may sit *on* your car. In each of these illustrations, *car* is the object of the italicized preposition. The word group containing the preposition and its object—*next to the car, in the car, under the car, on the car*—is called a *prepositional phrase.* You might wish to think of the preposition as asking a question that its object answers: a preposition must take an object; in other words, it must appear within a prepositional phrase.

As we noted at the beginning of this section, prepositions and prepositional phrases do not necessarily involve space.

> They plan to be away *until* Tuesday. (The preposition *until* links its object, *Tuesday,* to *away* and shows time.)
>
> The laws *of* nature sometimes contradict civil regulations. (The preposition *of* links its object, *nature,* to *laws* and shows possession.)
>
> Sally went *by* automobile. (The preposition *by* links its object, *automobile,* to *went* and shows means.)
>
> Wilfred bicycles *for* pleasure. (The preposition *for* links its object, *pleasure,* to *bicycles* and shows reason or purpose.)

Occasionally, and particularly in questions, a preposition may be separated from its object so that the prepositional phrase is disjointed and difficult to find.

> What are you looking *for?* (The object of the preposition *for* is *what.* The question could be reworded "For what are you looking?")
>
> *Sports Illustrated* is a magazine that I subscribe *to.* (The object of the preposition *to* is *Sports Illustrated.* The sentence could be reworded "I subscribe to *Sports Illustrated*" or "*Sports Illustrated* is a magazine to which I subscribe.")

EXERCISE

Underline the prepositions in the following sentences. Then circle the elements of each prepositional phrase.

1. The noise from the apartment above us made sleeping difficult.

2. The sign on the door said that the office was closed until noon.

3. He covered the dingy walls with brightly colored wallpaper.

4. The house next to ours has been for sale six months.

5. Is there anyone among you without guilt?

6. What are you writing with?

7. After a short nap, I felt ready for an evening of bowling.

8. Potatoes are usually sold by the bushel.

9. We have had three days of rain this week.

10. I'm not doing this for my health.

Conjunctions

Conjunctions join. They are used to connect the parts of sentences or to connect whole sentences. One group of conjunctions connects items of equal rank—words, word groups, and simple sentences. These conjunctions can occur singly (*and, but, or, nor, for, yet, so*) or in pairs (*either—or, neither—nor, both—and, not only—but also*). The single conjunctions are called *coordinating conjunctions;* the paired conjunctions are called *correlative conjunctions.*

> Tom *and* Jerry are opening a gas station. (The coordinating conjunction *and* connects the two nouns *Tom* and *Jerry.*)
>
> The old house looked dark *and* gloomy. (The coordinating conjunction *and* connects the two adjectives *dark* and *gloomy.*)
>
> Shall I call you at home *or* at your office? (The coordinating conjunction, *or*, connects the two prepositional phrases *at home* and *at your office.*)
>
> Sandra is *not only* intelligent *but also* popular. (The paired correlative conjunction *not only—but also* connects the two words *intelligent* and *popular.*)
>
> Bill applied to medical school, *but* he was not accepted. (The coordinating conjunction *but* connects two simple sentences.)
>
> *Either* take a nap now *or* sleep late tomorrow. (The paired correlative conjunction *either-or* connects two simple sentences.)

When two or more simple sentences are connected, the combination is called a *compound sentence.*

A second group of conjunctions (for example, *because, as if, even though, since, so that, while, whereas,* and *wherever*) is used to join elements of unequal rank—namely, *subordinate clauses* and *main clauses.* As we saw in the discussion of relative pronouns (p. 23), a subordinate clause contains a subject and a predicate but cannot stand as a complete sentence. In the following sentences, these clauses are subordinate *because* each is introduced by a connector which indicates that the idea expressed in that clause is subordinate to the idea expressed in the main clause—the part that can stand alone as an independent sentence. Accordingly, we call these connectors *subordinating conjunctions*.

> I am attracted to Velma *because* she is intelligent. (The conjunction *because* connects the subordinate clause *because she is intelligent* to the main clause.)
>
> Nero fiddled *while* Rome burned. (The conjunction *while* connects the subordinate clause *while Rome burned* to the rest of the sentence.)

In order to demonstrate how these connectors function, let us replace one subordinating conjunction with another. Notice the way in which this substitution changes the meaning of the clause, even though the main idea of the sentence remains unchanged.

> I am attracted to Velma *even though* she is intelligent.
>
> Nero fiddled *before* Rome burned.

A number of subordinating conjunctions (for example, *before, after, since, until*) can also serve as prepositions. As a result, the two are sometimes confused. However, if you remember that a preposition takes an object and that a subordinating conjunction introduces a subordinate clause that includes a subject and a predicate, you should have no trouble of this kind.

> They arrived *after* lunch. (*After* has an object, *lunch,* and is therefore a preposition.)
>
> They arrived *after* the movie had started. (*After* has a subject, *movie,* and a predicate, *had started,* and is therefore a subordinating conjunction.)

EXERCISE

Underline the conjunctions in the following sentences. In the blank to the left of each sentence, use the abbreviations below to indicate the type of conjunction you've underlined.

COOR = coordinating conjunction
CORR = correlative conjunction
SUB = subordinating conjunction

_____ 1. Raised together, a dog and cat will be friends.

_____ 2. I have three coats, but my sister has only one.

_____ 3. We employ both men and women in this factory.

_____ 4. George is a good friend even though we sometimes disagree.

_____ 5. Do you have time to talk, or should I phone you later?

_____ 6. Because we have classes at the same hour, let's form a car pool.

_____ 7. Neither her father nor her mother knew where she had gone.

_____ 8. Hilda has failed three times, yet she persists in trying.

_____ 9. Will you wait for me while I finish the dishes?

_____ 10. Molly didn't like the instructor even though she earned an *A* in the class.

_____ 11. Renée not only has a full-time job but also does all her own housework.

_____ 12. Stop by later, and we'll watch the ball game together.

_____ 13. Jim breezes through our math problems whereas I puzzle over them for hours.

_____ 14. I'm sure that either Gary or Jason could handle this job.

_____ 15. Kimberly felt especially energetic, so she walked to town instead of driving.

Interjections

An interjection is a word that is used to express strong feeling or to gain attention. It is followed by an exclamation point or a comma.

Hey! That's my coat you're taking. (strong interjection)
Oh, is it time to go now? (weak interjection)

Interjections are used less often than any other part of speech.

UNIT SELF-TEST

Each of the following sentences contains two italicized words. Identify the part of speech of each italicized word by writing in the blank to the left the correct abbreviation from the list below.

ADJ = adjective   C = conjunction
ADV = adverb   I = interjection
P = preposition

____C____   ____ADJ____   *Before* he could finish his question, the *angry* chairperson silenced him.

_____   _____   1. The *first* student answered the question *very* quickly.

_____   _____   2. People *usually* expect us to be *on* time.

_____   _____   3. We may be *tired when* we finish this work.

_____   _____   4. The tourists can see the entire valley *from* this *lookout* point.

_____   _____   5. He does his work *well, and* he can be depended upon.

_____   _____   6. *Help!* I'm about to fall *over* the cliff!

The answers are on page 442.

UNIT REVIEW EXERCISE 4A

Adjectives, Adverbs, Prepositions, Conjunctions, and Interjections

Each of the following sentences contains two italicized words. Identify the part of speech of each italicized word by writing in the blank to the left the correct abbreviation from the list below.

ADJ = adjective   C = conjunction
ADV = adverb   I = interjection
P = preposition

P   **ADV**   The man *in* the gray overcoat walked away *quickly.*

_____ _____ 1. *Five* actors auditioned *for* the lead in the new Neil Simon play.

_____ _____ 2. Sarah wanted most *of* the attention, *and* she got it.

_____ _____ 3. The *frightened* cat climbed *hurriedly* up the tree.

_____ _____ 4. I failed the test *because* I didn't study *hard* enough.

_____ _____ 5. *Without* a good marketing plan, we can't hope to sell our new product *successfully.*

_____ _____ 6. *The* flowers grew rapidly *after* he had fertilized them.

_____ _____ 7. *American* soldiers are guarding the visiting dignitary *now.*

_____ _____ 8. *Golly,* I never expected to win first prize *in* the contest.

43

————————— —————————   9. Cinderella lost her *glass* slipper, *and* the prince found it.

————————— ————————— 10. Mr. August is *too nervous* to be a good announcer.

————————— ————————— 11. The doors were locked *when* the *first* report was begun.

————————— ————————— 12. Each day the old man moved *more slowly.*

————————— ————————— 13. *Beneath* the overpass, the bandit waited *silently.*

————————— ————————— 14. *Each* Christmas season, prices are *higher.*

————————— ————————— 15. You take care *of* the refreshments, *and* I'll handle the invitations.

UNIT REVIEW EXERCISE 4B
Adjectives, Adverbs, Prepositions, Conjunctions, and Interjections

PART A

Write three sentences, each including at least two adjectives, and identify the adjectives by underlining them.

The <u>small</u> child bought <u>three</u>
<u>blue</u> balloons at the store.

1. _____

_____

2. _____

_____

3. _____

_____

PART B

Write three sentences, each including at least two adverbs, and identify the adverbs by underlining them.

The rain will <u>surely</u> stop <u>soon</u>.

1. _____

_____

2. _____

_____

3. _____

_____

PART C

Write three sentences, each including at least two prepositions, and identify the prepositions by underlining them.

_In_ the evening, we go _for_ walks
_in_ the woods.

1. _____

   _____

2. _____

   _____

3. _____

   _____

PART D

Write three sentences, each including at least two conjunctions. Use at least one correlative conjunction and one subordinating conjunction. Label each conjunction by underlining coordinating conjunctions once, correlative conjunctions twice, and subordinating conjunctions three times.

While the storm raged, the parents
and their children slept soundly.

1. _____

   _____

2. _____

   _____

3. _____

   _____

UNIT 5

Subordinate Clauses

As you have already learned, a clause is a group of words that includes both a subject and a predicate. You also know that there are two kinds of clauses—*main* (also called *independent*) and *subordinate* (also called *dependent*). A main clause expresses a complete thought and can stand alone as a simple sentence. A subordinate clause has a subject and a predicate but cannot stand alone (see pp. 23 and 38). A subordinate clause may function as a noun, as an adjective, or as an adverb.

Noun Clauses

A *noun clause* is a subordinate clause. It can begin with a pronoun (*who, whom, whose, that, which, what, whoever, whomever, whichever, whatever*) or a subordinating conjunction (*when, why, where, how, whether*). It can perform any of the functions of an ordinary noun.

> *What the neighbor told John* proved to be incorrect. (The noun clause is the subject of the sentence.)
>
> The woman asked *when the bus left for Spokane.* (The noun clause is the direct object of the sentence.)
>
> I'll give a reward to *whoever returns my billfold.* (The noun clause is the object of the preposition *to.*)

When the clause starts with *that* and serves as a direct object, the *that* can be omitted.

> Marybelle hoped *(that) she would graduate with honors.* (*That* is omitted but understood.)

There is an easy way to determine whether a clause serves as a noun. Simply replace it with *someone* or *something,* and ask yourself whether the sentence still makes sense. If the answer is yes, the clause is serving as a noun. If the answer is no, the clause is a different kind of subordinate clause. Notice that the above example sentence passes this test.

>Marybelle hoped *something*.

However, when we try the same trick with another kind of clause, the result is nonsense.

>The car *that won the race* belongs to my brother.
>The car *something* belongs to my brother. (The clause *that won the race* is in fact an *adjective clause* modifying *car*.)

EXERCISE

Underline the noun clause in each of the following sentences.

1. I wish I could fly like a bird.

2. Have you heard why the company failed?

3. Stuart couldn't decide which coat looked better on him.

4. Dr. Kant thinks that he knows everything.

5. The cup goes to whoever wins the race.

6. Don't tell me how the movie ended.

7. Home is where the heart lies.

8. I'll give half my kingdom to whichever knight slays the dragon.

9. Whether Melvin passes the course depends upon his score on the final.

10. Do you know who is making that racket?

Adjective Clauses

Like a noun clause, an *adjective clause* can begin with a pronoun (*who, whom, whose, that, which*) or a subordinating conjunction (*when, where, why, after, before*) (see pp. 23 and 38). Adjective clauses serve the same functions as ordinary adjectives, modifying nouns and pronouns.

> Our company is looking for someone *who has a background in data processing*. (The adjective clause modifies the pronoun *someone*.)
>
> I know a restaurant *where we can get good veal scallopini*. (The adjective clause modifies the noun *restaurant*.)

Sometimes the word that introduces the clause can be omitted.

> The chair *(that) we ordered last month* has just arrived. (The pronoun *that* can be omitted but understood.)
>
> The man *(whom) we were talking to* is a movie producer. (The pronoun *whom* can be omitted but understood.)

Sometimes, too, a preposition comes ahead of the introductory pronoun.

> The grace *with which Nelson danced* made the onlookers envious. (The clause begins with the preposition *with*.)

EXERCISE

Underline the adjective clause in each of the following sentences.

1. Harriet Thomas, who lives in Texas most of the year, spends January in Sun Valley, Idaho.

2. She wiped up the cereal that the baby had spilled.

3. I'll hire anyone Dr. Stone recommends.

4. The invitation to the party arrived the day after Henry had left for France.

5. Sylvia is a person whose opinion I value very highly.

6. Give me one reason why you feel the way you do.

7. Astrid's new car, which she bought yesterday, is a Volkswagen Rabbit.

8. The cake we ordered is ready.

9. This is the spot where we picnicked last week.

10. The candidate for whom I am voting is amply qualified for the office.

Adverb Clauses

An *adverb clause* is introduced by a subordinating conjunction (see p. 38). Like an ordinary adverb, this kind of clause may modify a verb, an adjective, another adverb, or a main clause. It answers such questions as "How?" "When?" "Where?" "Why?" "Under what conditions?" or "To what extent?"

The following list groups the most common subordinating conjunctions according to the questions their clauses answer.

When?

while
when
whenever
as
as soon as
before
after
since
until

Where?

where
wherever

How?

as if
as though

Why?

because
since
as
so that
now that

Under What Conditions?

if
once
unless
though
although
provided that

To What Extent?

than

He ate *as if he would never taste food again.* (The adverb clause modifies the verb *ate* and answers the question "How?")

You may start the projector *whenever you wish.* (The adverb clause modifies the verb *start* and answers the question "When?")

Wherever you go, I'll go too. (The adverb clause modifies the verb *go* and answers the question "Where?")

Sandra looked paler *than I had ever seen her look before.* (The adverb clause modifies the adjective *paler* and answers the question "To what extent?")

Albert worked rapidly *so that he could leave early.* (The adverb clause modifies the adverb *rapidly* and answers the question "Why?")

Unless everyone cooperates, we have little chance of success. (The adverb clause modifies the entire main clause and answers the question "Under what conditions?")

Occasionally, an adverb clause will omit one or more words that are not needed for an understanding of its meaning. Such a construction is called an *elliptical clause*.

While (he was) watching TV, Richard stuffed himself with potato chips. (*He was* can be omitted but understood.)

His car is more expensive *than mine* (*is*). (*Is* can be omitted but understood.)

Unlike noun and adjective clauses, adverb clauses can often be moved about in their sentences.

Richard stuffed himself with potato chips *while (he was) watching TV*.

EXERCISE

Underline the adverb clause in each of the following sentences.

1. I'm switching to Dr. Jekyll because I don't like Dr. Fell.

2. Provided that your father approves, you may stay in Las Vegas for two weeks.

3. I smile whenever I see your face.

4. The Nesbitts will attend the wedding if it takes place on Saturday.

5. Be sure to put your name on your paper before you turn it in.

6. Halfway through the party, Fenton started acting as though he felt ill.

7. Since the track meet took place, Bill has gained twenty pounds from inactivity.

8. Nick found several valuable books while rummaging through his attic.

9. Lend me two dollars so that I can attend the movies.

10. Earl behaves very snobbishly now that he has inherited a million dollars.

UNIT SELF-TEST

Each sentence contains an italicized subordinate clause. Identify the kind of clause by writing the correct abbreviation from the list below in the blank to the left.

N = noun clause
ADJ = adjective clause
ADV = adverb clause

**ADJ**   The student *who lives next door* owns a Mercedes convertible.

_____ 1. The children knew *that the dog did not belong to anyone in the neighborhood.*

_____ 2. He worked at a bank *that was robbed three times last year.*

_____ 3. *What to do about the problem* puzzles me.

_____ 4. *Whenever you've got time,* let's have a cup of coffee.

_____ 5. The baby cried *because he was hungry.*

The answers are on page 442.

UNIT REVIEW EXERCISE 5A
Subordinate Clauses

Each sentence following contains an italicized subordinate clause. Identify the kind of clause by writing the correct abbreviation from the list below in the blank to the left.

N = noun clause
ADJ = adjective clause
ADV = adverb clause

___N___ Henry knew *when the parade would start.*

_____ 1. *That she will return* seems unlikely to me.

_____ 2. We will leave *whenever everyone is ready.*

_____ 3. The store *that just went out of business* was the last independent grocery in town.

_____ 4. Sally approached the assignment *as if her life depended on it.*

_____ 5. *If the school is to buy new athletic equipment,* everyone on the board must approve.

_____ 6. He made an agreement *he could not carry out.*

_____ 7. Don recalled *where he had left the report.*

_____ 8. I'll give *whoever finishes first* a small prize.

_____ 9. George spoke loudly *because he wanted the people in the back of the auditorium to hear him.*

_____ 10. The problem *about which he spoke* did not exist two years ago.

_____ 11. At homecoming the town was more crowded *than I had ever seen it before.*

_____ 12. She asked to speak to *whoever was in charge.*

——————— 13. *Although he had once earned A's in literature,* Milton
            didn't understand the poem.

——————— 14. Life is *what you make it.*

——————— 15. It is she *whom you must ask about the job.*

UNIT REVIEW EXERCISE 5B
Subordinate Clauses

Change each subordinate clause into a complete sentence by adding an appropriate main clause.

After the dance was over, *Lizzie soaked her tired feet in hot water.*

1. When I was ten years old, _____

_____

_____

2. That he was no friend _____

_____

_____

3. _____ who wrote that novel _____

_____

_____

4. _____

_____

_____ as soon as you called.

5. _____ that he bought last Tuesday _____

_____

_____

6. _____

_____

_____ whatever she wants.

7. _____ when I saw her walking her dog in the

park _____

_____

8. _____

_____

_____ that the car stalled.

9. Because I can't complete the job on time, _____

_____

10. Whoever made that remark _____

_____

_____

UNIT 6

Noun, Adjective, and Adverb Phrases

A phrase is a group of words that, like a subordinate clause, serves as a single part of speech. Unlike such clauses, however, a phrase does not have a subject and a predicate. Phrases can function as verbs, nouns, adjectives, and adverbs. You are already familiar with verb phrases; this section will discuss noun, adjective, and adverb phrases.

Noun Phrases

The heart of a noun phrase is always a verb form. Some noun phrases are called *infinitive phrases* and are built around the infinitive—the form of the verb preceded by *to* (*to run, to see, to laugh,* and so forth). Keep in mind that "to" as part of a verb's infinitive has nothing to do with the preposition "to." Other noun phrases, called *gerund phrases,* are built around a verb form that functions as a noun and ends in *-ing* (*running, seeing, laughing,* and so forth). Not all verb forms ending in *-ing* are gerunds, and not all infinitives serve as the bases of noun phrases; to function as the basis of a noun phrase, the verb must serve as a noun. Like ordinary nouns, noun phrases can serve as subjects, direct objects, indirect objects, subject complements, and objects of prepositions.

> *Winning the Nobel Peace Prize* is the Secretary of State's ambition. (The gerund is the subject.)
> He likes *to repair automobiles.* (The infinitive phrase is the direct object.)
> Felice gave *writing the report* her full attention. (The gerund phrase is the indirect object.)

57

My purpose in taking this trip is *to visit my grandparents*. (The infinitive phrase is the subject complement.)

Fenton believes in *speaking his mind fearlessly*. (The gerund phrase is the object of the preposition *in*.)

The trick we used for identifying noun clauses will also work with noun phrases. Just substitute the word *something* for any phrase you are unsure of. If it's a noun phrase, the sentence will still make sense.

EXERCISE

Underline the noun phrase in each of the following examples.

1. Flying a crop-dusting plane is an exciting job.

2. Hank enjoys attending drag races.

3. I was surprised by his coming to the party.

4. Felice plans to become a doctor.

5. His hobby is restoring old cars.

6. Acme Auto Sales has built an enviable reputation by treating its customers fairly.

7. Russell's way of dieting was to give up carrots and spinach.

8. To become a skilled oboe player takes years of demanding practice.

9. Her goal was to major in environmental health.

10. Ben received a warning for driving an unsafe vehicle.

Adjective Phrases

Some adjective phrases are prepositional phrases in which the preposition and its object modify one or more nouns or pronouns.

The student *at the microscope* is examining a fly's wing. (The prepositional phrase *at the microscope* modifies the noun *student*.)

Other adjective phrases are built around the infinitive. We have already seen that this form of the verb can serve as a noun. However, the infinitive can also modify a noun or pronoun and serve as an adjective.

> That's no place *to visit in winter*. (The infinitive phrase *to visit in winter* modifies the noun *place* and therefore functions as an adjective.)

The bases of still other adjective phrases are verb forms known as *participles*. *Participles* are verb forms that can function as adjectives. Participles indicating present action, like gerunds, end in *-ing*. Most participles indicating past action end in *-ed*. Like infinitives, participles may take objects, complements, and modifiers. A participle plus an object, complement, or modifier is called a *participial phrase*.

> The chef *preparing dinner* trained in France. (The present participial phrase *preparing dinner* modifies the noun *chef* and functions as an adjective.)
>
> The fighter, *pounded by his opponent*, slumped to the canvas. (The past participial phrase *pounded by his opponent* modifies the noun *fighter* and functions as an adjective.)

Other participles showing past action can end in *-en* (beat*en*), *-n* (see*n*), *-t* (burn*t*), and *-d* (hear*d*).

Like other verb forms, participles may be used with helping verbs, which also have participial forms.

> *Having studied for a week*, Joanna felt confident about passing the exam. (The present participle of the verb *have* is *having* and it is here used with the past participle of *study—studied*. These participles, plus *for a week*, form a participial phrase that modifies the noun *Joanna* and accordingly functions as an adjective.)

EXERCISE

Underline the adjective phrase in each of the following sentences.

1. Having swum across Lake Louise, Jim wanted only to lie down.

2. The spacious veranda, swept by a summer breeze, soon attracted many people.

3. The excursion to visit Washington Irving's home will leave in ten minutes.

4. Give this package to the man in the blue suit.

5. The rain predicted for tomorrow is starting right now.

6. Swollen by the spring rains, Sutter's Creek rushed angrily past us.

7. Being a selfish child, young Francis Macomber ate the lion's share of the dessert.

8. Sweet Adeline, you're the darling of my heart.

9. Sworn to secrecy, Chester remained silent about his friend's plans.

10. Clem once owned the manuscript sold at yesterday's auction.

Adverb Phrases

Like their adjectival counterparts, some adverb phrases are prepositional phrases. Like ordinary adverbs, these prepositional phrases modify verbs, adjectives, and other adverbs.

> He bought ice skates *for himself*. (The prepositional phrase *for himself* modifies the verb *bought* and functions as an adverb.)
>
> The toddler was afraid *of the dog*. (The prepositional phrase *of the dog* modifies the adjective *afraid* and functions as an adverb.)
>
> Our visitor arrived late *in the day*. (The prepositional phrase *in the day* modifies the adverb *late* and functions as an adverb.)

Adverb phrases can also be built around the infinitive.

> Eve worked *to earn money* for college. (The infinitive phrase *to earn money* modifies the verb *worked* and functions as an adverb.)
>
> I am willing *to postpone our trip*. (The infinitive phrase *to postpone our trip* modifies the adjective *willing* and functions as an adverb.)
>
> Andrew ate too quickly *to enjoy the meal*. (The infinitive phrase *to enjoy the meal* modifies the adverb *quickly* and functions as an adverb.)

EXERCISE

Underline the adverb phrase in each of the following sentences.

1. The eclipse will take place soon after sunrise.

2. Jeremy studied every spare moment to make the dean's list.

3. Madge learned conversational Japanese by taking an extension course.

4. Mr. Leacock will see you after his next appointment.

5. Jonathan is too cowardly to ride the roller coaster.

6. The new GM compact car will be marketed in the spring.

7. My summer job helped me to buy a stereo.

8. He bought ice skates for his wife and himself.

9. The roaring of the wind died to a low mutter.

10. The people on the lawn scurried to escape the shower.

Verb Forms Not in Phrases

Verb forms can function as nouns, adjectives, and adverbs, even when they are not parts of phrases.

Pete wants *to leave.* (verb form as a noun)
Let *sleeping* dogs lie. (verb form as an adjective)
I'm ready *to quit.* (verb form as an adverb)
Swimming is my favorite sport. (verb form as a noun)

UNIT SELF-TEST

Each sentence contains an italicized phrase. Identify the kind of phrase by writing the correct abbreviation from the list below in the blank to the left.

N = noun phrase
ADJ = adjective phrase
ADV = adverb phrase

___ADJ___   *Wounded by the hunter,* the deer lay in the tall weeds.

_____ 1. I find it impossible *to follow your reasoning.*

_____ 2. Anyone *needing a ride to the polls* should call 794–4183.

_____ 3. What is your excuse *for this mistake?*

_____ 4. Brenda is running *for governor.*

_____ 5. *To embarrass you* was the last thing I wanted to do.

The answers are on page 442.

UNIT REVIEW EXERCISE 6A
Noun, Adjective, and Adverb Phrases

Each sentence contains an italicized phrase. Identify the kind of phrase by writing the correct abbreviation from the list below in the blank to the left.

N = noun phrase
ADJ = adjective phrase
ADV = adverb phrase

ADV   Little Tommy Tucker sings *for his supper.*

_____ 1. *Pleased by the applause,* the guitarist played two encores.

_____ 2. I hope *to attend next week's football game.*

_____ 3. *Visiting his hometown* was a saddening experience for Ed.

_____ 4. The airport limousine will arrive *in one hour.*

_____ 5. Thurber peered *through the microscope* but saw only the reflection of his own eye.

_____ 6. The mechanic *overhauling my car* was graduated from Clinton Technical Institute.

_____ 7. *Born on a Wednesday,* Wendy was full of woe.

_____ 8. They are very happy *with their Christmas presents.*

_____ 9. Reluctantly, I turned to my father-in-law *to borrow money.*

_____ 10. Anything *told by an idiot* is likely to be full of sound and fury.

_____ 11. She gave *managing the store* her full attention.

————   12. My first job was *testing samples of plastic.*

————   13. It's time *for a coffee break.*

————   14. They walked briskly *to keep warm.*

————   15. Listen to my plan *for solving the world's ills.*

UNIT REVIEW EXERCISE 6B
Noun, Adjective, and Adverb Phrases

Expand each phrase into a complete sentence.

The curtains _____, made of dark blue linen, dominated the whole living room.

1. In a tiny room off the main hall, _____

_____

2. Gathering wild blackberries _____

_____

3. _____

_____ to make his way in the world.

4. Burdened by mountainous debts and ill health, _____

_____

5. _____

_____ for the ground-breaking ceremonies tomorrow.

6. _____, to open a small grocery store, _____

_____

7. Opening the door a tiny crack, _____

_____

8. In the sudden, shocked silence, _____

_____

9. _____

_____ to get the other partygoers' attention.

10. _____ over the mantel _____

_____

Sharpening Your Usage Skills

Now that you are familiar with the "nuts and bolts" of grammar, you are equipped to understand and avoid common errors of usage. Avoiding these errors will clarify your writing and demonstrate that you are a careful communicator, which will in turn increase the chances that your messages will receive the responses you wish. That your reader should be favorably disposed toward a message in which you have evidently exercised care and thought makes obvious sense.

UNIT 7

Avoiding Sentence Fragments

A sentence fragment is not a complete sentence but rather a group of words that is capitalized and punctuated—incorrectly—as if it were a complete sentence. As you already know, to be considered a sentence a word group must pass two tests. First, it must have a subject and a verb. Second, it must express a complete thought. Following are two examples of fragments.

If you decide to go.
A home run in the first inning.

The first example has a subject and verb; the second, only a potential subject. Neither expresses a complete thought, and both leave the reader expecting more information.

Types of Fragments

Word groups mistakenly written as fragments include

phrases
subordinate clauses
verbs with their modifiers, objects, or complements (potential predicates)
the second halves of compound predicates
noun or noun substitutes with their modifiers.

The following sets of examples illustrate these kinds of fragments. In each case, the fragment is italicized.

Olga, a chemistry major, minored in bacteriology. *Hoping to improve her chances of working for a drug company.* (The fragment is an adjective phrase.)

Having been warned about the washed-out road. We took another route. (The fragment is an adjective phrase.)

Marco walked to the supermarket. *To buy a carton of milk.* (The fragment is an adverb phrase.)

I went to class. *Although I was not prepared.* (The fragment is an adverb clause.)

Whenever you ask. He will help you. (The fragment is an adverb clause.)

They've torn down the old house. *In which I grew up.* (The fragment is an adjective clause.)

We should never forget. *That experience is the best teacher.* (The fragment is a noun clause.)

John washed the windows. *And cleaned out the basement.* (The fragment is the second half of a compound predicate.)

That old gentleman sitting on the park bench and feeding the pigeons. (The fragment consists of a noun plus a modifying phrase—a potential *complete subject*.) *Was once the president of our largest bank.* (The fragment consists of a verb, its modifier, a complement, and its modifying phrase—a potential *complete predicate*.)

Independent clauses that start with a coordinating conjunction (*and, but, or, nor, for, yet, so*) are *not* sentence fragments although they are often mistakenly thought to be. The following are both complete sentences.

Phineas Phluff wanted the voters to send him to Washington. But they sent him to oblivion instead.

EXERCISE

Identify each of the following word groups as a sentence (S) or a fragment (F) by writing the correct letter in the blank to the left.

_____ 1. That he would ever have considered majoring in English.

_____ 2. Leaving the garden behind by jumping over the wall.

_____ 3. Having coronary artery surgery may prevent a fatal heart attack.

_____ 4. Because of the stiffness of his joints.

_____ 5. With which to purchase the shoes she needed for the dance.

_____ 6. To think of all the time I spent trying to entertain that child.

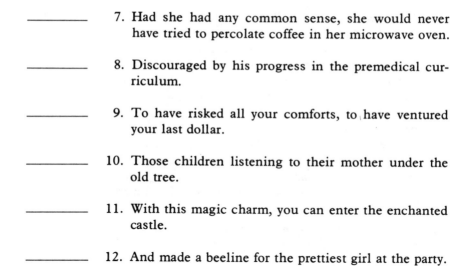

_____ 7. Had she had any common sense, she would never have tried to percolate coffee in her microwave oven.

_____ 8. Discouraged by his progress in the premedical curriculum.

_____ 9. To have risked all your comforts, to have ventured your last dollar.

_____ 10. Those children listening to their mother under the old tree.

_____ 11. With this magic charm, you can enter the enchanted castle.

_____ 12. And made a beeline for the prettiest girl at the party.

Getting rid of a sentence fragment in your writing is not difficult. Often, a fragment belongs either to the sentence that precedes it or to the sentence that follows it. In such cases, simply combine the fragment with the appropriate sentence. Consider the following example.

> Have a seat and look at the paper. *In the meantime.* I'll finish fixing the dinner.

In this instance, the statements make sense only if the fragment *in the meantime* is combined with the sentence that follows it.

> Have a seat and look at the paper. *In the meantime,* I'll finish fixing the dinner.

Sometimes you can convert a fragment into a sentence by adding or changing a word or phrase.

Observe how the example fragments we presented at the beginning of this unit have been corrected.

> Olga, a chemistry major, minored in bacteriology, *hoping to improve her chances of working for a drug company.* (The fragment has been joined to the preceding sentence.)
>
> Olga, a chemistry major, minored in bacteriology. *She hoped to improve her chances of working for a drug company.* (The fragment has been changed into a complete sentence.)
>
> *Having been warned about the washed-out road,* we took another route. (The fragment has been joined to the following sentence.)
>
> Marco walked to the supermarket *to buy a carton of milk.* (The fragment has been joined to the preceding sentence.)
>
> I went to class *although I was not prepared.* (The fragment has been joined to the preceding sentence.)

Whenever you ask, he will help you. (The fragment has been joined to the following sentence.)

They've torn down the old house *in which I grew up.* (The fragment has been joined to the preceding sentence.)

We should never forget *that experience is the best teacher.* (The fragment has been joined to the preceding sentence.)

John washed the windows *and cleaned the basement.* (The fragment has been joined to the preceding sentence.)

John washed the windows. *He also cleaned out the basement.* (The fragment has been changed into a complete sentence.)

That old gentleman sitting on the park bench and feeding the pigeons was once the president of our largest bank. (The fragments have been joined together.)

Note that two of our fragments—those about Olga and John—can be readily corrected by either method.

Punctuating Your Corrections

When combining a fragment and a sentence (a main clause), put a comma between them if the first element is an adverb clause or long phrase, or if the sense of the sentence calls for a distinct pause between the two elements.

Because we couldn't swim, we stayed in shallow water. (The comma separates the adverb clause from the following main clause.)

We stayed in shallow water *because we couldn't swim.* (No comma is needed because the adverb clause follows the main clause.)

Making his way stealthily through the underbrush, the hunter approached his quarry. (The comma separates a long phrase from the following main clause.)

The owner went home for the afternoon, *leaving me in charge of the store.* (The comma marks a distinct pause between two elements.)

He bought the car *advertised in the paper.* (No comma is needed because there is no pause between the elements.)

EXERCISE

Ten main clauses paired with fragments are presented below. In each case, join the fragment and the main clause to make a new, complete, correctly punctuated sentence.

1. In just about one minute. I'm going to lose patience completely with you.

2. Casey would waltz with the strawberry blonde. While the band played on.

3. Because I couldn't find my car keys. I had to take the bus.

4. If I leave for Cleveland in the next hour. I'll arrive at the auditorium in time for the start of the rock concert.

5. While in Chicago, I visited the Sears Tower. Which is the tallest building I've ever seen.

6. Living in an apartment house is pleasant. Unless one requires a great deal of privacy.

7. Gail and Olive Bates have gone to the Catskill Mountains. To spend a quiet weekend.

8. Dennis bought a pound of pecans. And ate them in one evening.

9. Frustrated by a boss he could never please. Clayton quit the company.

10. Panting and red-faced from his efforts. The runner staggered across the finish line.

UNIT SELF-TEST

Identify each of the following word groups as a sentence (S) or a fragment (F) by writing the correct letter in the blank to the left.

___F___   Zack, playing as a defensive linebacker for the Indians.

_____   1. A theory that he had previously developed while studying psychology.

_____   2. But the tape player needs repairs.

_____   3. Because he hadn't read the directions properly.

_____   4. To avoid hitting the car in front of me.

_____   5. Burned by the rays of the midday sun.

The answers are on page 443.

UNIT REVIEW EXERCISE 7A
Avoiding Sentence Fragments

Identify each of the following word groups as a sentence (S) or a fragment (F) by writing the correct letter in the blank to the left.

F   Even though he had to support his aged mother.

_____ 1. The men sat tensely on the nylon webbing.

_____ 2. Each listening to the drone of the engines and thinking of the events to come.

_____ 3. They were a strange and sinister-looking group.

_____ 4. With their camouflaged steel helmets snugly strapped to their heads and olive drab parachute packs strapped to their backs.

_____ 5. Two of them finished their cigarettes and crushed them out with the heels of their boots as the light changed color and warned of the impending jump.

_____ 6. The lieutenant silently noted how smoothly and effortlessly the conglomerate of straps, ropes, canvas, and rubber deployed when the rear door of the aircraft opened hydraulically and the three howitzers were eased out.

_____ 7. Then he and his men followed their guns, drifting slowly to earth in seeming defiance of gravity.

_____ 8. The ground rose to meet them.

_____ 9. They shucked their harnesses and quietly busied themselves with their first task.

_____ 10. To prepare the guns for movement to the preselected site.

_____ 11. Time was of concern now that they were on the ground.

_____ 12. But prior planning and anticipation of problems speeded the action of the crew, and soon the gun carriages were rapidly bumping over the underbrush.

_____ 13. Leaving the drop zone and the now useless and discarded parachutes behind.

_____ 14. The dust swirled and eddied as the once bleak knob of drifting blow sand was transformed by men and machines into Firebase Zulu.

_____ 15. Once beetles and lizards had roamed here.

_____ 16. But now tires, grease drippings, and cordite testified to the presence of men too purposeful about their work to bother with creatures that crawled.

_____ 17. Three cold, impersonal, sinister-looking gun tubes jutted their necks toward the horizon.

_____ 18. While nearby a quiet hum and eerie green lights marked the location of the mechanical brain housed in the fire-direction-control computer.

_____ 19. The soldier who fed and cared for this awesome device carried no heavy shells and pulled no lanyard.

_____ 20. His hands were soft and clean, and he read books on philosophy during slack hours while sticking close to his charge.

_____ 21. Overhead could be heard the soft, scarcely audible buzz of a small observation helicopter.

_____ 22. The hum of the computer was drowned when the squawk of the radio announced the first fire mission.

_____ 23. And quickened the pace of the ground crews.

_____ 24. The range, direction, elevation, wind velocity, and humidity were fed into the computer.

_____ 25. Which instantly determined the necessary deflection and elevation settings for the guns and the fuse settings for the shells.

_____ 26. What had once taken several minutes for the lieutenant to compute.

_____ 27. Was now completed in seconds.

_____ 28. The action climaxed as the guns began barking loudly.

_____ 29. Sending their cruel messages to an unsuspecting target.

_____ 30. The cannoneers never saw their enemy.

_____ 31. But they knew their efficiency in killing far surpassed that of the infantry.

_____ 32. This fact had at first bothered the new man with gun three, but he now loaded the gaping breech mechanically and unthinkingly.

_____ 33. No longer a troubled youth but now a seasoned soldier.

_____ 34. Struck by the thought of how unnatural the scene before him would appear to an early cannoneer.

_____ 35. The lieutenant paused on his way toward the mess tent.

_____ 36. The ancient artilleryman would recognize the guns and the trained crewmen.

_____ 37. But how, bred to a tradition of personal valor, would he react to the observation helicopter, the radio, the computer—and the impersonal, long-distance killing they make possible?

_____ 38. Shrugging the thought from his mind, the lieutenant continued his walk toward the mess tent and a hot cup of coffee.

This exercise is adapted from a composition by William Ewald, a student.

UNIT REVIEW EXERCISE 7B
Avoiding Sentence Fragments

PART A

Eight sentence fragments are presented below. In each case, the italicized fragment is accompanied by a complete sentence (a main clause). Join the two together to make a new, correctly punctuated sentence; then write another, similar sentence.

This is the best apartment. *That I have ever lived in.*

This is the best apartment that I have ever lived in.

They were the sweetest apricots that we had ever tasted,

1. The owner went to the bank. *Leaving me in charge of the filling station.*

_____

_____

_____

_____

2. Penny bought a new blouse. *Made in Hong Kong.*

_____

_____

_____

_____

3. *By shopping for presents in November.* We avoided the Christmas crowds.

_____

_____

_____

_____

4. They selected a Picasso print. *To hang over their couch.*

_____

_____

_____

_____

5. The angry tennis player threw his racket on the ground. *And strode furiously off the court.*

_____

_____

_____

_____

6. *Although he had promised to come home early.* Arthur stayed out until midnight.

_____

_____

_____

_____

7. Stanley told Harriet. *That he was retiring in August.*

_____

_____

_____

_____

8. I know the girl. *Who won the state chess championship.*

_____

_____

_____

_____

PART B

Expand each of the following fragments to a complete sentence by adding material at the indicated spot.

Hoping to reduce their fuel bill, _they insulated_ _the attic._

1. _____
   to settle the whole matter out of court.

2. When winter comes and the snow forms great drifts along the

   highways, _____

   _____

3. Through the crowded corridor, down the stairs, and out into the

   busy sunlit street _____

   _____

4. Horrified at what he had found in the basement of the old deserted

    house, _____

    _____ .

5. _____

    after finishing her test and checking her answers carefully.

6. Late at night, when the sounds of traffic cease and I am all alone,

    _____ .

7. Anyone who could possibly study on a fine fall day like this _____

    _____ .

8. Our new minister, a man who once served as an army chaplain,

    _____ .

9. _____

    despite frenzied efforts to complete the project by term's end.

10. That he would be eliminated in the first round of competition

    _____ .

Comma Splices and Run-on Sentences

A run-on (fused) sentence occurs when one sentence is run into another without any punctuation and beginning capital letters to separate them. A comma splice occurs when two complete sentences are separated by a comma. These similar errors are serious but easily avoided. Here are several examples.

The plumbers voted to strike the electricians voted to stay on the job. (run-on sentence)

The plumbers voted to strike, the electricians voted to stay on the job. (comma splice)

Sam failed to bring an umbrella he was drenched in the cloudburst. (run-on sentence)

Sam failed to bring an umbrella, he was drenched in the cloudburst. (comma splice)

Armadillos are quite common in this part of the country there goes **one** now. (run-on sentence)

Armadillos are quite common in this part of the country, there goes one now. (comma splice)

Sven refused to attend the concert he said he hated classical music. (run-on sentence)

Sven refused to attend the concert, he said he hated classical music. (comma splice)

Candice studied two hours each night she got only a $C-$ in economics. (run-on sentence)

Candice studied two hours each night, she got only a $C-$ in economics. (comma splice)

These two types of errors cause difficulty for your reader and create the impression that you are hasty and careless. They can be corrected several ways.

1. *Separate the sentences with a period and a capital.*

Armadillos are quite common in this part of the country. There goes one now.

Sven refused to attend the concert. He said he hated classical music.

2. *Separate the sentences with a semicolon.*

Armadillos are quite common in this part of the country; there goes one now.

Sven refused to attend the concert; he said he hated classical music.

3. *Separate the sentences with a comma plus a coordinating conjunction (and, but, or, nor, for, yet, so).*

Sam failed to bring an umbrella, *and* he was drenched in the cloudburst. Candice studied two hours each night, *but* she got only a $C-$ in economics.

4. *Separate the sentences with a semicolon and a conjunctive adverb.*

A *conjunctive adverb,* as its name suggests, is a special adverb that is partially a conjunction. Like conjunctions, conjunctive adverbs serve as linking devices. Like adverbs, they modify sentences and sentence elements, showing such things as similarity, contrast, result or effect, addition, emphasis or clarity, time, and example. Here are the more commonly used connecting words and phrases, grouped according to the things they show.

Similarity	consequently	in other words
likewise	hence	indeed
similarly	therefore	that is
Contrast	thus	**Time**
however	**Addition**	afterwards
nevertheless	also	later
on the contrary	furthermore	meanwhile
on the other hand	in addition	subsequently
otherwise	in the first place	**Example**
Result or Effect	moreover	for example
accordingly	**Emphasis or Clarity**	for instance
as a result	in fact	to illustrate

The following sentences show the use of conjunctive adverbs.

Sam failed to bring an umbrella; *consequently,* he was drenched by the cloudburst.

Armadillos are quite common in this part of the country; *in fact,* there goes one now.

Candice studied two hours each night; *nevertheless,* she got only a $C-$ in economics.

Sometimes the conjunctive adverb is preceded by a coordinating conjunction. In this case the semicolon is replaced by a comma.

Sam failed to bring an umbrella, *and consequently* he was drenched by the cloudburst.

Candice studied two hours each night, *but nevertheless* she got only a $C-$ in economics.

Conjunctive adverbs can occur *within,* as well as between, complete sentences. When they occur internally, they are not preceded by a semicolon. Instead, they are set off with a pair of commas. If you don't know whether to use a semicolon or commas, cover up the conjunctive adverb and read what comes on each side of it. If each set of words is a main clause, use a semicolon. Otherwise, use commas. Consider the following example:

Usually, I buy my clothes in Greeley. This time *however* I went to Denver.

Covering up the *however* gives us *this time* and *I went to Denver.* Because *this time* is not a main clause, the *however* is internal and must be set off with commas.

This time, *however,* I went to Denver.

5. *Make one of the sentences into a dependent clause introduced by a subordinating conjunction* (although, because, provided that, since, until, whenever, while, *and the like*).

Because Sam failed to bring an umbrella, he was drenched by the cloudburst.

Although Candice studied two hours each night, she got only a $C-$ in economics.

EXERCISE

Indicate, by writing the correct abbreviation in the blank to the left, whether the sentence is correct (C), is a run-on sentence (RO), or contains a comma splice (CS).

_____RO_____   1. Don't leave so soon the party is just starting to get interesting.

_____   2. I try to be helpful, however, sometimes I succeed only in making a nuisance of myself.

_____ 3. We are not on daylight saving time, therefore, darkness comes very early.

_____ 4. Sometimes I feel very ambitious at other times, though, I am pretty lazy.

_Ro_____ 5. I don't like this coffee it is too cold and bitter.

_C_____ 6. Harvey lived in Ecuador for five years; consequently, he is fluent in Spanish.

_CS_____ 7. Omar decided to become an accountant, Karen enrolled in surveying.

_CS_____ 8. I believe that chemistry is a very overcrowded profession, and many experts agree with me.

_C_____ 9. This weather is terrible; the rain never seems to let up.

_CS_____ 10. Our employee incentive program is simplicity itself, make one mistake and you're fired.

_____ 11. Mordecai was the hero in last night's game, for he scored the winning run.

_____ 12. Wesley was up all night that's why he's sleeping now.

_____ 13. Inge isn't at home, so Ole is very upset.

_____ 14. Joe is a college senior his sister owns a beauty shop.

_____ 15. Ramón lost his part-time job, and therefore he couldn't continue in school.

Picking Your Method of Correction

The method of correction to use will depend upon the particular sentence pairs. When the two ideas are not closely related, using a period and capital letter—or a semicolon—is often preferable, unless a choppy effect results. Sometimes, in fact—as with the sentences about Sven—no other method of correction will do.

For more closely related ideas, use the method of correction that best shows the relationship between the ideas. As the sentences about Sam show a cause-effect relationship (he didn't bring an umbrella; he got drenched), either the subordinating conjunction *because* or the conjunctive adverb *consequently* is preferable to the coordinating conjunction *and*. The fact that Candice made only a $C-$ is probably more important than the fact that she studied hard. Therefore, the sentences about her are probably best corrected with the subordinating conjunction *although*.

> Sam failed to bring an umbrella; *consequently,* he was drenched by the cloudburst.
>
> *Because* Sam failed to bring an umbrella, he was drenched by the cloudburst.
>
> *Although* Candice studied two hours each night, she got only a $C-$ in economics.

In some cases—the "strike" sentences are an example—any of the methods of correction are suitable.

> The plumbers voted to strike. The electricians voted to stay on the job.
>
> The plumbers voted to strike; the electricians voted to stay on the job.
>
> The plumbers voted to strike, but the electricians voted to stay on the job.
>
> The plumbers voted to strike; however, the electricians voted to stay on the job.
>
> Although the plumbers voted to strike, the electricians voted to stay on the job.

UNIT SELF-TEST

Indicate, by writing the correct abbreviation in the blank to the left, whether the sentence is correct (C), is a run-on sentence (RO), or contains a comma splice (CS).

____CS____   Jane laughed, she obviously enjoyed the gift that Ted had given her.

_____   1. Helen, Mark, and Angela played several games of Scrabble; then they watched the late movie on TV.

_____   2. Scott's Uncle Rockworth owns the largest hotel in town his cousin Mortimer works there as a bellboy.

_____   3. Happiness isn't the most important thing in life; after all, it can't buy money.

_____   4. The stunt driver crashed his car into the flaming barricade his audience gasped in suspense.

_____   5. The low road is flooded, you'll have to take the high road.

The answers are on page 443.

UNIT REVIEW EXERCISE 8A
Comma Splices and Run-on Sentences

Indicate, by writing the correct abbreviation in the blank to the left, whether the sentence is correct (C), is a run-on sentence (RO), or contains a comma splice (CS).

_RO_   The fishermen displayed their unusual catch the neighbors crowded curiously around.

————   1. I've enjoyed meeting you; can't we have dinner together some day soon?

————   2. The card catalog is an important library research tool, every student should know how to use it.

————   3. Captain Mountjoy is on vacation call back next week.

————   4. Here comes Mr. O'Malley he'll tell us who won the basketball game.

————   5. Taxes have hit a record high here, nevertheless, they are even higher in England and Sweden.

————   6. Count Dracula regrets that he can't serve as a blood donor; if you leave your name, however, he'll be glad to help your group with a cash contribution.

————   7. Jessica wanted to excel at figure skating, but she often neglected to practice.

————   8. I took careful lecture notes, and consequently I scored higher on the midterm than anyone else in the class.

————   9. There is no one here to answer your questions, call again in about an hour.

————   10. Shelley has been our mayor for six years she knows every voter in the village.

89

———————   11. Oliver could see no reason to limit his eating, consequently, he soon weighed sixty pounds more than Stanley.

———————   12. Modesty was not one of Morris's outstanding traits; on the contrary, he bragged constantly about his brains, charm, and influential connections.

———————   13. The nightwatchman made his usual rounds all seemed in order.

———————   14. Our Thanksgiving vacation lasts two weeks, so my roommates and I are going skiing in Colorado.

———————   15. Once he had bought the expensive telescope, however, he found that he seldom used it.

UNIT REVIEW EXERCISE 8B
Comma Splices and Run-on Sentences

Following is a series of sentences with no punctuation or with incorrect punctuation between the independent clauses. In each instance, correct the sentence by three of the methods discussed earlier.

We vacationed in New York City our friends spent their holiday at a small country lake.

We vacationed in New York City. Our friends spent their holiday at a small country lake. / We vacationed in New York City; our friends spent their holiday at a small country lake. / We vacationed in New York City, but our friends spent their holiday at a small country lake.

1. I can't come to the phone right now please take a message for me.

_____

_____

_____

_____

_____

_____

2. Gideon wanted to become a doctor, Hector chose engineering as his profession.

_____

_____

_____

_____

_____

_____

3. They arrived late at the theater, they missed the first act.

_____

_____

_____

_____

_____

4. I am not acquainted with Mr. Rodney I have never heard of him before.

_____

_____

_____

_____

_____

5. He didn't work hard, the boss didn't promote him.

_____

_____

_____

_____

6. Industrial accidents are a serious problem both management and labor must look for ways to reduce the number of injuries that occur each year.

7. First we must finish studying for our midterms, then we'll drop over to your place.

8. Teach me a few magic tricks I want to surprise my friends.

_____

_____

9. We couldn't hear the speaker very clearly, moreover the lighting was bad.

_____

_____

_____

_____

_____

_____

10. You'll like living in Midland there are cultural and recreational activities to suit every taste.

_____

_____

_____

_____

_____

_____

UNIT 9

Making Subjects and Verbs Agree

A verb must agree in number with its subject. Number indicates whether a word is singular (one) or plural (more than one). Singular subjects—*man, dog, he,* and so on—require singular verbs. Plural subjects—*men, dogs, they,* and so on—require plural verbs.

Ordinarily, making subjects and verbs agree causes no problems. Long before we were grown, we were aware of the following rules.

> *Have* becomes *has* when used with *he, she, it,* or a singular noun.
>
> Any verb form showing present action and used with *he, she,* or *it* ends in *-s* or *-es.*

The following examples illustrate these points.

> (I, You, We, They, The men) have, run, go.
>
> (He, She, It, The man) has, runs, goes.

We also know the irregular forms of the verb *to be.*

> (I) am, was.
>
> (You, We, They) are, were.
>
> (He, She, It) is, was.

And because we do know these things, almost no one ever makes mistakes like the ones shown below.

> That were an exciting baseball game.
>
> Ken and Myra is coming to dinner this evening.
>
> You is silly.

However, the following special situations can cause problems.

Subject and Verb Separated by a Word Group

Sometimes the subject is separated from the verb by a word group that includes a noun. When you write this sort of sentence, be sure that the verb agrees in number with the subject of the sentence, not a noun in the word group.

> Our supply of nails *was* inadequate. (The singular verb *was* agrees with the singular subject *supply*, not with the plural noun *nails* in the prepositional phrase *of nails*.)
>
> Several courses required for my major *are* not being offered this term. (The plural verb *are* agrees with the plural subject *courses*, not with the singular noun *major* in the prepositional phrase *for my major*.)
>
> The map that accompanied your directions *was* very helpful. (The singular verb *was* agrees with the singular subject *map*, not with the plural noun *directions* in the subordinate clause *that accompanied your directions*.)

The number of the verb is not affected by phrases that begin with such expressions as *along with, as well as, in addition to, together with,* and *like,* which can come between the subject and the verb. As always, make the verb agree with the subject of the sentence.

> Mr. Jones, along with his son and daughter, *operates* a repair shop. (The singular verb *operates* agrees with the singular subject *Mr. Jones*.)
>
> The walls, as well as the ceiling, *were* freshly painted. (The plural verb *were* agrees with the plural subject *walls*.)

EXERCISE

Choose the correct verb form from the pair of verb forms in parentheses, and write it in the blank to the left.

———————— 1. The rules for this contest (is, are) too complicated.

———————— 2. The students in my dormitory (plans, plan) to have a party next weekend.

———————— 3. My next door neighbor, together with two friends from across town, (is, are) opening a fruit market.

———————— 4. The nicotine in cigarettes (causes, cause) an increase in the blood pressure of smokers.

———————— 5. Hunting in areas with heavy deer populations (helps, help) cut the animals' competition for food.

_____   6. The Finsters, as well as their son, (has, have) bought bicycles for a trip through Michigan's Upper Peninsula.

Two Singular Subjects

Singular subjects joined by *and* usually require a plural verb.

The dog and the cat *are* friends. (The verb *are* is plural.)

Grading papers and preparing lectures *take* up most of my evenings. (The verb *take* is plural.)

Few of us would use *is* in the first of these two examples. However, when the subjects are word groups like *grading papers* and *preparing lectures,* singular verbs are often mistakenly used.

When two singular subjects joined by *and* are preceded by *each* or *every,* use a *singular,* rather than a plural, verb.

Every cup and saucer *was* badly chipped. (*Every* makes a singular verb necessary.)

Each watercolor and etching *has* been signed by the artist. (*Each* makes a singular verb necessary.)

Singular subjects joined by *or, either—or,* or *neither—nor* require a singular verb.

A doctor or a nurse *is* always on hand.

Neither his house nor his yard *was* in very good shape.

Either Dr. Miles or Ms. Reynolds *is* the speaker for tonight.

EXERCISE

Choose the correct verb form from the pair of verb forms in parentheses, and write it in the blank to the left.

_____   1. Neither the New Left nor the New Right (supports, support) this bill.

_____   2. Eating sensibly and exercising regularly (has, have) caused me to lose twenty pounds.

_____   3. Every car and truck on the road (seems, seem) to be speeding today.

_____   4. Either Kevin or Harley (is, are) sure to win this race.

_____ 5. Each sword and pistol in my collection (has, have) been owned by a famous person.

_____ 6. Clean air and pure water (makes, make) this a nice place to camp.

One Singular and One Plural Subject

When one singular and one plural subject are joined by *or,* *either—or,* or *neither—nor,* the verb agrees in number with the subject that is closer to it.

A novel *or* a few short stories *help* an otherwise dull evening pass pleasantly. (The verb *help* agrees with the plural subject *stories,* which is closer to the verb.)

A few short stories *or* a novel *helps* an otherwise dull evening pass pleasantly. (The verb *helps* agrees with the singular subject *novel,* which is closer to the verb.)

Neither the office manager *nor* the secretaries *were* there. (The verb *were* agrees with the plural subject *secretaries,* which is closer to the verb.)

Neither the secretaries *nor* the office manager *was* there. (The verb *was* agrees with the singular subject *manager,* which is closer to the verb.)

EXERCISE

Choose the correct verb form from the pair of verb forms in parentheses, and write it in the blank to the left.

_____ 1. Either the cats or the dog (has, have) been digging in the flower bed.

_____ 2. Neither Penelope nor her brothers (feel, feels) like joining the Photography Club.

_____ 3. Two apples or a sandwich (constitutes, constitute) my usual lunch.

_____ 4. Either the head gasket or the piston rings (is, are) responsible for our loss of power.

_____ 5. The principal or his two assistants (is, are) always available.

_____ 6. Neither the rooms nor the food (was, were) particularly good.

"Each," "Either," and "Neither" as Subjects

When the pronouns *each, either,* and *neither* are used as subjects, they always take singular verbs.

Each of the books *has* been favorably reviewed.
Neither *was* told about the meeting.
Neither of the men *was* told about the meeting.
Either of the plaques *makes* an attractive wall decoration.

Agreement errors are most likely to occur when the pronoun and the verb are separated by a word group. Other pronouns of this same sort (*anyone, everyone, someone, no one, nobody, nothing,* and so forth) almost never cause problems.

EXERCISE

Choose the correct verb form from the pair of verb forms in parentheses, and write it in the blank to the left.

——————— 1. Each of our employees (holds, hold) stock in the company.

——————— 2. Neither of the stolen cars (has, have) been recovered.

——————— 3. Either of these movies (is, are) well worth seeing.

——————— 4. Neither of our children (knows, know) how to swim.

——————— 5. Each (has, have) received an award for perfect attendance.

——————— 6. Either of these floor lamps (is, are) suitable for our living room.

Collective Nouns as Subjects

Collective nouns are nouns that are singular in form but stand for a group or collection of individuals or things. Here are some examples.

assembly	committee	crowd	group	mob	team
audience	company	family	herd	squad	tribe
class	convoy	flock	jury	staff	troop

In most instances, collective nouns are regarded as single units and therefore require singular verbs.

> The class *is* in the library. (*Class* is considered a unit.)
>
> The convoy *was* headed for the harbor. (*Convoy* is considered a unit.)

Occasionally, though, a collective noun is regarded as a group of individuals acting separately. In such cases, the collective noun takes a plural verb.

> The Thurston family *are* heavy drinkers. (*Family* in this instance is considered a collection of individuals, each of whom acts independently.)
>
> The panel *disagree* on who is to act as their spokesman. (In this sentence *panel* must take a plural verb because the individuals it includes are acting separately.)

EXERCISE

Choose the correct verb form from the pair of verb forms in parentheses, and write it in the blank to the left.

_____   1. The choir (is, are) practicing for the final concert of the season.

_____   2. The committee (is, are) drafting a final report.

_____   3. The staff (is, are) arguing about how to handle this problem.

_____   4. Our team (practices, practice) three hours each day.

Sentences in Which the Verb Comes Ahead of the Subject

Sentences that follow the pattern in which the verb comes ahead of the subject may begin with a phrase or such words as *here, there, how, what,* and *where.* In each case, the verb must agree in number with the subject that follows it.

> Beyond the blue horizon *lies* an enchanted land. (The singular verb *lies* agrees with the singular subject *land.*)
>
> Beyond the blue horizon *lie* cities of enchantment. (The plural verb *lie* agrees with the plural subject *cities.*)
>
> Where *is* my book? (The singular verb *is* agrees with the singular subject *book.*)
>
> Where *are* my books? (The plural verb *are* agrees with the plural subject *books.*)

There *is* no battery in that flashlight. (The singular verb *is* agrees with the singular subject *battery*.)

There *are* several ways of checking the answer. (The plural verb *are* agrees with the plural subject *ways*.)

EXERCISE

Choose the correct verb form from the pair of verb forms in parentheses, and write it in the blank to the left.

——————   1. There (is, are) many reasons for my becoming a vegetarian.

——————   2. How (is, are) Mrs. Johnson and her new baby?

——————   3. Here (comes, come) the Willetts and the Stokowskis now.

——————   4. There (is, are) a quick solution to this problem.

——————   5. After many a summer (dies, die) the swan.

——————   6. What (is, are) the reason for this racket?

——————   7. Where (is, are) the snows of yesteryear?

——————   8. Within this jungle (lurks, lurk) many dangerous beasts.

Sentences with Linking Verbs and Subject Complements

A linking verb agrees with its subject, not with the subject complement that follows it.

My favorite fruit *is* bananas. (The verb *is* agrees with the singular subject *fruit*.)

Bananas *are* my favorite fruit. (The verb *are* agrees with the plural subject *bananas*.)

EXERCISE

Choose the correct verb form from the pair of verb forms in parentheses, and write it in the blank to the left.

——————   1. The center of attention (was, were) the bride and groom.

_____   2. My favorite breakfast (is, are) ham, eggs, and toast.

_____   3. Rare coins (is, are) a good investment.

_____   4. Nursery rhymes (is, are) my little niece's favorite reading.

UNIT SELF-TEST

Choose the correct verb form from the pair of verb forms in parentheses, and write it in the blank to the left.

does   If the quality of the surveys (does, do) not improve, we may have to replace the entire crew.

_____   1. In the far corner of the room (was, were) an overturned chair and a shattered vase.

_____   2. The party for the retiring employees (was, were) held in a large rented hall near the office.

_____   3. Where (is, are) the books we got from the library?

_____   4. Their assessment of our difficulties (seems, seem) reasonable.

_____   5. Two plums or an orange (makes, make) a good midafternoon snack.

The answers are on page 443.

UNIT REVIEW EXERCISE 9A
Making Subjects and Verbs Agree

For each sentence below, choose the correct verb form from the pair of verb forms in parentheses, and write it in the blank to the left.

was   The man who designed these buildings (was, were) born in Japan.

_____ 1. There (was, were) hardly room to move in the crowded lounge.

_____ 2. The woman heading our staff of advertising copy-writers (hold, holds) degrees in journalism and English.

_____ 3. Each of the children (was, were) outstanding in school.

_____ 4. Neither Jim nor his friends (drives, drive) as much since gasoline prices have become so high.

_____ 5. Despite reports of enemy submarines, the convoy (was, were) preparing to depart.

_____ 6. Either the Bidwells or Marge Stevenson (is, are) responsible for the mixup in reservations.

_____ 7. Edward Finch, together with his two brothers, (is, are) on an automobile trip through Ontario.

_____ 8. Beyond the beach (grows, grow) a large oak tree and a clump of pines.

_____ 9. Raisins (is, are) an excellent source of iron.

_____ 10. Each car and truck (has, have) had an oil change.

_____ 11. The guests in the old Victorian hotel (was, were) evacuated after the fire was discovered.

_____ 12. A completely different set of results (has, have) been obtained this time.

_____ 13. Henry and Roberta Benson, along with their daughter Wilma, (has, have) joined Weight Watchers.

_____ 14. A shirt or some socks (makes, make) a nice Christmas gift.

_____ 15. Foolish investments and lavish entertaining (has, have) consumed much of their wealth.

UNIT REVIEW EXERCISE 9B
Making Subjects and Verbs Agree

Supply a proper verb for each of the following sentences, and then write a similar sentence.

The committee ___*are*___ unable to reach a decision.

Because the jury were unable to arrive at a verdict, the accused remained a free woman.

1. Look, there _____ old Mr. Grimes and his dog, Spot.

_____

_____

2. My father's pipe, as well as his slippers, _____ been missing since we moved.

_____

_____

3. Reaching the top of the rise, the members of the wagon train saw,

to their horror, that a large herd of buffalo _____ stampeding toward them.

_____

_____

4. Two muffins or a bowl of cold cereal _____ all Meg ever has for breakfast.

_____

_____

5. _____ either of these streets been scheduled for repaving?

_____

_____

6. Every door and window of the dilapidated old tenement _____ in need of replacement.

_____

_____

7. Either the butler or the two gardeners _____ guilty of murdering Sir Peregrine.

_____

_____

8. Where _____ my friends when I needed help?

_____

_____

9. Neither rain nor snow _____ ever stopped our mailman from making his deliveries.

_____

_____

10. Art prints _____ a good investment—sometimes!

_____

_____

UNIT 10

Choosing the Right Verb Form

Using a verb that does not agree in number with its subject is not the only kind of error involving verb forms. Several other types of verb errors occur so frequently that they merit special attention. These errors include using the wrong *principal part*, confusing *lie* with *lay* and *sit* with *set*, omitting the final *-d* from certain verbs, and using *nonstandard verb forms*.

Using Principal Parts

All verbs have three *principal parts*—the *present*, the *past*, and the *past participle*. The present principal part is used to show present and future time.

> I *go* to the beach once a week. (The verb *go* shows present, repeated action.)
>
> She *is* the speaker today. (The verb *is* shows a present state of being.)
>
> I *shall go* to the beach tomorrow. (The verb phrase *shall go* shows future action.)
>
> She *will be* the speaker at our next meeting. (The verb phrase *will be* shows a future state of being.)

Sentences in which the *present* form of the verb appears without a helping verb are in the *present tense*. Sentences in which the *present* form of the verb appears with *shall* or *will* are in the *future tense*.

The past principal part of a verb is its *past tense*, and it shows that an action or a state of being occurred at a particular time in the past.

> Maria *completed* her computer program yesterday. (The verb *completed* shows a past action.)
>
> Robert *was* unhappy about his performance on the test. (The verb *was* shows a past state of being.)
>
> I *came* to college a year ago. (The verb *came* shows a past action.)

Past participles can perform two different functions in sentences. As we have already seen (p. 59), participles and the phrases built around them can function as adjectives. However, when past participles appear with forms of the helping verb *to have,* they are elements of verb phrases and are considered verbs. When used with *has* or *have,* the past participle shows that an action, a state of being, or the effects of either have begun in the past and continue until the present.

> Norman *has worked* as a laboratory technician for five years. (An action begun five years ago continues in the present.)
>
> William *has finished* his report. (The effect of the past action continues in the present.)
>
> The players *have been* irritable since they lost the homecoming game. (The state of being, begun in the past, continues in the present.)

Verb phrases formed by *has* or *have* and the *past participle* are in the *present perfect tense.*

When used with *had,* the past participle shows that one past action or state of being ended before or after another past action or state of being.

> He *had been* sick for several years before he died. (The italicized state of being occurred first.)
>
> Michele bought a new typewriter. She *had wanted* one for years. (The italicized action occurred first.)
>
> Ten seconds after the bell, the classroom *had emptied* completely. (The italicized action occurred last.)

Verb phrases formed by *had* and the *past participle* are in the *past perfect tense.*

When used with *shall have* or *will have,* the past participle form shows that an action or a condition will be completed at some specified future time.

> I *shall have satisfied* the requirements for my degree by next June. (The future action will have been completed.)
>
> In two weeks, our president *will have been* with the company twenty-five years. (The future state of being will have been completed.)

Verb phrases formed by *shall have* or *will have* and the *past participle* are in the *future perfect tense.*

Past participles of active verbs also appear in combination with forms of the verb *to be.* These combinations are discussed on page 59.

Most verbs have the same past and past participle forms (for example, I *walked,* I have *walked*; she *heard,* she has *heard*). However, a sizable number of verbs have different past and past participle forms, and many usage problems result from confusing these forms (for example, I have *went* for I have *gone*). Following are forty common verbs that are especially likely to cause this sort of difficulty.

Present	Past	Past Participle
arise	arose	arisen
bear	bore	borne
become	became	become
begin	began	begun
bite	bit	bitten
blow	blew	blown
break	broke	broken
choose	chose	chosen
come	came	come
do	did	done
draw	drew	drawn
drink	drank	drunk
drive	drove	driven
eat	ate	eaten
fall	fell	fallen
fly	flew	flown
forget	forgot	forgotten
freeze	froze	frozen
give	gave	given
go	went	gone
grow	grew	grown
know	knew	known
ride	rode	ridden
ring	rang	rung
rise	rose	risen
run	ran	run
see	saw	seen
shake	shook	shaken
sing	sang	sung
sink	sank	sunk
speak	spoke	spoken
spring	sprang	sprung
steal	stole	stolen
swear	swore	sworn
swim	swam	swum
take	took	taken
tear	tore	torn
throw	threw	thrown
wear	wore	worn
write	wrote	written

Memorizing the principal parts of any verb that gives you trouble will help prevent this kind of error. Until you have the parts down pat, check this list or consult a good desk (not pocket) dictionary whenever you can't decide which form is right.

EXERCISE

Choose the correct principal part from the pair of verbs in parentheses and write it in the blank to the left.

_____   1. The price of gasoline has (rose, risen) every year since the Arab oil embargo.

_____   2. I have (tore, torn) my dress at the collar.

_____   3. The children (sang, sung) the songs they had learned in school.

_____   4. Our dog (eat, ate) the meat we had planned to cook for dinner.

_____   5. We haven't (spoke, spoken) to each other since our big argument.

_____   6. Marge (saw, seen) the bank robbers make their getaway.

_____   7. A man (come, came) into the gas station and asked for directions to the football stadium.

_____   8. The tornado has (blew, blown) our house down.

_____   9. Tom thought he had (gave, given) the right answer.

_____   10. Mrs. Peters said she had (went, gone) to London twice before.

_____   11. The phone (rang, rung) several times before someone answered it.

_____   12. Tatiana has not (wore, worn) that bracelet before.

_____   13. Have you ever (drove, driven) to New York?

_____ 14. My bicycle tire (sprang, sprung) a leak last evening.

_____ 15. She has (forgot, forgotten) her keys.

Confusing "Lie" and "Lay" and "Sit" and "Set"

The use of *lay* for *lie* is very common in informal spoken English ("I'm going to lay down."). Nonetheless, this usage is incorrect and when you write or speak in formal situations, as in class or on the job, you will need to make careful distinctions between these verbs.

To *lie* means "to be or to remain in a horizontal position." Because we can't remain things, this verb never takes a direct object: it is an *intransitive* verb. The following sentences illustrate the three principal parts of *lie*.

> I *lie* down for a nap each afternoon. (present)
> I *lay* down for a nap yesterday afternoon. (past)
> I have *lain* down for a nap every afternoon this week. (past participle)

To *lay* means "to place." Because we do place things, this verb always takes a direct object: it is a *transitive* verb. The following sentences illustrate the verb's principal parts.

> Those two men *lay* bricks for a living. (present)
> Those two men *laid* over twelve hundred bricks yesterday. (past)
> Those two men have *laid* an average of twelve hundred bricks every day this month. (past participle)

Notice that the past principal part of *lie* and the present principal part of *lay* are identical—a fact that goes a long way toward explaining the confusion between the two verbs.

Sit and *set* do not cause as much trouble as *lie* and *lay*. Nevertheless, they too are often confused, as shown by such errors as "Come in and set awhile" and "I sat the dish on the sideboard."

To *sit* means "to rest on one's haunches" as in a chair. Like *lie*, it is intransitive. The following sentences illustrate the verb's principal parts.

> Sometimes I *sit* on the floor when I watch TV. (present)
> We *sat* on the floor when we ate at that Japanese restaurant. (past)
> I have *sat* through some pretty terrible movies in my time. (past participle)

To *set* means "to place in position." Except in a few special cases, it is always transitive. Notice that the verb's three principal parts are identical.

I *set* my briefcase on the desk when I come home at night. (present)

I *set* my briefcase on the desk when I came home last evening. (past)

I have *set* the package on the desk. (past participle)

Set occasionally functions as an intransitive verb, such as when it is governed by the subject *sun*.

The sun *set* behind the hills.

Whenever you have trouble choosing between *lie* and *lay* or *sit* and *set*, check to see whether the sentence has a direct object. If there is none, the intransitive *lie* or *sit* is the right verb. If there is a direct object, the transitive *lay* or *set* is required. To determine the right form of the verb, check to see whether it is accompanied by a helping verb. If it is, use the past participle form. If it isn't, check the time of the action or condition. For present or future time, use the present form. For past time, use the past form. Now let's apply these guidelines to the following sentences.

Barry _____ in the sun because he wants a tan. (Is the correct verb *lie* or *lay*? Which form of the correct verb is required?)

I _____ close to the stage at last night's play. (Is the correct verb *sit* or *set*? Which form of the correct verb is required?)

Joanna has _____ the new carpet in her living room. (Is the correct verb *lie* or *lay*? Which form of the correct verb is required?)

The first two sentences have no direct object, and so the correct verbs are *lie* and *sit*. The third sentence does have a direct object, and so the correct verb is *lay*. The first sentence is talking about present action ("he wants a tan") and the second about past action ("at last night's play"). These two sentences should therefore read as follows:

Barry *lies* in the sun because he wants a tan.

I *sat* close to the stage at last night's play.

The final sentence includes the helping verb *has,* and therefore it should read as follows:

Joanna has *laid* the new carpet in her living room.

EXERCISE

Choose the correct verb form from the pair of forms in parentheses, and write it in the blank to the left.

_____   1. Our cat was so sick it just (lay, laid) on the floor even when we offered it some fish.

_____   2. Harold (set, sat) waiting for us until we arrived home.

_____ 3. Don't (lie, lay) the book on that hot radiator.

_____ 4. This treaty has (laid, lain) the groundwork for greater cooperation between our two countries.

_____ 5. (Sit, Set) the vase down, and I'll put these flowers in it.

_____ 6. If you expect to get well, you must (lie, lay) down and rest.

_____ 7. (Sit, Set) on the couch; it's more comfortable than that chair.

_____ 8. The clerk (sat, set) the pile of shirts on the counter.

_____ 9. Those lazy people have (laid, lain) in bed all morning.

_____ 10. In the morning, (set, sit) the trash out by the curb.

_____ 11. For his summer job, Rupert (lay, laid) pipe for a building contractor.

_____ 12. You have (set, sat) around long enough; get up and go to work.

Omitting Endings from Certain Verbs

Omitting endings involves dropping the -d or -ed from verbs that have the same past and past participle principal parts. The most common errors include the use of _ask_ for _asked, prejudice_ for _prejudiced, suppose_ for _supposed,_ and _use_ for _used._ These errors are shown below.

I _ask_ my roommate yesterday to lend me his tweed jacket.

The governor's reputation as an alcoholic _has prejudice_ his chances for reelection.

Lucinda mistakenly _suppose_ that she would receive an invitation to the party.

Henry _use_ to work for General Motors.

Although such omissions are generally difficult to detect in an individual's speech—for example, there is very little difference between the sound of _suppose to_ and _supposed to_—the error is considered serious, and you should be careful to avoid it in your writing. The correct verb forms of the sentences given above follow.

> I *asked* my roommate yesterday to lend me his tweed jacket.
>
> The governor's reputation as an alcoholic *has prejudiced* his chances for reelection.
>
> Lucinda mistakenly *supposed* that she would receive an invitation to the party.
>
> Henry *used* to work for General Motors.

EXERCISE

Write the correct form of the italicized verb in the blank to the left.

————————————— 1. I had *suppose* that my uncle would meet us at 7 P.M., but he never showed up.

————————————— 2. I *use* to collect coins, but now I collect stamps.

————————————— 3. When Bonnie *ask* for more pie, her mother said no.

————————————— 4. William's lies have *prejudice* everyone against Burton.

Use of Nonstandard Verb Forms

Some usages are considered nonstandard and should be avoided whenever you speak or write. Common errors include the use of *busted* for *broke, broken,* and *burst; drownded* for *drowned; swang* for *swung* and *throwed* for *threw* and *thrown.* Here are four examples of these errors.

> The balloon *busted* when Sam tried to blow it up.
>
> My typewriter is *busted.*
>
> When ten years old, I nearly *drownded.*
>
> The children *swang* all afternoon in the park.

The correct verb forms are as follows:

> The balloon *burst* when Sam tried to blow it up.
>
> My typewriter is *broken.*
>
> When ten years old, I nearly *drowned.*
>
> The children *swung* all afternoon in the park.

EXERCISE

Write the correct form of the italicized verb in the blank to the left.

———————— 1. The children *throwed* a tantrum when their parents refused them more candy.

———————— 2. That's the third plate you've *busted* today.

———————— 3. Tarzan, pursuing Jane's kidnappers, *swang* through the jungle trees.

———————— 4. Ten sailors *drownded* when the ship sank.

———————— 5. The flask *busted* because the pressure in it became too high.

UNIT SELF-TEST

Choose the correct verb form from the pair of verb forms in parentheses, and write it in the blank to the left.

written Your brother has (wrote, written) me directions on how to get to his cottage.

———————— 1. Each Saturday morning, I (lie, lay) around the house and read the papers.

———————— 2. Because of the subzero temperatures, our water pipes have frozen and (burst, busted)

———————— 3. He couldn't finish the article because someone had (tore, torn) the last page out of the magazine.

———————— 4. Pam has (rode, ridden) her bike to work every day this week.

———————— 5. Manfred (suppose, supposed) he would win a spot on the first team.

The answers are on pages 443 and 444.

UNIT REVIEW EXERCISE 10B
Choosing the Right Verb Form

Each of the following sentences is written with the basic form of a verb. Write the correct principal part of the verb in the blank to the left; then write a similar, correct sentence using this principal part.

swum I have *swim* out to the raft and back several times.

I have swum the 500 - meter freestyle and the 1500 - meter backstroke in competition.

_____ 1. When he had *finish* his speech, he was roundly applauded.

_____ 2. Although I *ring* the bell several times, no one answered.

_____ 3. It was so cold the car battery had *freeze*.

_____ 4. The foundations of the electrical generation building *sink* three inches in the first year.

119

——————   5. They *lay* the hero to rest last Friday.

——————   6. Because of the stormy weather yesterday, most people *choose* to stay home.

——————   7. Father gave me a cookie because I had *eat* all of my vegetables.

——————   8. When the children had *ride* the Ferris wheel, they were ready to go home.

——————   9. The pitcher *throw* the runner out at second base.

——————   10. Sims has just *break* the world record for the 100-yard dash.

UNIT 11

Avoiding Errors in Showing Time

Errors in showing time include unwarranted shifts in time (tense) and failure to make clear the order in which two past events occurred.

Unwarranted Shifts in Time

When describing a series of events or a past situation, beginning writers sometimes make unwarranted and confusing shifts from past to present time and vice versa. Such shifts are especially likely in summaries of the plots of plays, movies, and stories. The following paragraph contains two unwarranted shifts in time.

> When Framton Nuttel first *arrives* at Mrs. Sappleton's home, he *is* greeted by her niece, Vera, who *announces* that she *will entertain* him until her aunt *comes* downstairs. Vera, a compulsive storyteller, *proceeded* [shift from present to past tense] to tell Framton a beautifully tragic but completely false tale about the death of her aunt's husband and two brothers. She *said* that three years before, the three *had gone* hunting and *perished* in a bog, and that their bodies *were* never *recovered*. Framton *believes* [shift from past back to present tense] her.

To prevent such shifts, you must pay close attention to the time frame of the events or situation you are describing and shift time only when the narrative time changes. Here is a corrected version of the above paragraph, in the present tense.

> When Framton Nuttel first *arrives* at Mrs. Sappleton's home, he *is* greeted by her niece, Vera, who *announces* that she *will entertain* him until her aunt *comes* downstairs. Vera, a compulsive storyteller, *proceeds*

121

to tell Framton a beautifully tragic but completely false tale about the death of her aunt's husband and two brothers. She *says* that three years before, the three *went* hunting and *perished* in a bog, and that their bodies *were* never *recovered*. Framton *believes* her.

The future *will entertain* in the first sentence is correct because the entertainment must follow the announcement. The next-to-last sentence retains the past tense because it deals with an event that supposedly occurred before Framton's visit to Mrs. Sappleton. Alternatively, this paragraph may be rewritten in the past tense.

When Framton Nuttel first *arrived* at Mrs. Sappleton's home, he *was greeted* by her niece, Vera, who *announced* that she *would entertain* him until her aunt *came* downstairs. Vera, a compulsive storyteller, *proceeded* to tell Framton a beautifully tragic but completely false tale about the death of her aunt's husband and two brothers. She *said* that three years before, the three *had gone* hunting and *had perished* in a bog, and that their bodies *had* never *been recovered*. Framton *believed* her.

Note the use of the helping verb *had* in the next-to-last sentence with the past participles *gone, perished,* and *recovered*. This sentence deals with events that supposedly occurred earlier than the events of the narrative as a whole, and is therefore written in the past perfect tense.

Other unwarranted time shifts can also occasionally occur. The following example includes an unwarranted shift to future time. As a result, the sentence says that Mr. Gotrox has bought a car that is not yet on the market.

Mr. Gotrox *has bought* the 1933 Bugatti sedan that *will go* on sale today.

EXERCISE

Indicate, by writing the correct letter in the blank to the left, whether the sentence is correct (C) or contains an unwarranted shift in time (S).

_____   1. Do you remember the interesting toys you have when you were a child?

_____   2. I have been working as a landscape architect this summer, and I found the work very satisfying.

_____   3. Students who wish to reduce the costs for their books will find they will pay less at the off-campus book store.

_____   4. Mary closes her eyes and after what seems like a few minutes found that morning had come.

———————— 5. As we open the door to go outside, we received a blast of sleet in the face.

———————— 6. The doorbell rang, and Nora turned off her radio before she answers the door.

———————— 7. All night long the waves buffeted my boat, and I think I'll never live through the storm.

———————— 8. Last year, Lawrence ran for sheriff but failed to win.

———————— 9. We wanted everything that we'll see on this shopping trip.

———————— 10. When Laura started to play her harp, everyone has stopped to listen.

Past Times Not Shown Properly

Often, as in the second corrected version of the paragraph about Framton Nuttel, you will need to indicate that one past action or condition ended before or after another past action or condition occurred. To do so, use the past tense of one main verb and the past perfect tense (*had* plus the past participle) of the other main verb, as in the following sentence.

Bob *bought* a new lamp because he *had broken* the old one.

Failure to do so can cause you to misstate the time relationship of the events, as in the following sentences.

The team *scored* two touchdowns when the first quarter *ended*.
Fifteen minutes after the store *closed* all the shoppers *left*.

The first of these sentences indicates that the team scored two touchdowns at the moment the first quarter ended. The second indicates that all the shoppers in the store at closing time left exactly fifteen minutes later. The first situation is impossible; the second is at best highly unlikely. When misstatements of this sort occur in your writing, you must decide which verb needs to be changed in order to correct the situation. Usually, it will be the verb for the earlier event, but sometimes it will be the verb for the later event.

The team *had scored* two touchdowns when the first quarter ended. (The verb indicating the earlier action has been changed.)
Fifteen minutes after the store *closed* all the shoppers *had left*. (The verb indicating the later action has been changed.)

If two past events occurred at the same time or nearly the same time, then use the past form for both verbs. Similarly, if you wish to show that two actions occurred in the past—rather than that one occurred and that the other was completed—use the past tense for both verbs.

When the bell *rang,* the students *rushed* out the door.
Every time Bill *started* his homework, someone *interrupted* him.

EXERCISE

Indicate, by writing the correct letter in the blank to the left, whether the sentence is correct (C) or presents past sequences incorrectly (I). If the sentence is incorrect, circle the error.

_____   1. Phyllis sold the car that she had bought two weeks before.

_____   2. William wore a flower that he picked from his garden.

_____   3. When I made the coffee, I sat down and drank a cup.

_____   4. Last week he visited the town where he had lived as a child.

_____   5. The judges awarded Shannon a prize for the novel she wrote.

_____   6. General Gung Ho decorated his walls with weapons that he captured during his last campaign.

_____   7. Darrin and Tammy said that they made two hundred dollars at their garage sale.

_____   8. As thunder crashed and lightning dazzled the night sky, the children cowered fearfully in the living room.

_____   9. Two hours after the cruise ship sank, twenty bodies washed ashore.

_____   10. Seth married the woman he had courted for five years.

UNIT SELF-TEST

Indicate, by writing the correct letter in the blank to the left, whether the sentence is correct or contains an error in showing time.

C = correct
S = unwarranted shift in time
I = incorrect past time sequence

___S___   The assembly line starts operating at 7 A.M. and usually ran until 6 P.M.

_____ 1. Last year Altman played lead guitar in a rock band and sings most of the vocals.

_____ 2. After the patient had undressed, the doctor began the examination.

_____ 3. The three men entered the bank furtively, and after quick glances in all directions they draw guns and announced a holdup.

_____ 4. She told the instructor that she finished the test ten minutes ago.

_____ 5. Yesterday I washed the curtains and waxed the kitchen floor.

The answers are on page 444.

UNIT REVIEW EXERCISE 11A
Avoiding Errors in Showing Time

Indicate, by writing the correct letter from the list below in the blank to the left, whether the sentence is correct or contains an error in showing time.

C = correct
S = unwarranted shift in time
I = incorrect past time sequence

____C____ The cat darted toward the squirrel that had come into the front yard.

_____ 1. Before they read the bad reviews, they decided to skip the movie.

_____ 2. As the weeks pass, Columbus's men became more and more frightened and talked of turning back.

_____ 3. Strolling the streets of Calcutta, we saw beggars so starved they are hardly able to hold their heads up.

_____ 4. Today is the day for my big job interview; after breakfast I rushed to my car and try to start it—only to fail completely.

_____ 5. The men piled on trucks and left hurriedly for higher ground, knowing that they did all they could to keep the dike from breaking.

_____ 6. After she had completed the report, she relaxed by listening to a record.

_____ 7. When Lucy walks into the shop, the first thing she saw was the proprietor dusting his objets d'art.

_____ 8. Dishes rattled and the skillet clanged against the stove as my parents hurry to prepare the evening meal.

_____ 9. Wherever Ramonda looked in the bazaar, she saw pottery, leather goods, and brass ornaments that she wishes to buy.

127

_____ 10. Because I heard so much about Houston, I felt delighted about my forthcoming visit there.

_____ 11. Have you received the bonus the company will give its employees?

_____ 12. As the speaker finished, her audience broke into applause.

_____ 13. As I approached the office door, the first thing I heard is the secretary tap-tapping on the typewriter.

_____ 14. The Rotary Club had sold all the tickets to the play three days before it opened.

_____ 15. The students listened intently as the instructor lectured on the comma.

UNIT REVIEW EXERCISE 11B
Avoiding Errors in Showing Time

Rewrite the following sentences to correct the errors in showing time.

During the 1960s, the connection between smoking and lung cancer becomes generally accepted by tobacco researchers.

During the 1960s, the connection between smoking and lung cancer became generally accepted by tobacco researchers.

1. After Tammie has carefully read the instructions for assembling the swing, she got her tools and set to work.

2. Marilyn worked for the company six months when she received her first promotion.

3. As the careering car headed for the sidewalk, pedestrians shouted and scurry to get out of the way.

4. I have jogged for about six months and notice that I was much less tense now.

_____

_____

_____

5. Paul hadn't received the graduation present that his parents are going to give him.

_____

_____

_____

6. The rooms in the old castle were dark and gloomy, and it is easy to imagine that ghosts prowl the midnight corridors.

_____

_____

_____

7. Sally told Tim that she wrote her mother an hour before.

_____

_____

_____

8. Once the instructor had worked the problem in class, I see my mistake.

_____

_____

_____

9. One hour after I went to bed, lightning struck the tree in my front yard.

_____

_____

_____

10. After he rested awhile, he began studying again.

_____

_____

_____

The Passive Voice

Transitive verbs have two *voices: active* and *passive*. A verb is in the *active voice* when the subject of the sentence performs the action named by the verb.

> Teresa planned a party. (The subject *Teresa* performs an action; the verb *planned* is in the active voice.)

A verb is in the *passive voice* when the subject of the sentence receives the action described by the verb. The noun or pronoun that tells who performed the action may appear in a prepositional phrase or remain unmentioned. The following sentences illustrate the passive voice.

> A party was planned by Teresa. (The subject *party* receives an action; the verb phrase *was planned* is in the passive voice.)
>
> The party *has been postponed*. (The verb phrase *has been postponed* is in the passive voice.)
>
> The party is *to be held* next week instead. (The infinitive phrase *to be held* is in the passive voice.)

The first of these sentences includes a prepositional phrase that names the person who performed the action. In the second and third sentences, the performer is not identified.

A passive verb consists of some form of *be* followed by the past participle of a transitive verb. Sometimes a helping verb such as *can, may, shall,* or *will* accompanies the passive phrase. Like the verb forms we studied on page 107, passive verbs may show past, present, or future time.

> I *am awakened* by my clock radio each morning. (present, repeated action; present tense)

I *was awakened* by a violent thunderstorm last night. (past action; past tense)

I *will be given* the details of the new sales plan tomorrow. (future action; future tense)

I *have been hired* for a one-year trial period. (The effect of a past action continues until present; present perfect tense)

I *had been told* about Professor Schmidt's retirement before he announced it. (The past action occurred before the earlier past action; past perfect tense)

In just two more days, a new president *will have been elected.* (The future action will have been completed; future perfect tense)

EXERCISE

Indicate, by writing the correct letter in the blank to the left, whether the italicized portions of the following sentences are in the active (A) or the passive (P) voice.

_____ 1. That woman over there *has been accused* of shoplifting, but she emphatically denies the charge.

_____ 2. Nadine Perry *was struck* by a car last evening.

_____ 3. Her parents *gave* Wendy a new watch for her birthday.

_____ 4. Witnesses said that the getaway car *had been driven* by Chester Stark.

_____ 5. The members of our club *have chosen* Maxine Willoughby as their new president.

_____ 6. By 7 P.M., I *shall have finished* my term paper.

_____ 7. He *is humiliated* constantly by his supposed friends.

_____ 8. You *will be informed* of our decision within three days.

_____ 9. I *have loved* you from the very day I first met you.

_____ 10. In six more weeks, I *will have been employed* by this company for twenty years.

Drawbacks of the Passive Voice

The passive voice gives your writing a flat, impersonal tone and almost always requires more words than the active voice. Consider the following paragraph, written largely in the passive voice.

Graft becomes possible when gifts are given to police officers or favors are done for them by persons who expect preferential treatment in return. Gifts of many kinds may be received by officers. Often free meals are given to officers by the owners of restaurants on their beats. During the Christmas season, officers may be given liquor, food, or theater tickets by merchants. If favored treatment is not received by the donors, no great harm is done. But when traffic offenses, safety code violations, and the like are overlooked by the officers, corruption results. When such corruption is exposed by the newspapers, faith is lost in the law and law enforcement agencies.

Note the livelier tone of the following revised version, which is written largely in the active voice.

Graft becomes possible when police officers accept gifts or favors from persons who expect preferential treatment in return. Officers may receive gifts of many kinds. Often restaurant owners provide free meals for officers on local patrol. During the Christmas season, merchants make gifts of liquor, food, or theater tickets. If donors do not receive favored treatment, no great harm is done. But when officers overlook traffic offenses, safety code violations, and the like, corruption results. When the newspapers expose such corruption, citizens lose faith in the law and law enforcement agencies.

This version has twenty-three fewer words than the earlier version, and is livelier as well.

Situations Where the Passive Voice Is Preferable

Because of its livelier, more emphatic tone, the active voice is usually more effective. Nonetheless, there are certain situations where the passive voice is better. Occasionally, for instance, it may be desirable to conceal someone's identity. Consider this memorandum from a supervisor to a group of employees who have consistently taken overly long coffee breaks.

At the monthly supervisors' meeting, it was suggested that coffee breaks be suspended permanently unless employees immediately limit them to ten minutes. The suggestion was approved. Please observe the ten-minute limit from now on so that such action will not be necessary.

To prevent hostile comments and harassment, the supervisor deliberately uses the passive voice to conceal the name of the person who made the suggestion.

Technical and scientific writing commonly makes use of the passive voice to explain how processes are or were carried out. In such descriptions the action, not the actor, is important, and an objective, impersonal tone is desirable.

> To obtain a water sample for dissolved oxygen analysis, a B.O.D. bottle is completely filled and then capped so no air is trapped inside. Next, 2 ml of manganese sulfate solution is added, well below the surface of the sample, and this is followed by 2 ml of alkali-iodine-oxide agent. The bottle is then stoppered carefully, so as to exclude air bubbles, and the contents are mixed by inverting the bottle at least 15 times.

There are times when the passive voice is preferable in everyday writing.

> The garbage is collected once a week—on Monday.
> The aircraft carrier was commissioned last August.

In these sentences, just as in the scientific example above, what was done, rather than who did it, is the important thing. Omitting the name of the doer gives the action the necessary emphasis.

Except in such special situations, however, you should try to use the active voice.

UNIT SELF-TEST

Indicate, by writing the correct letter in the blank, whether the sentence is in the active (A) or the passive (P) voice.

___P___   The instructions have been followed by Todd.

_____ 1. These new rules will apply to all our employees.

_____ 2. Your suggestion has been adopted by the committee.

_____ 3. Mr. Gilbert's lecture on Saudi Arabia was announced last week.

_____ 4. Ned is known for his skill in storytelling.

_____ 5. They are trying a new approach to the problem.

The answers are on page 444.

UNIT REVIEW EXERCISE 12A
The Passive Voice

Indicate, by writing the correct letter in the blank to the left, whether the sentence is in the active (A) or the passive (P) voice.

___P___ The surveyor's transit has been locked in the cupboard.

_____ 1. The high rate of absenteeism among the employees was discussed by the supervisors.

_____ 2. The leaky faucet has been repaired.

_____ 3. In a few days, everyone will be told the details of our new vacation policy.

_____ 4. The guests had not been told about the burnt roast.

_____ 5. She has not learned how to be assertive.

_____ 6. Sheldon is looking for a way out of his financial difficulties.

_____ 7. Several old warehouses have been converted into low-cost apartment buildings.

_____ 8. You will be given an award for your safety suggestion.

_____ 9. The rules for use of the gymnasium will be reviewed by the recreation committee.

_____ 10. As soon as the spare tire had been put on, the flat was taken to the nearest service station.

_____ 11. The switch is attached to the wall with four screws.

_____ 12. He has overcome all his father's objections to the trip.

137

_____ 13. Corn was introduced to the Pilgrims by friendly American Indians.

_____ 14. If we are lucky, the car will have been repaired by this time tomorrow.

_____ 15. I have been looking for you all afternoon.

UNIT REVIEW EXERCISE 12B
The Passive Voice

Rewrite each of the following sentences, converting those that are in the active voice to the passive voice and those that are in the passive voice to the active voice.

On Christmas morning, the presents were opened by the family.

On Christmas morning, the family opened the presents.

1. Copper is being replaced by aluminum as an electrical conductor for high-temperature service.

_____

_____

2. We have scraped all the old putty and dirt from the window frame.

_____

_____

3. The new ice arena will be opened by the city in about two weeks.

_____

_____

4. We have just installed a new computer in our main office.

_____

_____

5. New fire extinguishers have been purchased for the building.

_____

_____

6. Two hours after its disappearance, the stolen auto was returned by the thieves.

_____

_____

7. The start of the game was signaled by a loud buzzer.

_____

_____

8. All of the prizes in the contest will be furnished by Mid-State Chevrolet, Incorporated.

_____

_____

9. The city has just repaired the pavement in front of my house.

_____

_____

10. Donna's party was enjoyed by all the guests.

_____

_____

UNIT 13

Making Pronouns and Antecedents Agree

At one time or another in your reading, you may have come across a sentence such as this: "Governor Winkoop's antecedents were English and French." The term *Antecedent* means "ancestors," but not just human ancestors. Pronouns also have antecedents—the nouns and noun substitutes to which they refer. Ordinarily, the antecedent comes ahead of the pronoun, just as our ancestors have come ahead of us. Occasionally, though, the antecedent follows the pronoun.

> Eleanor fixed *her* bicycle. (The antecedent *Eleanor* precedes the pronoun *her.*)
>
> After *he* had eaten, Father played with the puppies. (The antecedent *Father* follows the pronoun *he.*)

Like verbs with their subjects, pronouns should agree in number with their antecedents. If the antecedent is singular, the pronoun should be singular. If the antecedent is plural, the pronoun should be plural. The following pointers will help in the special situations that are most likely to cause problems.

Indefinite Pronouns as Antecedents

When we discussed pronouns on page 23, we mentioned a group that do not refer to specific persons or things. These are the indefinite pronouns. When the following indefinite pronouns are used as antecedents, the pronouns that refer to them should be singular.

each	anyone	someone
each one	anybody	somebody
either	anything	something
either one	everyone	no one
neither	everybody	nobody
neither one	everything	nothing

> Anyone who has finished *his* test may leave. (The singular pronoun *his* refers to the indefinite pronoun *anyone*.)
>
> Neither of the salesmen had met *his* quota. (The singular pronoun *his* refers to the indefinite pronoun *neither*.)

Recently, the use of *his or her* has become common when the sex of the antecedent is unknown, as in the first sentence above.

> Anyone who has finished *his or her* test may leave.

Don't, however, use the *his or her* construction so often that your writing becomes awkward and distracting to your reader. The use of *he* as a general reference (the so-called generic *he*) is standard in English and should not necessarily be considered sexist. However, sometimes one can rewrite the sentence in the plural and avoid apparent sexism.

> *Those* who have finished *their* tests may leave.

Occasionally, a ridiculous result occurs when a singular pronoun refers to an indefinite pronoun that is obviously plural in meaning.

> Everybody complained that the test was too hard, but I didn't agree with *him*. (*Everybody* is plural in meaning; the singular *him* makes the sentence ridiculous.)
>
> Everyone was talking, so I told *him* to quiet down. (*Everyone* is plural in meaning; the singular *him* makes the sentence ridiculous.)

In such cases, recast the sentence to eliminate the problem.

> Everybody complained that the test was too hard, but I didn't think so. (The sentence has been recast.)
>
> Everyone was talking, so I asked for silence. (The sentence has been recast.)

In informal writing and speaking, there is an increasing tendency to use plural pronouns with indefinite pronoun antecedents.

> Each of the players took *their* turn.
>
> Someone has left *their* muddy footprints on the floor.

However, because many people object to this practice, you should avoid it in your own writing and speaking.

EXERCISE

Choose the correct pronoun from the pair in parentheses, and write it in the blank to the left.

—————— 1. Anyone wanting a successful college career must devote much of (his, their) time to studying.

—————— 2. The general realized that everyone in the audience had (his, their) idea of what a just war is.

—————— 3. No one should force (his or her, their) interests on other members of the family.

—————— 4. The fortune-teller said that somebody in the room would lose (his, their) life before the evening ended.

—————— 5. In an ideal world, everyone should be (his, their) own confessor.

—————— 6. The sheriff asked each one of the witnesses whether (he, they) could describe the robber.

—————— 7. The secretary of the ski club urged everybody to pay (his, their) dues before the end of the month.

Two Singular Antecedents

Two or more antecedents joined by *and* usually require a plural pronoun.

His car and boat were left in *their* usual places.

Harold, Norman, and Lucinda finished *their* joint presentation ten minutes early.

However, when the antecedents are preceded by *each* or *every*, the pronoun should be singular.

Every family and business must do *its* part to conserve energy. (*Every* makes a singular pronoun necessary.)

Each college and university sent *its* budget request to the legislature. (*Each* makes a singular pronoun necessary.)

Singular antecedents joined by *or, either—or,* or *neither—nor* require singular pronouns.

Has either John or Bill finished *his* report?

Neither Margaret nor Jane has completed *her* preparations for the trip.

A badger or a fox has made *its* home in this burrow.

Applying this rule will sometimes result in an awkward or ridiculous sentence. In such cases, recast the sentences to avoid the problem.

Neither Sharon nor Roger has written *his or her* thank-you note. (The sentence is not only awkward but also ambiguous.)

Sharon and Roger have not written thank-you notes. (The sentence has been recast.)

Neither Sharon nor Roger has written a thank-you note. (The sentence has been recast.)

Sharon has not written a thank-you note, and neither has Roger. (The sentence has been recast.)

EXERCISE

Choose the correct pronoun from the pair in parentheses, and write it in the blank to the left.

_____ 1. Neither Orland nor Jake volunteered (his, their) services for the Campus Cleanup Campaign.

_____ 2. Each supervisor and superintendent agreed that (he, they) would contribute to the local Red Cross drive.

_____ 3. When asked to make statements, Shannon and Zula insisted on (her, their) right to remain silent.

_____ 4. Having opened the refrigerator, Tammy and Delia helped (herself, themselves) to the caviar I'd been hoarding.

_____ 5. Questioned by the reporter, neither Doreen nor Madge would reveal (her, their) political affiliation.

_____ 6. To cope with tornadoes, each city and town set up (its, their) special warning system.

_____ 7. I've been told that either Orville or Wilbur will fly (his, their) unique plane in next Saturday's race.

_____ 8. The instructor praised Ian and Wesley for (his, their) fine work during the term.

Singular and Plural Antecedents

If one singular and one plural antecedent are joined by *or, either—or,* or *neither—nor,* the pronoun agrees in number with the closer antecedent.

Either Jim Forbes or the *Mastersons* will lend us *their* car. (The pronoun *their* agrees with the plural antecedent *Mastersons.*)

Either the Mastersons or *Jim Forbes* will lend us *his* car. (The pronoun *his* agrees with the singular antecedent *Jim Forbes.*)

Sometimes you must write the antecedents in one particular order to express the desired meaning.

Neither the superintendent nor the *workers* recognized their peril. (The pronoun *their* agrees with the plural antecedent *workers.*)

Neither the workers nor the superintendent recognized *his* peril. (The pronoun *his* agrees with the singular antecedent *superintendent.*)

Notice that the meaning is different in these sentences. In the first, the peril is to everyone. In the second the peril is to the superintendent only.

EXERCISE

Choose the correct pronoun from the pair in parentheses, and write it in the blank to the left.

_____ 1. I'm told that neither Betty Myers nor the Engels filed (her, their) income taxes on time.

_____ 2. As of last week, neither his cousins nor Adam had decided on (his, their) vacation itinerary.

_____ 3. A dog or two cats could maintain (itself, themselves) quite well on our family's table scraps.

_____   4. Either the Borum brothers or Ronald Drag will show (his, their) travel slides at the meeting.

_____   5. Every time I glanced out the window, I saw Tim's parents or Tim sunning (himself, themselves) on the roof deck.

_____   6. The hostess asked that either Fran Jones or the Gibsons move (her, their) car.

Collective Nouns as Antecedents

On page 99 we learned that collective nouns (*assembly, committee, squad,* and so forth) are singular in form but stand for a group of individuals or things.

If a collective noun is regarded as a single unit, the pronoun that refers to it should be singular. If the collective noun is regarded as a group of individuals acting separately, then the pronoun should be plural.

> The group presented *its* resolution. (The group is acting as a unit.)
>
> The flock of geese returned to *its* nesting place. (The flock is acting as a unit.)
>
> The council debated whether *they* should pass or reject the new parking ordinance. (The council is acting as a group of individuals.)
>
> Yesterday the team signed *their* contracts for the coming season. (The team is acting as a group of individuals.)

EXERCISE

Choose the correct pronoun form from the pair in parentheses, and write it in the blank to the left.

_____   1. The board will announce (its, their) decision next week.

_____   2. The faculty couldn't agree on rules for (itself, themselves).

_____   3. Our new club held (its, their) first meeting right after New Year's.

_____   4. We watched the crowd leaving the theater and scattering toward (its, their) homes.

_____ 5. Having completed the survey, the committee voted (itself, themselves) out of existence.

_____ 6. The flotilla weighed anchor and steamed toward (its, their) destination.

_____ 7. The mob roared (its, their) approval of the speaker's remarks.

_____ 8. The squad of police took (its, their) positions around the building housing the terrorists.

UNIT SELF-TEST

Choose the correct pronoun from the pair in parentheses, and write it in the blank to the left.

___*his*___ Everyone should turn in (his, their) term papers on Friday of this week.

_____ 1. The Drama Club had (its, their) picture taken for the high school yearbook.

_____ 2. Notwithstanding the cold and rainy weekend, both Harold and Norman seemed to be in (his, their) usual cheery mood.

_____ 3. Every man, woman, and child had (his or her, their) eyes glued on the tall fin slicing swiftly through the water.

_____ 4. I challenge anyone who thinks (he, they) can beat me at chess.

_____ 5. The president and the sales manager, like any other employee of the company, had to serve (himself, themselves) in the cafeteria.

The answers are on page 444.

UNIT REVIEW EXERCISE 13A
Making Pronouns and Antecedents Agree

Choose the correct pronoun form from the pair in parentheses, and write it in the blank to the left.

him or her   If anyone objects to this proposal, now is the time for (him or her, them) to speak up.

_____ 1. The committee debated the proposal vigorously, but at day's end (it, they) had reached no decision.

_____ 2. Nobody should leave valuables in (his, their) car without locking the door.

_____ 3. Neither Joan nor Mary had reason to complain about the treatment (she, they) received after the boating accident.

_____ 4. Despite the acute distress of many in the audience, no one was allowed to leave (his or her, their) seat until the three-hour television show had been taped.

_____ 5. If you see William or his brother, tell (him, them) to get in touch with me.

_____ 6. Neither of the two hoboes looked as if (he, they) had ever had a bath.

_____ 7. The graduating class was unanimous in (its, their) choice of Ralph Nader as commencement speaker.

_____ 8. Each of the actors in the school play has been given tickets for (his or her, their) parents.

_____ 9. Someone in the restaurant has blocked the exit from the parking lot with (his, their) car.

149

_____ 10. After a day of sightseeing, neither Roberta nor Donna felt much like spending (her, their) evening at a disco.

_____ 11. Everyone, like it or not, remembers (his, their) most embarrassing moments.

_____ 12. The school will furnish the beverage, but each boy and girl must bring (his or her, their) own food to the picnic.

_____ 13. The squad of soldiers set about performing (its, their) different duties.

_____ 14. Neither Mr. Lovett nor his sons had finished (his, their) breakfast when I arrived.

_____ 15. Each waiter and busboy said that (he, they) would attend the employees' Christmas party.

UNIT REVIEW EXERCISE 13B
Making Pronouns and Antecedents Agree

Supply the proper pronoun for each of the following sentences; then write a similar correct sentence.

Anyone who contributes $100.00 to the building fund will have

___*his*___ name engraved on the plaque in the lobby.

Anybody who wants transportation to the actresses' workshop should sign her name on the circulating sheet.

1. Everyone drove _____ own car to the party.

_____

_____

_____

2. Neither Elmer nor Monte has had _____ research proposal approved.

_____

_____

_____

3. Each of the members of the school band will be held responsible

for _____ uniform.

_____

_____

_____

4. Anyone who believes hockey is easy should try it _____ .

_____

_____

_____

5. His slide rule and calculator were missing from _____ usual spot.

_____

_____

_____

6. Neither Mavis nor her friends had made _____ vacation plans.

_____

_____

_____

7. Everyone participating in the dog show expected to have

_____ entry singled out for Best of Show.

_____

_____

_____

8. After four hours, the city council still had not reached agreement

on the size of _____ salary increase.

_____

_____

_____

9. Every bus and truck in our organization must have

   _____ tires replaced.

   _____

   _____

   _____

10. If everyone does _____ duty, we will win this battle.

    _____

    _____

    _____

UNIT 14

Avoiding Faulty Pronoun Reference

Except for indefinite pronouns, every pronoun you write should refer clearly and unmistakably to one particular noun or noun substitute—its antecedent. Note the following example.

> After checking out the books from the library, Arlie put *them* in the car. (The pronoun *them* clearly refers to the noun *books.*)

Unfortunately, it is all too easy to produce sentences without clearly evident antecedents. Reference can be faulty because the pronoun has more than one possible antecedent, a hidden antecedent, or no antecedent at all. Such errors slow the pace of reading and can cause your reader to misunderstand your meaning. In addition, ridiculous sentences sometimes result. Here are some suggestions to help you correct these errors.

More Than One Antecedent

The following sentences are unclear because they include more than one possible antecedent.

> Take the radio out of the car and sell *it*. (It is unclear whether the radio or the car should be sold.)
>
> The supervisors told the sheet-metal workers that *they* would receive a bonus. (It is unclear whether supervisors or workers will receive a bonus.)

Sometimes writers will produce a sentence like the one below.

> If the fans don't buy all the pennants, pack *them* away until the next game. (*Pennants* is clearly the antecedent, but the presence of *fans* makes the sentence sound ridiculous.)

You can correct both of these kinds of faults by substituting a noun for the pronoun or by rephrasing the sentence.

> Take the radio out of the car, and then sell the car. (A noun has been substituted for the pronoun.)
>
> The supervisors told the sheet-metal workers, "Congratulations, you have won a merit bonus." (The sentence has been rephrased as a quotation to make its meaning clear.)
>
> The supervisors complimented the sheet-metal workers on receiving a merit bonus. (The sentence has been rephrased to make its meaning clear.)
>
> The supervisors told the sheet-metal workers to expect a bonus. (The sentence has been rephrased to make its meaning clear.)
>
> The supervisors told the sheet-metal workers that they themselves were expecting a bonus. (The sentence has been rephrased to make its meaning clear.)
>
> Pack away any unsold pennants, and save them for the next game. (The sentence has been rephrased so that it is no longer ridiculous.)

EXERCISE

Indicate, by writing the correct letter in the blank to the left, whether the sentence is correct (C) or contains a faulty pronoun reference (F).

_____   1. Millie asked Suzanne how she liked her new hat.

_____   2. Nobody is ready for the test, so I'll postpone it a week.

_____   3. Move the car out of the garage and paint it.

_____   4. When children won't pick up their toys, pack them away in boxes.

_____   5. Mother asked me whether I thought she had been impolite.

_____   6. After Jeff had paid Brad, he looked relieved.

_____   7. Because my parents like oysters, I served them as an appetizer.

_____ 8. Jack told Henry that he was getting gray hair.

_____ 9. Albert told Sue that she was tired and needed to rest.

_____ 10. When the ladies had finished making the quilts, they were boxed for distribution to needy people.

_____ 11. Mary visited Sally while she was in town.

_____ 12. The instructor reminded the students that their themes were due on Friday.

_____ 13. Take the screens off the windows and wash them.

Hidden Antecedents

An antecedent is hidden if it is serving as an adjective rather than as a noun. Here are two sentences with hidden antecedents.

> When I removed the table's finish, _it_ proved to be oak. (_It_ ought to refer to _table_, which in this sentence appears as the adjective _table's_.)
>
> The popcorn bowl was empty, but we were tired of eating _it_ anyhow. (_It_ ought to refer to _popcorn_, which in this sentence is an adjective.)

To correct this error, substitute a noun for the pronoun, or switch the positions of the adjective and the pronoun, and then make whatever changes are required by correct English.

> When I removed its finish, the table proved to be oak. (The adjective and the pronoun have been switched and their forms have been changed accordingly.)
>
> The popcorn bowl was empty, but we were tired of eating popcorn anyhow. (The noun has been substituted for the pronoun.)

EXERCISE

Indicate, by writing the correct letter in the blank to the left, whether the sentence is correct (C) or contains a faulty pronoun reference (F).

_____ 1. Oboe playing can be very relaxing, but it is a difficult instrument to master.

_____ 2. Jack's father felt proud when he received a promotion to manager.

_____ 3. An inspection of the soldiers' barracks revealed that they had done a thorough job of cleaning and straightening up.

_____ 4. While I was dishing up its food, the cat kept meowing constantly.

_____ 5. As the wolf approached the sheep paddock, they moved to its far side.

_____ 6. When the clown appeared at the children's party, they clapped and shouted.

_____ 7. He called Thelma's house three times, but she never answered the phone.

_____ 8. Five minutes after our arrival at their dock, the Shotwells were taking us for a boat ride.

No Antecedent at All

A no-antecedent sentence is one without any noun to which the pronoun can refer. Sentences of this sort are common in informal speech, but you should avoid them in formal writing or speaking. The following sentences show this error.

> The street is bustling with activity because *they* are doing their Christmas shopping.
> I have always wanted a garden, and last summer I did *it.*
> *It* says in this article on leukemia that many cases are now being cured.

To correct such a sentence, substitute an appropriate noun for the pronoun, or reword it to avoid the problem.

> The street is bustling with activity because people are doing their Christmas shopping. (A noun has been substituted for the pronoun.)
> I have always wanted a garden, and last summer I finally grew one. (The sentence has been reworded to avoid the problem.)
> This article on leukemia says that many cases are now being cured. (The sentence has been reworded to avoid the problem.)

Sometimes a *this, that, it,* or *which* will refer not to a single noun but to a whole idea. This usage is perfectly acceptable as long as the writer's meaning is obvious, as in the following sentence.

> The instructor lost our midterm exams, *which* meant we had to take the test again.

Problems can arise, however, when the reader can't figure out which of two or more ideas the pronoun refers to. Consider this faulty example.

> Harry called Bert two hours after the agreed-upon time and canceled their next-day's fishing trip. *This* made Bert very angry.

Here, we cannot tell whether the late call, the cancellation of the fishing trip, or both caused Bert's anger. Again, the problem can be corrected by the addition of a clarifying word or phrase or by rewording.

> Harry called Bert two hours after the agreed-upon time and canceled their next-day's fishing trip. This *tardiness* made Bert very angry. (The clarifying word *tardiness* has been added.)

> Harry called Bert two hours after the agreed-upon time and canceled their next-day's fishing trip. *Harry's change of plans* made Bert very angry. (The sentence has been reworded to avoid the problem.)

EXERCISE

Indicate, by writing the correct letter in the blank to the left, whether the sentence is correct (C) or contains a faulty pronoun reference (F).

_____   1. Roger called the emergency room, but they didn't answer.

_____   2. I called the newspaper and told them I wished to advertise a used shotgun.

_____   3. Caught cheating on the examination, Pam tried to lie her way out of it.

_____   4. Because we had blown a tire, it caused us to arrive one hour behind schedule.

_____   5. When the cars collided, they screamed.

_____   6. The instructor insisted that his students attend the lecture and write a summary of it, which irritated them greatly.

_____   7. Nowadays they let everybody graduate from high school.

_____   8. Armbruster thought that acting would be an easy profession, but since becoming one he has changed his mind.

———————— 9. The locker room was very noisy because the players were celebrating their victory.

———————— 10. My father spoke to me severely, which hurt my feelings.

———————— 11. Some people are financially able to retire at sixty-five, but for others it brings hardship.

———————— 12. The boss told Sheila's associates that she had written an excellent report. This made Sheila feel good.

UNIT SELF-TEST

Indicate, by writing the correct letter in the blank to the left, whether the sentence is correct (C) or contains a faulty pronoun reference (F).

__F__ We called the police station and told them there had been a car accident.

———————— 1. The receptionists told the typists that they should be making more money.

———————— 2. The energy crisis will not ease soon, so any effort to conserve it will benefit everyone.

———————— 3. The street was very quiet after the riot because they were all inside.

———————— 4. Nobody is ready for the test, so it will be postponed.

———————— 5. They say that more than half of all auto accidents involve drunken drivers.

The answers are on pages 444 and 445.

UNIT REVIEW EXERCISE 14A
Avoiding Faulty Pronoun Reference

Indicate, by writing the correct letter in the blank to the left, whether the sentence is correct (C) or contains a faulty pronoun reference (F).

___F___ Every Saturday evening, Neville would go to a nearby disco and dance until they closed.

_____ 1. I have never seen a crocodile, but I have read about them in school.

_____ 2. Mary called Carolyn and asked if she thought she should go to the party.

_____ 3. William plans to work for a brokerage house as that is his father's occupation.

_____ 4. The young man was unemployed, and it made him sad.

_____ 5. Bob called his mother and asked her whether his girl friend could come to dinner.

_____ 6. Alvin found that the Craftwell Corporation had excellent fringe benefits and paid its employees very well, which improved his morale greatly.

_____ 7. Always remove the rug from the room before cleaning it.

_____ 8. When Malcolm accidentally walked into the ladies' room, they burst out laughing.

_____ 9. NOW is a prominent organization, and they work actively for women's rights.

_____ 10. This is Marion's sister and her husband, Mike.

_____ 11. If the guests don't eat all the appetizers, put them in the refrigerator.

_____ 12. I discussed my plans with several friends, and they all said they approved.

_____ 13. If raw milk disagrees with the baby, it should be boiled.

_____ 14. It says in the paper that this winter will be colder than normal.

_____ 15. Tom's brother asked him to go fishing because he enjoyed the sport.

UNIT REVIEW EXERCISE 14B
Avoiding Faulty Pronoun Reference

Rewrite each of the following sentences to correct the faulty pronoun reference.

Jessica's mother was delighted when her first novel was accepted for publication.

Jessica's mother was delighted when her daughter's first novel was accepted for publication.

1. When Norbert entered the faculty lounge, they all stopped talking.

_____

_____

2. This restaurant serves good food, but they don't get much business.

_____

_____

3. Jean's cousin moved away when she was a little girl.

_____

_____

4. Delbert told his father that he needed to buy new shoes.

_____

_____

5. As soon as the tube in my bicycle tire was patched, I rode it home.

_____

_____

6. Tommy insisted loudly on playing his new opera records for his friends, which bothered them greatly.

_____

_____

7. When Mildred talked to her sister, she said the temperature in Minneapolis was twenty degrees below zero.

_____

_____

8. During the Mardi Gras, they all put on outlandish costumes.

_____

_____

9. When Charles poked the snake's cage, it hissed.

_____

_____

10. Because the cat did not get along well with the dog, Joan's parents gave it away.

_____

_____

UNIT 15

Avoiding Unwarranted Shifts in Person

Pronouns can be in the first person, second person, or third person. First person pronouns (for example, *I, me, mine, we, us, ourselves*) identify people who are speaking or writing about themselves. Second person pronouns (*you, your, yours, yourself, yourselves*) identify people who are being addressed directly. Third person pronouns (for example, *he, she, it, his, hers, its, they, theirs, himself*, and any indefinite pronoun) identify people or things that are being spoken or written about. You will notice that there are singular and plural forms for each person, although in the case of *you, your*, and *yours*, the singular and plural forms are identical.

> *I* invited *my* neighbors to spend a week with *me* at *my* cottage. (*I, my*, and *me* refer to the speaker and are first person singular pronouns.)
>
> *You* are perfectly capable of fixing *your* breakfast *yourself*. (*You, your*, and *yourself* refer to the person being addressed directly and are second person singular.)
>
> *They* told *themselves* that *someone* would recognize *their* plight and save *them*. (*They, themselves, someone, their*, and *them* refer to persons being spoken about and are third person plural pronouns.)

Beginning writers often shift carelessly from one person to another, usually from the third person to the second. The following examples illustrate unwarranted shifts.

> If an employee works hard, *he* has many opportunities for advancement, and eventually *you* might become a department supervisor. (The shift is from third to second person.)
>
> An understanding roommate is one *you* can tell *your* personal problems to. This kind of roommate knows when *I* want to be alone and respects *my* wish. (The shift is from second to first person.)

165

After working as a cashier for six months, *I* welcomed a promotion to bookkeeper with *her* own office. (The shift is from first to third person.)

You can avoid such errors by paying careful attention to the pronouns you use in each sentence and by making sure that no shifts occur as you go from one sentence to the next. Notice the improved smoothness and clarity of the corrected examples.

If an employee works hard, *he* has many opportunities for advancement, and eventually *he* might become a department supervisor. (The sentence uses the third person only.)

An understanding roommate is one *you* can tell *your* personal problems to. This type of roommate knows when *you* want to be alone and respects *your* wish. (The sentence uses the second person only.)

After working as a cashier for six months, *I* welcomed a promotion to bookkeeper with *my* own office. (The sentence uses the first person only.)

Not all shifts in person are unwarranted. Consider, for example, the following correct sentences.

I would like *you* to take this sales report to Ms. Carter's office. *She* asked to borrow it.

Here the speaker identifies himself or herself (*I*) while speaking directly to a listener (*you*) about someone else (*she*). In such cases, shifts are necessary in order to get the message across.

EXERCISE

Indicate, by writing the appropriate letter in the blank to the left, whether the sentence is correct (C) or contains an unwarranted shift in person (S).

_____   1. Participants in the meeting should come prepared to discuss the items on the agenda and to bring up any other matter you consider important.

_____   2. Ask John whether he will lend me his biology textbook this afternoon.

_____   3. Students in the laboratory must handle the transformers carefully, and please use your voltmeter when checking them.

_____   4. Anyone wishing to attend the departmental luncheon should sign your name on this sheet.

_____   5. Have you found out why they didn't invite you to their party?

_____   6. When I ask Rochelle to help me with my homework, sometimes she turns you down.

_____   7. A child is likely to reject a new food that is markedly different from the usual fare, but as we grow older we become more willing to experiment.

_____   8. For safer winter driving, drivers should put snow tires on their cars.

_____   9. I buy a lottery ticket every week even though I know your chances of winning a big prize are very slim.

_____   10. Unless you have a good grounding in grammar, nobody can hope to succeed as a technical writer.

UNIT SELF-TEST

Indicate, by writing the appropriate letter in the blank to the left, whether the sentence is correct (C) or contains an unwarranted shift in person (S).

___S___   We are well aware that you can't depend on Langley for any help.

_____   1. When a person smokes, you inhale cancer-producing chemicals with every puff.

_____   2. According to the theory of reincarnation, your subconscious mind carries the memories of all our previous lives.

_____   3. While participating in a track meet, a runner shouldn't think of what you're doing.

_____   4. After Dmitri had finished the day's work, he walked to the commissary, where he ate a bowl of borscht soup.

_____   5. In August everyone welcomes a cool day, but you know that the relief from the heat is only temporary.

The answers are on page 445.

UNIT REVIEW EXERCISE 15A
Avoiding Unwarranted Shifts in Person

Indicate, by writing the correct letter in the blank to the left, whether the sentence is correct (C) or contains an unwarranted shift in person (S).

___S___ When I told the employees that the factory would close for a month, you could see the shock in their faces.

_____ 1. If you'll promise never to cut down another cherry tree, George, I'll let you keep your hatchet.

_____ 2. When we weren't on duty, employees could use any recreational facility at the resort.

_____ 3. Everyone should eat an adequate, nutritionally balanced breakfast so you will have the energy to work at full capacity during the morning.

_____ 4. Failure to secure hotel reservations is one of the worst mistakes anyone can make while you are planning a vacation.

_____ 5. Every customer who buys a stove or refrigerator during our twentieth anniversary sale is eligible to compete for the Florida vacation we are offering.

_____ 6. We think our boss is wonderful; he is always ready to help you with problems that arise on the job.

_____ 7. Students who wish to save money on their books will find that you will pay less for them at the Off-Campus Book Emporium.

_____ 8. If you are planning to visit New York City, be sure to read *The New Yorker*'s "Goings on About Town" section just before you go; it will tell you what interesting events will be taking place while you are there.

169

—————   9. Once a person has learned to ride a bicycle, you never forget how.

—————   10. Mary's ability to make others smile merely by smiling herself and to make you laugh when things go wrong has earned her many friends.

—————   11. If one compares the statistics for automobiles and firearms, you will see that each year twenty-five times more people are killed by cars.

—————   12. How peaceful everything seems when you are walking in the country, and how quickly life becomes hectic again when you return to the city.

—————   13. No one can hope to write successful themes unless you know your purpose before you begin.

—————   14. If anybody is finished, you can turn in your papers and leave.

—————   15. As soon as we entered the room, you could sense the tension in the atmosphere.

UNIT REVIEW EXERCISE 15B
Avoiding Unwarranted Shifts in Person

Rewrite the following sentences to correct the shifts in person.

The fog closed in on our campsite, and soon you couldn't see more than a few feet.

The fog closed in on our campsite, and soon we couldn't see more than a few feet.

1. Our house was situated in a grove of trees, and you couldn't see the highway from our front window.

_____

_____

_____

2. Every smoker should cut down on our consumption of tobacco and thus decrease our chances of developing lung cancer.

_____

_____

_____

3. If you take lessons and practice conscientiously, almost anyone can become a competent swimmer.

_____

_____

_____

4. This company has got to recognize that its biggest asset is our employees.

_____

_____

_____

5. Students should see their advisers before making out your schedules for next term.

_____

_____

_____

6. When one is moving, you must expect some things to become temporarily misplaced.

_____

_____

_____

7. We are now on daylight saving time; therefore, you have one more hour of daylight each evening.

_____

_____

_____

8. Once we are committed to a course of action, it is often difficult for people to change their views.

_____

_____

_____

9. We must pay careful attention to this detective show; otherwise, a person can miss important clues.

_____

_____

_____

10. Many people are feeling angry and frustrated right now; the time has come when I must file my income tax return.

_____

_____

_____

UNIT 16

Choosing the Right Pronoun Case

The term "case" refers to the changes in form that a noun or a pronoun undergoes to show its function in a sentence. There are three cases in English: the *subjective*, the *objective*, and the *possessive*. The subjective case is used for subjects and subject complements. The objective case is used for direct objects, indirect objects, and objects of prepositions. The possessive case shows ownership or possession.

Nouns and most indefinite pronouns (*anyone, someone, no one, everyone,* and the like) undergo changes in form for the possessive case only.

> *John* knows *Douglas. Douglas* knows *John.* (The forms are identical in both the subjective and objective cases.)
>
> *John's* college program is very difficult. (The *'s* is added to *John* to show possession.)
>
> *Anyone's* guess is as good as mine. (The *'s* is added to *anyone* to show possession.)

However, several of the most common pronouns have different forms for each case.

Subjective	Objective	Possessive
I	me	my, mine
you	you	your, yours
he	him	his
she	her	her, hers
we	us	our, ours
they	them	their, theirs
who	whom	whose

175

Ordinarily, people have no difficulty choosing the right case form. A few constructions, however, can conceal the function of the pronoun and cause mistakes to be made. The following pointers will help you to choose the proper case form.

"We" and "Us" Preceding Nouns

Nouns that serve as subjects take the pronoun *we*. Those that serve as objects take the pronoun *us*.

> *We* managers must set a good example for the employees. (The pronoun *we* precedes the subject of the sentence, *managers*.)
>
> The guide took *us* visitors through the nuclear installation. (The pronoun *us* precedes the object of the sentence, *visitors*.)
>
> The master of ceremonies said that *we* contestants could win as much as one thousand dollars each. (The pronoun *we* precedes the subject of the noun clause, *contestants*.)

If you have difficulty choosing the right pronoun, mentally omit the noun and read the sentence to yourself, first with one pronoun and then with the other. The incorrect pronoun will sound wrong, and the correct one will sound right.

> Father gave (we, us) girls two large chocolate hearts for Valentine's Day.

Omitting *girls* reveals at once that *us* is the correct choice.

EXERCISE

Choose the right pronoun form from the pair in parentheses, and write it in the blank to the left.

_____ 1. (We, Us) boys will mow your lawn for a dollar.

_____ 2. Let (we, us) girls watch the game with you.

_____ 3. The recruiter said that (we, us) fellows would enjoy army life.

_____ 4. The farmer angrily told (we, us) hunters that we were trespassing.

_____ 5. (We, Us) cigarette smokers would rather cough than quit.

_____ 6. What fools (we, us) humans are!

_____ 7. Father said he had a present for (we, us) children.

_____ 8. The high cost of gasoline is causing (we, us) commuters a great deal of concern.

Compound Subjects, Objects, and Appositives

Pronouns in compound subjects of sentences and dependent clauses should be in the subjective case. Those in compound objects should be in the objective case.

> Sam and *I* plan to work in public health. (The pronoun *I* is part of the compound subject.)
> The school awarded Marcia and *her* certificates of academic excellence. (The pronoun *her* is part of the compound indirect object.)
> A monsoon forced the guide and *them* to postpone for a day their trip into the jungle. (The pronoun *them* is part of the compound direct object.)
> The school awarded certificates of academic excellence to Marcia and *her*. (The pronoun *her* is part of the compound object of the preposition.)
> Between John and *me,* we finished the job in one hour. (The pronoun *me* is part of the compound object of the preposition.)

An appositive is a noun or noun substitute—and any associated words—that follows another noun or noun substitute and tells something about it. The case of a pronoun in a compound appositive depends on the case of the noun or noun substitute it describes. When the appositive accompanies the subject of the sentence, the pronoun should be in the subjective case. When it accompanies an object, the pronoun should be in the objective case.

> The superintendent selected two people, Loretta and *me,* to receive merit increases. (The pronoun *me* is the appositive of the noun *people,* which functions as the direct object.)
> We, Loretta and *I,* received merit increases. (The pronoun *I* is the appositive of the pronoun *we,* which functions as the subject.)

Again the technique of mental omission can help you to pick the right pronouns. Consider these examples.

> Wallace and (she, her) will compete in the state finals.
> His rebuke made us, Bob and (I, me), blush with shame.

Omission of the appropriate words gives us the following.

(She, her) will compete in the state finals.
His rebuke made (I, me) blush with shame.

Reading the two versions of each example reveals that *she* and *me* are the right choices.

EXERCISE

Choose the right pronoun form from the pair in parentheses, and write it in the blank to the left.

_____ 1. Terry and (I, me) have been told to expect promotions early next year.

_____ 2. High interest rates have forced our neighbors and (we, us) to postpone buying new homes.

_____ 3. The zoning commission has selected two people, Neal and (I, me), to submit rezoning proposals to the city council.

_____ 4. Let Gerard and (I, me) settle our disagreement by ourselves.

_____ 5. Can you really teach Rachel and (I, me) the hustle?

_____ 6. The threatening weather frightened John and (they, them) into postponing their trip.

_____ 7. When did you discover that Ann and (he, him) had started dating?

_____ 8. The boss threatened two employees, Grigsby and (I, me), with dismissal for doing poor work.

Pronouns in Subordinate Clauses

A pronoun that serves as the subject of a subordinate clause must be in the subjective case. A pronoun that serves as an object must be in the objective case. In the following sentence, the pronoun *who* is the subject of its clause and is therefore in the subjective case.

The recruiter will see all students *who* request a job interview.

On the other hand, in the next sentence the pronoun *whom* is the direct object of its clause and is therefore in the objective case.

Sheila is the student *whom* we voted most likely to succeed.

Once again there is a simple trick to help you decide whether *who* or *whom* is correct. First, mentally isolate the subordinate clause. Second, block out the pronoun in question, and then insert *he* and *him* at the appropriate spot in the remaining part of the clause. If *he* sounds better, *who* is the correct case form. If *him* sounds better, *whom* is correct. Now let's apply this trick to the following sentence.

The man who(m) I met last night is a well-known art critic.

Examination of the sentence shows the clause to be *who(m) I met last night*. Isolating the clause, blocking the pronoun, and inserting *he* and *him* gives us *I met he last night* and *I met him last night*. Clearly, the second version is the correct one, and therefore *whom* is the proper form.

Sometimes the pronoun in a clause is preceded by a preposition. In such instances, you must reposition the preposition before inserting the *he* and *him*.

The man *from who(m) I bought my camera* has won many prizes for his pictures. *I bought my camera from (he, him).*

Here, too, *whom* is the correct form.

EXERCISE

Choose the right pronoun form from the pair in parentheses, and write it in the blank to the left.

_____ 1. Tell me (who, whom) you want to go along with us.

_____ 2. Mary is the sort of person (who, whom) excels at everything she does.

_____ 3. Give the package to (whoever, whomever) is at home.

_____ 4. I regret to announce that Mr. Martinez, with (who, whom) most of you are well acquainted, has decided to retire next month.

_____ 5. He had a jovial greeting for (whoever, whomever) came into the office.

_____ 6. It doesn't matter (who, whom) you marry; the next day you'll find it was someone else!

———————— 7. (Whoever, Whomever) you choose is my choice, too.

———————— 8. Morgan is the man (who, whom) I believe most deserves promotion.

Comparisons Using "than" or "as . . . as"

Sentences that make comparisons and include the expressions *than* or *as . . . as* often provide no direct statement about the second item of comparison.

John is as qualified as Bill.

When both naming words are nouns, this kind of sentence presents no case problems. However, when the second naming word is a pronoun, you may have trouble choosing the proper one.

She is taller than (they, them).
The explanation amazed my classmates as much as (I, me).

If such a problem arises, expand the sentence by mentally supplying the omitted material. Next read the sentence with one pronoun and then the other, and see which sounds right.

She is taller than (they, them) are.
The explanation amazed my classmates as much as it did (I, me).

Applying this test to our two examples shows that *they* is the right choice for the first sentence and *me* is the right choice for the second one.

Some sentences that make comparisons may have two possible meanings, one requiring the subjective form of the pronoun and the other requiring the objective form.

Harriet disliked her social-climbing neighbors as thoroughly as *I* (disliked them).
Harriet disliked her social-climbing neighbors as thoroughly as (she disliked) *me*.

EXERCISE

Choose the right pronoun form from the pair in parentheses, and write it in the blank to the left.

———————— 1. Marvin's wife has more artistic talent than (he, him), despite his great success as an illustrator.

_____ 2. Because my brother is smaller than (I, me), he escapes many household chores.

_____ 3. They didn't buy as much as (we, us) at the supermarket.

_____ 4. His excuses angered me more than (they, them).

_____ 5. Although all three of us worked equally hard, our boss praised Sam more than (we, us).

_____ 6. He's an expert poker player, so you can't expect to win as much as (he, him).

_____ 7. Do you think I'll be able to finish this test as quickly as (they, them)?

_____ 8. Pam is more popular than (she, her).

Pronouns Preceding Gerunds

When we discussed noun phrases (page 57), we mentioned that one kind is based on verb forms ending in -ing (*running, sleeping, laughing,* and so forth) and that we call such verbal nouns *gerunds.*

A pronoun that precedes a gerund should be in the possessive case.

> I don't understand *his* failing the course.
>
> I dislike *her* constant bickering.

Use of the possessive case shows that it is the *failing* that you don't understand and the *bickering* that you dislike, rather than the person who failed and the person who bickers. *Failing* and *bickering* are gerunds, or verbal nouns, and are the direct objects of *understand* and *dislike.* We can say that the emphasis is on the actions rather than on the actors.

Now consider the following sentence.

> William caught *them* sneaking out of the house.

Here, the use of the objective rather than the possessive case shows that William caught the persons doing the sneaking rather than the sneaking itself. *Sneaking* is a participle, or verbal adjective, modifying the direct object *them.* The emphasis is on the actors rather than on their actions.

Whenever you have trouble deciding between the objective and the possessive cases in such sentences, check to see whether the emphasis is on the action or on the actor. When the emphasis is on the

action, the word ending in *-ing* will be a gerund and will require a possessive; when the emphasis is on the actor, the word ending in *-ing* will be a participle modifying the object—a pronoun in the objective case.

EXERCISE

Choose the right pronoun form from the pair in parentheses, and write it in the blank to the left.

_____ 1. I object to (them, their) dropping by without phoning first.

_____ 2. They met (him, his) coming out of the bank.

_____ 3. The Bidwells enjoyed (him, his) playing but wondered who had composed the music.

_____ 4. The sheriff told us that (us, our) noticing the license plate on the getaway car had led to the arrest of the robbers.

_____ 5. I saw (them, their) walking toward town.

_____ 6. Wendy said that (she, her) winning the year's most valuable player award had taken her completely by surprise.

_____ 7. My friends watched (me, my) fixing my car.

_____ 8. There are several reasons for (me, my) leaving school temporarily.

Pronouns as Subject Complements

In formal writing and speaking, the subject complement should always be in the subjective case.

It is *I*.

It is *he* who is most responsible for this company's success.

However, this rule is often ignored in conversation and informal writing.

It's *me*.

That's *him* working in the garden.

EXERCISE

Choose the right pronoun form from the pair in parentheses, and write it in the blank to the left. Assume that all the sentences are formal.

_____ 1. Can it be (she, her) who will win the contest?

_____ 2. Our chief antagonists in this stockholders' battle are (they, them).

_____ 3. No one doubted that it was (he, him) who had caused the accident.

_____ 4. That is (he, him) talking to the boss.

UNIT SELF-TEST

Choose the right pronoun form from the pair in parentheses, and write it in the blank to the left.

whoever The customer asked to speak to (whoever, whomever) was in charge of handling complaints.

_____ 1. The teacher chose (we, us) two students to run the projector.

_____ 2. The Mafia Godfather made her partner and (she, her) an offer they couldn't refuse.

_____ 3. The weather report warned everyone (who, whom) was planning to travel that weekend.

_____ 4. Mrs. Taylor gave Alice and (I, me) extra time to complete our term project.

_____ 5. The two finalists, Chester Malloy and (she, her), will be judged by a three-person panel.

The answers are on page 445.

UNIT REVIEW EXERCISE 16A
Choosing the Right Pronoun Case

Choose the right pronoun form from the pair in parentheses, and write it in the blank to the left.

___*I*___   Two football players, Randy and (I, me), were sidelined with injuries.

_____   1. The operator who relayed the call to the fire station was (she, her).

_____   2. Blanche Emory is the one (who, whom) our laboratory director has chosen to head the new research team.

_____   3. The office manager knows she can rely on (we, us) typists for fast, accurate work.

_____   4. The scientist (who, whom) the class admires most is Madame Curie.

_____   5. Norbert is a more dedicated jogger than (I, me).

_____   6. Mary and (I, me) plan to take summer jobs on Nantucket Island.

_____   7. (We, Us) delegates feel confident that our candidate will win the presidential nomination.

_____   8. Is this the service manager to (who, whom) I am speaking?

_____   9. Joseph and (they, them) are officers in the local branch of the steam fitters' union.

_____   10. Martha invited two classmates, Mary and (I, me), to her birthday party.

_____   11. Our accounting instructor will grade you as fairly as (I, me).

185

_____   12. Erin knew (who, whom) was calling because she recognized his voice.

_____   13. The MacPhersons told Eileen and (I, me) about their trip to Scotland.

_____   14. This will be the last chance for you and (I, me) to take advantage of the low excursion rates.

_____   15. The prize money will be divided between Althea Grant and (I, me).

UNIT REVIEW EXERCISE 16B
Choosing the Right Pronoun Case

Supply the right pronoun for each of the following sentences; then write a similar correct sentence.

Anyone __*who*__ is chosen secretary of this organization can expect to spend many hours each week on club business.

Everyone who is a good citizen is
willing to serve on juries.

1. Naomi is the only person _____ I believe has the necessary qualifications to be our office manager.

   _____

   _____

2. Two friendly natives told _____ tourists that we had taken the wrong turn several miles back.

   _____

   _____

3. Although Alan had just started working as a reporter, it was _____ who scored the biggest scoop of the year.

   _____

   _____

4. Two of us, Eloise and _____ , have sold poems to several mass-circulation magazines.

   _____

   _____

187

5. _____ Worthwells consider ourselves to be several cuts above the common herd.

_____

_____

6. Mary Beth and _____ plan to spend our vacation camping on the shore of Crooked Lake.

_____

_____

7. The administrators can't understand why _____ students should have any opportunity to air our grievances.

_____

_____

8. Margie told her friends that she was as puzzled as _____ by her failure to win even an honorable mention in the contest.

_____

_____

9. Tell me _____ you invited to your birthday party.

_____

_____

10. The ringmaster gave Billy and _____ two passes to the big top as payment for carrying water for the circus animals.

_____

_____

UNIT 17

Avoiding Errors with Adjectives and Adverbs

As we noted before, adjectives modify nouns and noun substitutes, whereas adverbs modify verbs, adjectives, and other adverbs. Although there are exceptions (for example, *here, never, often, quite, soon, then,* and *too*), most adverbs end in -*ly.* In fact, most adverbs are formed by adding -*ly* to adjectives.

> Mary is a *happy* child. (*Happy* is the adjective modifying *child.*)
> She smiled *happily* as she opened the gift. (*Happily* is the adverb modifying *smiled.*)

Ordinarily, adjectives and adverbs cause little trouble when we speak and write. None of us, for instance, would ever commit such errors as these.

> The view from the hill was *beautifully.*
> He made a *greatly* fuss over the lukewarm coffee.

Three kinds of errors do crop up with some frequency, however. These errors are misusing adjectives for adverbs, misusing adverbs for adjectives in subject complements, and using the wrong forms to make comparisons.

Misusing Adjectives for Adverbs

Although almost any adjective can be mistakenly used for the corresponding adverb, the word pairs listed below are most likely to cause problems. For each pair, the adjective comes first.

awful—awfully	good—well
bad—badly	real—really
considerable—considerably	sure—surely

The following faulty sentences illustrate the sorts of errors that can occur.

> Nelson did *good* in his first tennis lesson. (The adjective *good* is used mistakenly to modify the verb *did*.)
>
> His explanation for the mistake seems *awful* weak to me. (The adjective *awful* is used mistakenly to modify the adjective *weak*.)
>
> We came *real* close to having a bad accident. (The adjective *real* is used mistakenly to modify the adverb *close*.)

In each of these cases, the adverb is needed. Here are the above sentences rewritten in correct form.

> Nelson did *well* in his first tennis lesson.
>
> His explanation for the mistake seems *awfully* weak to me.
>
> We came *really* close to having a bad accident. (In this case, *very* might be used in place of *really*.)

Whenever you don't know whether an adjective or adverb is needed, check the word being modified. If the word is a noun or a pronoun, use an adjective. If it is a verb, adjective, or adverb, use an adverb.

EXERCISE

Choose the correct form of the word from the pair in parentheses, and write it in the blank to the left.

_____   1. The dog sniffed (eager, eagerly) at the food.

_____   2. Speak (clear, clearly), or don't speak at all.

_____   3. If I do this assignment (good, well), I'll get a good grade for the course.

_____   4. My Aunt Mildred makes (real, really) good fudge.

_____   5. The veterinarian handled the sick animal as (gentle, gently) as he could.

_____   6. Last winter was cold, but this winter has been (considerable, considerably) colder.

_____   7. Be sure your name is written (legible, legibly) on the contract.

_____ 8. Senator Conwell ran (bad, badly) in the last election, but he nevertheless won a narrow victory.

_____ 9. By now, you're (sure, surely) aware there's no such thing as a sure bet in a horse race.

_____ 10. A car stopped very (sudden, suddenly) in front of us.

Misusing Adverbs as Adjectives in Subject Complements

An adjective used as a subject complement follows a linking verb and describes the subject of the sentence. Linking verbs fall into two groups. The first group includes the different forms of the verb *be* (*is, are, am, was, were, be, been*). The second group includes such words as *seem, remain, feel, look, smell, sound,* and *taste*—words that can also function as action verbs.

When used as linking verbs, words in the second group, in effect, function as forms of the verb *be*. They must, therefore, be followed by an adjective rather than an adverb.

The soup tastes *terrible.*
Wanda felt *uncertain* about changing her job.
My boss looked *angry.*

When the linking verbs in the second group stand for physical actions, they function as action verbs and must be followed by adverbs.

The customer tasted the soup *carefully.*
Wanda felt *uncertainly* in the grass for her lost ring.
My boss looked *angrily* at me.

If you are having trouble deciding whether such a verb should be followed by an adjective or an adverb, the following trick will show you which to use. Start with the adjective, substitute the appropriate form of *be* for the verb you have used, and then see whether the sentence still makes sense. If the answer is yes, the verb is a linking verb and the adjective is correct. If the result is nonsense, the verb is showing action, and you should use an adverb. Let's try this trick on the following two sentences, which have been written with adjectives.

The roast beef tastes delicious.
The watchman sounded the alarm quick.

Replacing *tastes* with *is* and *sounded* with *was* gives us these sentences:

> The roast beef *is* delicious.
> The watchman *was* the alarm quick.

The first of these rewritten sentences still makes sense, and therefore *delicious* is correct. The second rewritten sentence is now nonsense and therefore requires the adverb *quickly* to modify the action verb *sounded*.

The verb *feel* presents a couple of complications. For one thing it may be used properly with either *good* or *well*, as in the sentences below.

> I feel *good* about giving ten dollars to the Red Cross.
> I feel *well* today; I was sick yesterday.

The first of these sentences indicates that the speaker is morally and spiritually satisfied. The second sentence means, "I am in good health," and shows that *well* is not only an adverb for *good* but also an adjective meaning "in health."

Feel is also commonly used with *badly*, rather than *bad*, in such sentences as these:

> I am feeling *badly* today.
> Sheila feels *badly* about her parents' divorce.

Although such usage is acceptable in informal speech, it is incorrect in formal speaking and writing. Use *bad* instead, as illustrated in the following rewritten sentences.

> I am feeling *bad* today.
> Sheila feels *bad* about her parents' divorce.

EXERCISE

Choose the correct form of the word from the pair in parentheses, and write it in the blank to the left.

_____   1. Ms. Jones looked (stern, sternly) at the loud, unruly students.

_____   2. The bouquet of flowers smelled very (fragrant, fragrantly).

_____   3. The bell sounded the alarm (loud, loudly).

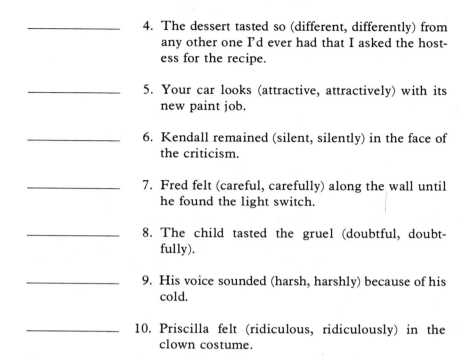

_____ 4. The dessert tasted so (different, differently) from any other one I'd ever had that I asked the hostess for the recipe.

_____ 5. Your car looks (attractive, attractively) with its new paint job.

_____ 6. Kendall remained (silent, silently) in the face of the criticism.

_____ 7. Fred felt (careful, carefully) along the wall until he found the light switch.

_____ 8. The child tasted the gruel (doubtful, doubtfully).

_____ 9. His voice sounded (harsh, harshly) because of his cold.

_____ 10. Priscilla felt (ridiculous, ridiculously) in the clown costume.

Using the Wrong Forms to Make Comparisons

Adjectives and adverbs change form to show comparison. When one thing is compared with another, short adjectives usually add *-er;* longer adjectives and most adverbs add *more* (for example, *high, higher; defective, more defective; slowly, more slowly*). When something is compared with two or more other things, *-est* is added to short adjectives, and *most* is used with longer adjectives as well as with adverbs (*highest, most defective, most slowly*). A few adjectives and adverbs—for example, those shown below—have irregular forms.

Adjectives	Adverbs
good—better—best	well—better—best
bad—worse—worst	badly—worse—worst
much—more—most	much—more—most

In making comparisons, a person may mistakenly use a double form, as illustrated by these two faulty sentences.

My lamb chop seems *more tenderer* than yours.
That is the *most stupidest* idea he's ever had!

Here are the sentences rewritten correctly.

My lamb chop seems *more tender* than yours.

That is the *stupidest* idea he's ever had!

A second problem involves using the form for three or more things when only two things are being compared.

Eva is the *smartest* of the two girls.

The Spanish bungalow was the *most* expensive of the two houses I looked at.

Although such usage sometimes occurs in informal writing, it is incorrect. Use -*est* and *most* only when you actually compare something with two or more other things, as in these sentences.

Wendell is the *richest* of the three brothers.

The Mummy Awakes proved to be the most frightening of the four movies I saw last weekend.

EXERCISE

Choose the correct expression from the pair in parentheses, and write it in the blank to the left.

_____ 1. Roger is the (taller, tallest) boy in his gym class.

_____ 2. As the body becomes (healthier, more healthier), the emotions also improve.

_____ 3. The performance will be (later, more late) in the evening.

_____ 4. Killer McGurk clearly proved the (better, best) fighter in that bout.

_____ 5. Which is the (closer, closest) of the two towns?

_____ 6. I feel (confidenter, more confident) of winning the prize than I've ever felt before.

_____ 7. This novel is the (more, most) readable of the pair.

_____ 8. That's the (sickest, most sickest) joke I've ever heard.

UNIT SELF-TEST

Choose the correct form of the word from each pair in parentheses, and write it in the blank to the left.

clearly   Hilda doesn't speak her lines (clear, clearly) at all.

_____ 1. The candy tasted so (sweet, sweetly) that I couldn't eat it.

_____ 2. I am feeling (considerable, considerably) better than I did last week.

_____ 3. Marie is the (older, oldest) of the two sisters.

_____ 4. Father looked (cross, crossly) when I asked to borrow the car.

_____ 5. We are (real, really) pleased to see you here.

The answers are on page 445.

UNIT REVIEW EXERCISE 17A
Avoiding Errors with Adjectives and Adverbs

Choose the correct form of the word from the pair in parentheses, and write it in the blank to the left.

carefully   The child looked (careful, carefully) in all directions, then stepped onto the roadway.

_____ 1. Don't feel (bad, badly) about failing to win the prize.

_____ 2. Susan plays the piano exceptionally (good, well).

_____ 3. The new station wagon handles (easy, easily) even when it is fully loaded.

_____ 4. The senator reacted very (bitter, bitterly) to the news of his defeat.

_____ 5. Because he behaved (rude, rudely), he was never invited back to the neighbor's house.

_____ 6. His decision to return the lost wallet to its owner speaks (good, well) of his character.

_____ 7. The coach believes Bob is the (faster, fastest) of the two swimmers.

_____ 8. The birds' songs sound (beautiful, beautifully) in the clear morning air.

_____ 9. Of the twelve students in the automotive class, Rhonda is the (better, best) mechanic.

_____ 10. We were afraid to eat the fish because it smelled so (strong, strongly).

_____ 11. He did (poor, poorly) on his final exam.

197

————————— 12. That skit was (more clever, more cleverer) than the one we saw last week.

————————— 13. We feel (sure, surely) you have misjudged us.

————————— 14. Lucy has a dog and a cat, but she likes the cat (better, best).

————————— 15. Your sins will (sure, surely) find you out.

UNIT REVIEW EXERCISE 17B
Avoiding Errors with Adjectives and Adverbs

Circle any incorrect adjective or adverb in the following sentences, and write the correct form in the blank to the left. Write "C" in the blank to the left for any sentence that is correct. Finally, write a similar, correct sentence below each sentence in the exercise.

strange   The driver's actions appeared strangely to the policeman.

Burning sugar smells strange.

_____ 1. He felt his way careful in the dark.

_____

_____

_____ 2. That pie doesn't taste as good as it looks.

_____

_____

_____ 3. Carlos sings too harsh and spoils the song.

_____

_____

_____ 4. Whenever Mother has a headache, she feels miserably.

_____

_____

_____   5. Kirsten is the smartest girl in this school.

_____

_____

_____   6. Fred played so bad he was dropped from the basketball team.

_____

_____

_____   7. Please divide the tasks equally among the workers.

_____

_____

_____   8. Ted thought the test was really difficult.

_____

_____

_____   9. If you follow Man Mountain Manzoni's body-building program, you will be more stronger within a month.

_____

_____

_____   10. You have done a real fine job restoring this painting.

_____

_____

UNIT 18

Avoiding Misplaced Modifiers

A misplaced modifier is a word, phrase, or clause that is improperly separated from the word it modifies. Because of the separation, sentences with this fault often sound awkward, ridiculous, or confusing. Furthermore, they can be downright illogical.

Misplaced modifiers can be corrected by shifting the modifier to a more sensible place in the sentence, generally next to the word modified. Occasionally, small changes in phrasing are also necessary. The following sections illustrate the different kinds of misplaced elements and tell how to correct them.

Misplaced Adjectives and Adverbs

Misplaced adjectives almost always distort the meaning the writer intends to convey. Consider, for example, these two incorrect sentences:

I ate a *cold* dish of cereal for breakfast today.

While walking near her home, Sherry found a *gold* man's watch.

The first sentence conveys the idea that the *dish,* not the *cereal,* was cold. The second sentence refers to a *gold man* rather than a *gold watch.* Sentences like these are quite common in everyday speech and ordinarily cause their hearers no trouble. Nevertheless, they are imprecise, and for this reason they should have no place in your writing. With such sentences, positioning the adjective next to the noun it modifies clears up the difficulty.

I ate a dish of *cold* cereal for breakfast today.

While walking near her home, Sherry found a man's *gold* watch.

Although an adjective must be positioned as closely as possible to the word it modifies, an adverb can often be shifted around in a sentence without causing a change in meaning.

Nervously, he glanced upward at the shaky scaffolding.
He glanced *nervously* upward at the shaky scaffolding.
He glanced upward *nervously* at the shaky scaffolding.
He glanced upward at the shaky scaffolding *nervously.*

Such flexibility is not always possible, though, as the following sentences show.

Just John was picked to MC the first half of the program. (No one else was picked.)
John was *just* picked to MC the first half of the program. (John was recently picked.)
John was picked to MC *just* the first half of the program. (John will not MC the second half of the program.)

Each of these sentences says something logical but quite different, and its correctness or incorrectness depends upon what the writer had in mind.

Often, misplacing an adverb not only alters the intended meaning but also yields one that is highly unlikely or completely ridiculous.

We ate the lunch that we had brought *hurriedly.* (*Brought hurriedly* is probably not the intended meaning.)
I *only* brought ten dollars with me. (*Only brought*—suggesting "I brought it, but I didn't engrave and print it"—is probably not the intended meaning.)

Like adjectives, adverbs are often misplaced in everyday speech, but they should be precisely positioned in any writing you do. Proper positioning yields sentences that accurately reflect the meaning you intend.

We ate *hurriedly* the lunch that we had brought.
I brought *only* ten dollars with me.

EXERCISE

Indicate, by writing the correct abbreviation in the blank to the left, whether the sentence is correct (C) or contains a misplaced modifer (MM).

_____   1. Winter seems all but over; we've just had one cold day all week.

_____ 2. Everyone enjoyed seeing the Martha Graham dancers immensely.

_____ 3. I have made nearly fifty dollars this week.

_____ 4. When we opened the canvas woman's purse that we had found, we saw that it was empty.

_____ 5. The instructor told the students that they would only have to write three papers that term.

_____ 6. The baby ate nearly all of her lunch.

_____ 7. The job scarcely took an hour to complete.

_____ 8. The striking Volkswagen's paint job drew a throng of admiring viewers.

_____ 9. Most readers have misunderstood the significance of this report completely.

_____ 10. Mr. Chung could hear scarcely a word of what the speaker was saying.

Misplaced Phrases and Clauses

Like single words, phrases and clauses can be misplaced. The following sentences illustrate this kind of fault.

The dealer sold the Mercedes to the banker _with leather seats._ (The banker appears to have leather seats.)

The two men talked quietly in the corner _smoking pipes._ (The corner appears to be smoking pipes.)

There is a fence behind the house _made of barbed wire._ (The house appears to be made of barbed wire.)

The hostess served toast to her guest _that was lightly buttered._ (The guest appears to be lightly buttered.)

Here are corrected versions of the above sentences.

The dealer sold the Mercedes _with leather seats_ to the banker.

The two men _smoking pipes_ talked quietly in the corner.

Behind the house, there is a fence _made of barbed wire._

There is a _barbed wire_ fence behind the house. (Note the change of wording in this corrected version.)

The hostess served toast _that was lightly buttered_ to her guest.

In attempting to make a correction, don't reposition the modifier so as to create a second erroneous or ridiculous meaning.

The girl went to the door to meet her boyfriend *wearing a pink dress.* (The boyfriend appears to be wearing a dress.)

The girl went to the door *wearing a pink dress* to meet her boyfriend. (The door appears to be wearing a dress in anticipation of the boyfriend's visit.)

Wearing a pink dress, the girl went to the door to meet her boyfriend. (This version is correct.)

EXERCISE

Indicate, by writing the correct abbreviation in the blank to the left, whether the sentence is correct (C) or contains a misplaced modifier (MM).

_____ 1. We hiked over the hills wearing only light shirts and trousers.

_____ 2. We gave the old clothes to the pauper that had been rotting in the basement.

_____ 3. The Ambersons stood in line to buy tickets to the show for twenty minutes.

_____ 4. Shelley read an interesting article in *The New York Times* about cerebral palsy.

_____ 5. Frances complained about the tough roast to her butcher.

_____ 6. The clerk sold the picture to the tall lady in the gold frame.

_____ 7. Hillary whistled to the dog on the way to the movies.

_____ 8. Clayton uses a pen with a gold cap in writing his reports.

_____ 9. I found a photograph in the attic that Father had given to Mother.

_____ 10. The President made some vigorous remarks about inflation during his news conference.

Squinting Modifiers

A squinting modifier is a modifier that is positioned so that the reader can't tell whether it is intended to modify the part of the sentence that precedes it or the part that follows it.

The teacher said *on Monday* she would return our tests.

As this sentence is written, we can't tell whether the teacher made the statement on Monday or intends to return the tests on Monday.

This kind of error can be corrected by repositioning the modifier so that the sentence has just one meaning.

On Monday, the teacher said she would return our tests.

The teacher said she would return our tests *on Monday.*

EXERCISE

Indicate, by placing the correct abbreviation in the blank to the left, whether the sentence is correct (C) or contains a squinting modifier (SM).

_____ 1. We decided that evening to visit my mother.

_____ 2. Dr. Steinmetz said on Tuesday the world would come to an end.

_____ 3. My brother told me after the dance to drive right home.

_____ 4. Clarissa worked steadily at the task.

_____ 5. The man who had entered noisily tripped over the carpet.

_____ 6. Workers who are tardy usually don't keep their jobs very long.

Awkward Separation of Sentence Elements

In the section on phrases (pages 57–66), we noted that some of them are built around the word *to* followed by the basic form of a verb (*to run, to see, to call*) and that such word pairs are called *infinitives.* At one time or another someone has probably told you that it is wrong to split an infinitive—that is, to insert modifying words between its two parts. Although this assertion doesn't always hold true, it is nevertheless undesirable to split an infinitive when doing so would create an awkward sentence.

> I plan *to,* if my passport has been renewed by then, *visit* England next month. (awkward splitting of an infinitive)

Similarly, you should avoid separating subjects from verbs and verbs from objects when awkwardness would result.

> The *investigators,* after checking the company's financial records carefully, *concluded* that its tax returns were accurate. (awkward separation of subject and verb)
>
> They *found,* after two hours of driving down a rutted country road, *the entrance* to the abandoned mine. (awkward separation of verb and direct object)

Notice the improvement in smoothness when the awkwardly placed interrupting modifiers are repositioned.

> I plan to visit England next month, *if my passport has been renewed by then.*
>
> *After checking the company's financial records carefully,* the investigators concluded that its tax returns were accurate.
>
> They found the entrance to the abandoned mine *after two hours of driving down a rutted country road.*

EXERCISE

Indicate, by placing the correct abbreviation in the blank to the left, whether the sentence is correct (C) or contains an awkward separation of elements (AWK).

_____ 1. It is bad financial practice to, when you see something you can't afford, buy it anyway.

_____ 2. The Robertsons had their car checked thoroughly before leaving on their vacation.

_____ 3. Mrs. Ames, upon seeing the empty cookie jar and the crumb-covered rug, decided to spank her son Willie.

_____ 4. We know, now that we have examined all the alternatives, that we have made the right decision.

——————   5. I would like, providing my parents will agree with my plans, to spend this summer in Arizona.

——————   6. After hoeing the huge garden, Harvey was ready for a bath and a nap.

UNIT SELF-TEST

Indicate, by writing the correct abbreviation in the blank to the left, whether the sentence is correct (C) or contains a misplaced modifier (MM).

_MM_   The robber surprised the grocer wearing a stocking mask.

——————   1. This hot cup of camomile tea will settle your stomach, Peter.

——————   2. Thank Heaven that Christmas comes just once a year.

——————   3. I've only watched that TV show three times.

——————   4. People who brag about their accomplishments continually irritate their friends and acquaintances.

——————   5. The child was rescued from the tornado before she was injured by her mother.

The answers are on pages 445 and 446.

UNIT REVIEW EXERCISE 18A
Avoiding Misplaced Modifiers

Indicate, by writing the correct abbreviation in the blank to the left, whether the sentence is correct (C) or contains any of the several types of misplaced modifiers (MM).

_MM_ A stranger came to the house where we lived asking directions.

———————— 1. The ambassador's wife wore gold clips in her ears from Vienna.

———————— 2. Carmen and I were the only teachers present at the school board meeting.

———————— 3. She found a suitcase near the lake that had a hole in it.

———————— 4. Let's, before we leave for Chicago, phone the Palmer House and reserve a room.

———————— 5. Located on a lakeshore, the vacationing couple stayed in a furnished cabin.

———————— 6. The baby-sitter and her boyfriend argued while we stared loudly.

———————— 7. Dr. Mitty only needed ten minutes to remove the brain tumor.

———————— 8. Our car was carefully checked by two mechanics before our trip to Tulsa.

———————— 9. I only ate out twice last week.

———————— 10. I hope you will try to, when you have the time, come in for a conference.

———————— 11. How the speaker silenced his hecklers completely amazes me.

_____ 12. All of us wished our team would win ardently.

_____ 13. I composed the whole speech in my head while on the way to the meeting.

_____ 14. Dora wrapped the present on the bed using gold paper and red ribbon.

_____ 15. She found a woolen child's mitten on the sidewalk.

UNIT REVIEW EXERCISE 18B
Avoiding Misplaced Modifiers

Rewrite each of the following sentences to correct the misplaced modifiers.

A wind blew across the prairie that was hot and strong.

A wind that was hot and strong blew across the prairie.

1. Elsie had made up her mind to be a music teacher before she was twelve years old.

2. Denise almost sold all her sculptures at the local handicrafts fair.

3. He struck the goldfish bowl with his head, which fortunately was empty.

4. Our parents talked together while we listened mysteriously.

211

5. I told Delbert when my new telescope arrived I would let him see Saturn's rings.

   _____

   _____

6. We only have two more miles to go before reaching the coast.

   _____

   _____

7. The instructor said that everyone in the class should not expect to pass.

   _____

   _____

8. Sharon found a cake mix that didn't require eggs at the supermarket.

   _____

   _____

9. I would like to, if I can find one on sale, buy a new overcoat.

   _____

   _____

10. Throw that spoiled package of fish into the garbage can.

    _____

    _____

UNIT 19

Avoiding Dangling Modifiers

A dangling modifier is a phrase or clause that is not clearly and logically related to the word or words it modifies. In most cases, the modifier appears at the beginning of the sentence, although it can also come at the end. Sometimes the error occurs because the sentence fails to specify anything to which the modifier can logically refer. At other times, the modifier is positioned next to the wrong noun or noun substitute.

> *Looking toward the horizon,* a funnel-shaped cloud was stirring up the dust.
>
> *Tossing the candy wrapper* on the sidewalk, a policeman ticketed me for littering.

The first of these sentences is faulty because it does not specify anything to which *Looking toward the horizon* can logically refer. In other words, the looker is not identified in any way. In the second sentence, the modifier is incorrectly positioned next to *policeman.* And because those two elements are together, the policeman appears to have tossed the wrapper away—and then ticketed the writer for doing so! As these examples show, dangling modifiers result in inaccurate and sometimes ludicrous statements. Other examples of dangling constructions are shown below.

> *Walking to the movies,* a cloudburst drenched me. (The *cloudburst* appears to be walking to the movies.)
>
> *Not being sure of the directions,* it took him two hours to reach my house. (*It* appears to be unsure of the directions.)
>
> A string broke *while playing the cello.* (The *string* appears to have been playing the cello.)
>
> *Having been fixed the night before,* Priscilla could use the car. (*Priscilla* appears to have been fixed the night before.)

213

Fatigued by the long walk, the lemonade was refreshing. (The *lemonade* appears to have been fatigued by the long walk.)

After filling my gas tank, a nail punctured my tire. (The *nail* appears to have filled the gas tank.)

When nine years old, my mother enrolled in medical school. (*Mother* appears to have enrolled when she was nine years old.)

Dangling modifiers may be corrected in two general ways. First, the modifier may be left as it is and the main part of the sentence rewritten so that it begins with the term actually modified. Second, the dangling part of the sentence can be expanded into a complete subordinate clause with both a subject and a verb. With certain sentences, either method will work equally well. With others, one of the two will be preferable, or only one will be feasible. Here are corrected versions of the above set of sentences.

Walking to the movie, *I was drenched by a cloudburst.* (The main part of the sentence has been rewritten.)

While I was walking to the movie, a cloudburst drenched me. (The modifier has been expanded into a subordinate clause.)

Not being sure of the directions, *he took two hours to reach my house.* (The main part of the sentence has been rewritten.)

Because he was unsure of the directions, it took him two hours to reach my house. (The modifier has been expanded into a subordinate clause.)

A string broke *while Lana was playing the cello.* (The modifier, an elliptical adverb clause, has been expanded into a subordinate clause with an expressed subject.)

Because the car had been fixed the night before, Priscilla could use it. (The modifier has been expanded into a subordinate clause, and the word *car* in the main clause has been changed to a pronoun for better English form.)

Because I was fatigued by the long walk, the lemonade was refreshing. (The modifier has been expanded into a subordinate clause.)

Fatigued by the long walk, I found the lemonade refreshing. (The main part of the sentence has been rewritten.)

After I had filled my gas tank, a nail punctured my tire. (The modifier has been expanded into a subordinate clause.)

When I was nine years old, my mother enrolled in medical school. (The modifier has been expanded into a subordinate clause with an expressed subject.)

Notice that we have corrected the sentences about the cello, Priscilla, the nail, and the mother by just one of the two general methods. Rewriting the main part of the "Priscilla" sentence gives us an undesirable passive (see pages 133–140) construction: "Having been fixed the night before, the car could be used by Priscilla." There is no way to correct the other sentences by rewriting their main clauses.

EXERCISE

Indicate, by writing the correct abbreviation in the blank to the left,
whether the sentence is correct (C) or contains a dangling modifier (DM).

_____   1. At the age of ten, my parents took me to Disney
              World.

_____   2. While reading the *Ladies' Home Journal,* an article
              on reducing home heating costs caught my eye.

_____   3. Having competed in football and track, Phil has a
              well-muscled body.

_____   4. When born, we know a baby cannot care for itself.

_____   5. If planted too early, cold weather can kill peas.

_____   6. Now a senior in college, the Boston Celtics have
              signed Scaffold Smith to a three-year contract.

_____   7. Standing on the corner, I watched the fire engines
              race by.

_____   8. Rubber fins are necessary when skin diving.

_____   9. As an important political writer, his views are widely
              accepted.

_____   10. After changing a flat tire, it should be repaired at the
               nearest service station.

UNIT SELF-TEST

Indicate, by writing the correct abbreviation in the blank to the left,
whether the sentence is correct (C) or contains a dangling modifier (DM).

_DM_   After finishing the ice arena, it will be opened to the
             public.

_____   1. From under a rock, a snake appeared unexpectedly.

_DM_   2. Reaching the middle of the lake, a stiff <u>breeze</u> <u>caught</u> our sails and blew us toward the opposite shore.

_Dm_   3. Playing soccer for the first time, the <u>game</u> <u>was</u> too strenuous for Gerald.

_____   4. To excel in college, <u>you</u> must <u>attend</u> your classes regularly and study hard.

_Dm_   5. Having done the dishes and made the beds, the <u>house</u> was presentable again.

The answers are on page 446.

UNIT REVIEW EXERCISE 19A
Avoiding Dangling Modifiers

Indicate, by writing the correct abbreviation in the blank to the left, whether the sentence is correct (C) or contains a dangling modifier (DM).

DM   Feeling happy at meeting again after so many years, our long plane trip seemed to pass quickly.

_____ 1. Glancing to my left, a fast-flowing stream wound its way through the meadow.

_____ 2. After an hour in jail with a shoplifter and a drunk, my cousin came and bailed me out.

_____ 3. As a budding high school athlete, one of my goals was to be a football hero.

_____ 4. While we were talking, the fire alarm sounded.

_____ 5. While smoking my last cigarette, a deer darted past my blind and disappeared in the woods.

_____ 6. To drive safely, the car must have a clean windshield.

_____ 7. Not being aware of what had happened, the confusion puzzled Jill.

_____ 8. By brushing every day, teeth will develop fewer cavities.

_____ 9. Remembering that he had a test the next day, the student left to study at the library.

_____ 10. To be a successful salesperson, a pleasant personality is vital.

_____ 11. After sitting in my stalled car for an hour, a policeman arrived and gave me a lift back to town.

217

_____ 12. My dog slept at my feet while grading papers last night.

_____ 13. In order to repair this engine, a special wrench is needed.

_____ 14. Rewritten for the third time, the essay received a much higher grade.

_____ 15. Having heard the violin soloist, Howard wanted to take violin lessons.

UNIT REVIEW EXERCISE 19B
Avoiding Dangling Modifiers

Rewrite each of the following sentences to correct the dangling modifier.

When flying over the Rockies, the peaks were snow-covered and partly hidden by clouds.

When we flew over the Rockies, the peaks were snow-covered and partly hidden by clouds.

1. Once filled with ink, you can write for several hours before the pen runs dry.

_____

_____

_____

2. The mercury in the thermometer must be shaken down before taking a patient's temperature.

_____

_____

_____

3. By inserting a nail into a potato, the time required to bake it can be reduced.

_____

_____

_____

219

4. As a secretary, certain responsibilities were delegated to me.

_____

_____

_____

5. By writing a letter to the editor, the public will know your views on a particular issue.

_____

_____

_____

6. Owing to lack of experience, the job was lost by Millicent.

_____

_____

_____

7. To compose good examples of dangling modifiers, a sense of humor is necessary.

_____

_____

_____

8. Driving up the long, tree-lined approach, the mansion loomed above us.

_____

_____

_____

9. As a supervisor, it was difficult to find fault with Richard.

_____

_____

_____

10. After explaining that I had lost my billfold, the hotel allowed me to pay by check.

_____

_____

_____

UNIT 20

Avoiding Nonparallelism and Faulty Comparisons

To write effective prose, you must use similar grammatical forms to express similar ideas and you must compare only like things. Otherwise, your sentences will lack smoothness and will not properly emphasize the relationship between the ideas.

Nonparallelism

Nonparallelism results when different grammatical forms are used to express two or more equivalent ideas. In other words, the parallel ideas are not presented with parallel structure. This error can occur with elements in pairs or in series as well as with elements following correlative conjunctions.

Elements in Pairs or in Series

Elements in pairs or in series may include words, phrases, and clauses. The following faulty sentences illustrate some of the many possible nonparallel combinations.

We called the meeting *to present* our new vacation policy, *to discuss* last week's accident, and *for reporting* on the status of our XR-1 project. (The phrases are different in form.)

James's outfit was *wrinkled, mismatched,* and *he needed to wash it.* (The adjectives do not parallel the main clause.)

The instructor complimented the student *for taking part in classroom discussions* and *because she had written a superb library research paper.* (The phrase does not parallel the subordinate clause.)

223

Winkelmann believes *in the health benefits of exercise* and *that meditation aids thinking.* (The phrase does not parallel the subordinate clause.)

Note the improvement in smoothness and clarity when the sentences are revised so that the ideas in them are expressed by parallel structure.

We called the meeting *to present* our new vacation policy, *to discuss* last week's accident, and *to review* the status of our XR-1 project. (All the phrases begin with infinitives.)

James's outfit was *wrinkled, mismatched,* and *dirty.* (Three adjectives describe the noun *outfit.*)

The instructor complimented the student *for taking part in classroom discussions* and *for writing a superb library research paper.* (The two phrases begin with the preposition *for.*)

Winkelmann believes *that exercise benefits health* and *that meditation aids thinking.* (The two subordinate clauses are parallel.)

Parallelism is achieved in the first and third examples with phrases that are identical in form, in the second example with the same part of speech repeated throughout a series, and in the fourth example with two matched clauses. Note that mixing phrases and clauses does not produce parallelism.

EXERCISE

Indicate, by writing the appropriate abbreviation in the blank to the left, whether the sentence is correct (C) or nonparallel (NP).

_____   1. The room was dark, gloomy, and dusty.

_____   2. Our honors program emphasizes independent study, stimulates creative thinking, and the creative capacities of the students are developed.

_____   3. Some of the principal reasons for going to college are to receive an education, to learn independent living, and getting a better job.

_____   4. Bob performs his tasks quickly, willingly, and with accuracy.

_____   5. The novel's chief character peers through a tangle of long hair, slouches along in a shambling gait, and gets into trouble constantly.

_____   6. Oscar liked reading books, attending plays, and to search for antiques.

_____   7. Joe's problem is not that he earns too little money but spending it foolishly.

_____   8. Several members of my class have quit school to take jobs, join the armed forces, or so that they could get married.

_____   9. Lisa's paper was not accepted because it was late, it was too short, and it was written in pencil.

_____   10. The procedure for assembling this model consists of painting the pieces, glueing them together, and you must touch up the finished model.

Elements Following Correlative Conjunctions

Correlative conjunctions (*either . . . or, neither . . . nor, both . . . and, not only . . . but also*) emphasize the ideas that they link. Nonparallelism occurs when the correlative conjunctions are followed by unlike grammatical elements. Once again, awkwardness and decreased effectiveness are the result. Here are four sentences that show nonparallelism. In each case the conjunctions are underlined once, and the elements that follow them are underlined twice.

He is either sick or he is drunk. (adjective, main clause)

When asked whether she would pledge a sorority, Edith replied that she neither had the time nor the inclination. (verb plus direct object, noun)

Jenny not only has bought a watercolor but also a lithograph. (verb plus direct object, noun)

The play was both well-acted and had beautiful stage sets. (adjective, verb plus direct object)

Ordinarily, repositioning one of the correlative conjunctions will eliminate the problem. Sometimes, however, one of the grammatical elements must be rewritten. Here are revised versions of the four sentences shown above.

Either he is sick, or he is drunk. (two main clauses)

When asked whether she would pledge a sorority, Edith replied that she had neither the time nor the inclination. (two nouns)

Jenny has bought not only a lithograph but also a watercolor. (two nouns)

The play was both well-acted and beautifully staged. (two past participles modified by adverbs)

The first three sentences were corrected by repositioning the first correlative conjunction; the last one was corrected by rewriting the part following the second correlative conjunction.

EXERCISE

Indicate, by writing the appropriate abbreviation in the blank to the left, whether the sentence is correct (C) or nonparallel (NP).

_____ 1. Edith could neither recall the purse snatcher's height nor build.

_____ 2. Uncle Solomon not only flies planes but also fixes them.

_____ 3. He wishes either to major in industrial hygiene or environmental health.

_____ 4. Boris is both a clever mimic and a skilled magician.

_____ 5. I not only lack the time but also the talent to sing in your barbershop quartet.

_____ 6. Professor Jensen was neither a good lecturer nor a careful grader.

_____ 7. My mother was asked to bring either a dish of baked beans or a gallon of ice cream to the potluck.

_____ 8. Dominique both vacuumed the living room and the den.

Faulty Comparisons

A faulty comparison results when a writer fails to mention one of the items being compared, omits words needed to clarify the relationship, or compares unlike items.

Failure to Mention Both Items

Writers of advertisements often produce sentences like the following:

Our renter's insurance provides more liberal benefits.
Snapi-Krak Cereal is a better nutritional value.

Whatever their merits in advertising, such sentences have no place in formal writing because they fail to specify exactly what their writers mean. For example, does the insurance company mean that its policies are more liberal than those of any competitor or those of just one particular company? With what other cereal or cereals is Snapi-Krak being compared? Mentioning the second term of a comparison eliminates guesswork and ensures that the reader receives the intended message.

> Our renter's insurance provides more liberal benefits than those offered by all other insurance companies.
>
> Snapi-Krak Cereal is a better nutritional value than any competitive sweetened cereal.

EXERCISE

Indicate, by writing the appropriate abbreviation in the blank to the left, whether the sentence is correct (C) or contains a faulty comparison (FC).

_____ 1. Café Endicott offers you a more varied and unusual menu.

_____ 2. The trees in California are much larger.

_____ 3. City life is considerably more hectic than country life.

_____ 4. Spitball Collins proved to be considerably less belligerent toward umpires.

_____ 5. Compared with her sister Maxine, Sybil has a better sense of humor.

_____ 6. This photographer's work covers a narrower range of subject matter.

_____ 7. Over the years, the Hotray microwave oven will provide more carefree service.

_____ 8. The movie playing this week is better than last week's film.

Omission of Clarifying Words

Two words, *other* and *else*, are especially likely to be omitted from comparisons. Doing so results in illogical sentences like the two that follow.

Mr. Smothers, my history instructor, is more conscientious than any instructor I have had.

Grigsby has more merit badges than anyone in his scout troop.

The first sentence is illogical because Smothers is one of the writer's instructors and, therefore, cannot be more conscientious than any instructor the writer has had. Similarly, because Grigsby is a member of his scout troop, he cannot have more badges than anyone in the troop. Adding *other* to the first sentence and *else* to the second clears up these logical difficulties.

Mr. Smothers, my history instructor, is more conscientious than any *other* instructor I have had.

Grigsby has more merit badges than anyone *else* in his scout troop.

Another common error of omission is the failure to include the second element of the word pair *as . . . as* in sentences that make double comparisons. Here is an example of this kind of error.

The house looked just *as* decrepit, if not more decrepit than, the barn.

The two comparisons in this sentence are *as decrepit as* and *more decrepit than*. Because of the omission of the second *as*, however, the first comparison reads as follows: "The house looked just as decrepit the barn." Supplying the missing *as* corrects this error and gives us the following sentence.

The house looked just *as* decrepit *as*, if not more decrepit than, the barn.

Sentences of this sort are often smoother when written so that the second comparison follows the name of the second item.

The house looked just as decrepit as the barn, if not more decrepit.

EXERCISE

Indicate, by writing the correct abbreviation in the blank to the left, whether the sentence is correct (C) or contains a faulty comparison (FC).

_____ 1. I found San Francisco more interesting than any city I've been in.

_____ 2. This physics class beats anything I'm taking this term.

_____ 3. His yacht is as expensive, if not more expensive than, his private jet.

_____ 4. Elroy seems more at home on a dance floor than anywhere.

_____ 5. Kimberly works as hard as, if not harder than, the other trainees.

_____ 6. The advertisement said that Spain attracts a greater number of tourists than any country in Europe.

_____ 7. The offset printing process is more widely used than any other printing process.

_____ 8. Unfortunately for us voters, Candidate Tweedledumb is as stupid, if not more stupid than, Candidate Tweedledim.

Comparison of Unlike Items

To make a sentence of comparison logical, we must compare similar items. We can compare two or more insurance policies, cereals, instructors, Boy Scouts, or buildings; but we can't logically compare Boy Scouts and insurance policies or cereals and buildings. Nevertheless, beginning writers often unintentionally compare unlike items. The following sentences illustrate this error.

> Beth's _photography_ is like a _professional_. (The sentence compares _photography_ and _professional_.)
>
> The electronics _graduates_ from Acme College get better job offers than _Apex College_. (The sentence compares _graduates_ and _Apex College_.)

This problem can be corrected by changing the sentences so that things of the same kind are compared.

> Beth's photography is like that of a _professional_.
>
> Beth's photography is like a _professional's_ (photography). (The word _photography_ is omitted but understood.)
>
> The electronics _graduates_ from Acme College get better job offers than do electronics _graduates_ from Apex College.

EXERCISE

Indicate, by writing the correct abbreviation in the blank to the left, whether the sentence is correct (C) or contains a faulty comparison (FC).

_____ 1. Kathy's voice is like an opera star's.

_____ 2. My job as a typist was very different from working as a probation officer for the Mountvale County juvenile court.

_____ 3. Unlike Covent Garden or any other European opera house, there is no champagne bar in the Grand Ole Opry Building.

_____ 4. His clothing is different from anyone else I've ever met.

_____ 5. The skills required for clowning are very different from those required for other kinds of comedy.

_____ 6. Studies show that children whose parents smoke are much more prone to respiratory illness than non-smoking families.

_____ 7. Fresh vegetables from one's own garden cost almost nothing compared with supermarket prices.

_____ 8. Unlike my job at the restaurant, I received two weeks' vacation each year when I worked in Grady's Department Store.

_____ 9. A hardback novel published today costs much more than one published twenty years ago.

_____ 10. The students at Passwell College earn better grades than Flunkwell University.

UNIT SELF-TEST

Indicate, by writing the appropriate abbreviation in the blank to the left, whether the sentence is correct (C), nonparallel (NP), or an example of faulty comparison (FC).

_____ Unlike real life, characters in novels often have exciting adventures.

_____ 1. My hobbies are reading, bicycling, and to ski.

_____ 2. Harold believed that he was a literary genius, that he was writing the Great American Novel, and that it was going to make him a millionaire.

_____ 3. In order to pass my course, not only must you prepare a long research report but also write five shorter papers.

_____ 4. American business has invested much more heavily in the Far East.

_____ 5. Hermione has a better background in accounting than any person in the office where she works.

The answers are on page 446.

UNIT REVIEW EXERCISE 20A
Avoiding Nonparallelism and Faulty Comparisons

Indicate, by writing the appropriate abbreviation in the blank to the left, whether the sentence is correct (C), nonparallel (NP), or an example of faulty comparison (FC)

NP   Pam is interested in meditation, acupuncture, and becoming a vegetarian.

_____ 1. Reading requires much more concentration than to watch TV.

_____ 2. Inge proved less qualified than anyone who applied for the position she wanted.

_____ 3. My automobile is neither comfortable nor will it go very fast.

_____ 4. Riding a bicycle through Kansas is easy compared to the mountains and the desert.

_____ 5. Jerry-Bilt Homebuilders, Incorporated, has more satisfied customers.

_____ 6. That comedian's jokes are neither funny nor new.

_____ 7. He was tall, broad-shouldered, and had red hair.

_____ 8. Uncle Jethro's latest get-rich-quick scheme not only is very foolish but also very costly.

_____ 9. Unlike Dean's shyness, Bryce is sociable and feels comfortable with others.

_____ 10. Your job will involve maintaining our parts inventory, the repair of air conditioners, and installing furnaces.

_____ 11. The apparition glided through the wall, across the room, and up the fireplace chimney.

233

————————   12. Barry County has had more cases of measles than any county in the whole state.

————————   13. Like Williamsburg, we still have huge amounts of snow to cope with in Bay Ridge.

————————   14. I enjoy helping students, counseling advisees, and participation in faculty meetings.

————————   15. In contrast to Harriet's neatness, test tubes and inoculating needles cluttered Sam's desk.

UNIT REVIEW EXERCISE 20B
Avoiding Nonparallelism and Faulty Comparisons

Rewrite each of the following sentences to correct the nonparallelism or faulty comparison.

Hinduism has fewer followers than Christians.

Hinduism has fewer followers than Christianity.

1. The night life of Port Arthur is much more varied and exciting than Crestburg.

_____

_____

_____

2. Suzanne is more dedicated than any dancer in her ballet troupe.

_____

_____

_____

3. Professor Segovia not only is modest but also scholarly.

_____

_____

_____

4. Swindell Pre-Owned Cars, Incorporated, always offers its customers better deals.

_____

_____

_____

5. I like fishing, hunting, and to live in the country.

_____

_____

_____

6. His plane is as fast, or faster than, any other plane entered in the cross-country race.

_____

_____

_____

7. If you buy a Silver Arrow auto, you'll get 20 percent better gasoline mileage.

_____

_____

_____

8. Dick's cousin begins the day by rising around 10 A.M., followed by a leisurely shower.

_____

_____

_____

9. The mountains in California are higher than Massachusetts or North Carolina.

_____

_____

_____

10. My brother is as tough, if not tougher than, any other kid on this block.

_____

_____

_____

UNIT 21

Avoiding Wordiness

Wordiness is an especially common fault with beginning writers. It results in papers that are long-winded, awkward, boring, and often difficult to follow. One form of wordiness is often called "deadwood." This term refers to words and phrases that do nothing but take up space and clutter the writing. In the following passage, the deadwood is enclosed in brackets.

> Responsible parents [of today] do not allow their children [to have] absolute freedom [to do as they please], but neither do they severely restrict their children's activities. For an illustration, let's see how one set of responsible parents, the McVeys, react to their son's request for permission to attend a party at a friend's house. When he asks [his parents] whether he can attend [the party], his parents say that he may [do so] but tell him that he must be home by a particular time. [By telling their son to be home by a particular time, the parents place restrictions on him.] If he does not [pay] heed [to] the restrictions and comes home late, he is punished: [to punish him,] his parents refuse to let him go out the next time he asks.

Deleting the paragraph's deadwood not only reduces it by 30 percent—from 135 words to 94—but also increases the clarity of the writing.

Deadwood can result because a writer says something unnecessary, uses too many words to express an idea, or says the same thing twice. The writer of our unedited paragraph has made all of these mistakes. For example, "of today" is unnecessary. The phrase "pay heed to" can be replaced with just "heed." And "by telling their son to be home by a particular time" repeats what is said in the last part of the preceding sentence.

The following list includes twenty-eight common wordy expressions and corrections for them.

Expression	**Correction**
absolutely essential	essential
at this point in time	at this time, now
audible to the ear	audible
combine together	combine
commute back and forth	commute
completely eliminate	eliminate
completely unanimous	unanimous
in the vicinity of	near
in the modern world of today	today
in this day and age	today
in view of the fact that	because, since
large in size	large
personally, I believe	I believe
red in color	red
due to the fact that	because, since
final outcome	outcome
four different times	four times
four in number	four
important essentials	essentials
in my opinion, I believe	I believe
in the event that	if
repeat again	repeat
round in shape	round
true facts	facts
usual custom	custom
very unique	unique
visible to the eye	visible
with the exception of	except for

EXERCISE

Indicate, by writing the appropriate abbreviation in the blank to the left, whether the sentence is correct (C) or wordy (W).

_____ 1. Mark had long arms that were heavily muscled and broad shoulders that had a pronounced slope to them.

_____ 2. Sam has many interests; he likes to swim, he likes to play tennis, and he likes to ski.

_____ 3. Our country is entering a new age, rich with opportunity.

_____ 4. It is absolutely essential that we completely eliminate this problem within a time span of two days.

_____ 5. Due to the fact that our town uses paper ballots, we won't know the final outcome of the election until morning.

_____ 6. The tanks crashed through the barbed wire while the infantry advanced behind them.

_____ 7. After crawling over a fence and through a tunnel, the boys found themselves in a small garden.

_____ 8. Our neighbor who lives in the house next door has been the recipient of an invitation to the governor's ball.

_____ 9. Henry Luce published _Time_ Magazine, and the same man also published _Life_ and _Fortune_.

_____ 10. With the exception of Barry, everyone in the course received a _B_ or better.

UNIT SELF-TEST

In each case indicate, by writing the appropriate abbreviation in the blank to the left, whether the sentence is correct (C) or wordy (W).

__W__ As a rule, I am usually up and about by 9 A.M. in the morning.

_____ 1. Modern houses of today are much better insulated than older houses years ago.

_____ 2. The sarcastic remarks that Linda delivered had the effect of causing everyone to become very angry.

————————— 3. At this point in time, I am planning to pursue a major in the field of environmental health.

————————— 4. Disturbed by the screaming jets, the animals fled into the wilderness surrounding the airport.

————————— 5. Because the bag was too full, the vacuum backfired and left the room dirtier than before.

The answers are on page 446.

UNIT REVIEW EXERCISE 21A
Avoiding Wordiness

Indicate, by writing the appropriate abbreviation in the blank to the left, whether the sentence or sentence pair is correct (C) or wordy (W).

_W_   During the course of her lecture the speaker paused several times. Each time she paused, she asked whether the audience had any questions.

————— 1. Personally, I am of the opinion that the final results of our membership drive will prove to be disappointing to all of us.

————— 2. Fillmore's proposal that a committee be set up to study the proposed merger was adopted unanimously.

————— 3. We regret and are truly sorry for any trouble and inconvenience you have experienced because the directions for assembling our backyard carousel were not written more clearly.

————— 4. The profession of surgery is a profession that demands great manual dexterity.

————— 5. It was brought to the supervisor's attention that many workers were taking coffee breaks that were too long.

————— 6. Without exception, I catch several colds every winter.

————— 7. Take the red wire and connect it to the positive pole of the battery.

————— 8. It is my position that you should completely abandon your acting career.

————— 9. Whenever you are in Oshkosh, be sure to visit my Aunt Ethel's candy store.

_____ 10. The campers finally found a level spot where they could pitch their tent.

_____ 11. When you have become aware of the true facts of this case, you will come to the realization that Roger is clearly guilty.

_____ 12. My program provides excellent training for management positions in health institutions. The program combines business and science courses, providing students with the background needed to manage health institutions.

_____ 13. James wanted to see the new play very badly, but he hated to spend fifteen dollars for a ticket.

_____ 14. On four different occasions, Devlin tried unsuccessfully to call his parents but couldn't reach them.

_____ 15. Whenever I feel ambitious, I lie down until the feeling goes away.

UNIT REVIEW EXERCISE 21B
Avoiding Wordiness

Rewrite each of the following sentences to eliminate the wordiness.

Last summer I engaged in the repair of railroad cars.

Last summer I repaired railroad cars.

1. Commuting back and forth to work in the morning and evening costs my father $20.00 a week.

2. In view of the fact that rain had been predicted, Prudence was of the opinion that it would be a wise course of action to take an umbrella when she went shopping.

3. Kim and Kerry disagree on many things. The chief thing they disagree on is legalized abortion, which Kim strongly opposes.

245

4. Marilyn turned in her library research paper two days late. John was also two days late getting his in, and so was Jake.

_____

_____

_____

5. Each day following supper in the evening our family carries on a discussion of the day's events.

_____

_____

_____

6. It is our hope that in the future years to come you will look back with fondness on the time you spent here at this school.

_____

_____

_____

7. There are two main species of jellyfish. These two main species are the blue manaets and the red manaets.

_____

_____

_____

8. By 2:30 P.M. in the afternoon, we had reached our destination, an old Victorian house, gray in color, that sat atop a tall, high hill.

_____

_____

_____

9. This restaurant offers a varied menu. The kinds of food you can get here include French, Italian, and German dishes.

    _____

    _____

    _____

10. At the present time, I am preparing for a trip that I will soon be going to make to Dubuque.

    _____

    _____

    _____

Learning to Punctuate and Use Mechanics Properly

Whenever you *talk*, you use a number of vocal cues to help make your meaning clear. Depending upon what you wish to say and what the particular situation is, you may pause momentarily, raise or lower your voice, or speak with greater-than-usual emphasis. When you *write*, you use punctuation marks to show such pauses and intonations as well as to indicate the relationships between different sentence elements. As a result, punctuation marks play a key role in making sure that your message receives the proper emphasis and is not temporarily misread. A knowledge of mechanics—knowing when to use capitals, italics, and abbreviations and how to show numbers—will help you to identify words used in special ways and to avoid distracting inconsistencies. Thus, proper punctuation and the appropriate use of mechanics will help you write with greater clarity, precision, and emphasis.

Let's see how punctuation and mechanics can affect meaning. Read the following sentences.

What are you trying to tell me I'm hard of hearing.

What! Are you trying to tell me I'm hard of hearing?

What are you trying to tell me? I'm hard of hearing.

The first of these examples conveys no real meaning at all. The second expresses indignation at a suggestion that the writer may be somewhat deaf. The third not only admits to some deafness but also suggests that whoever is talking to the writer will have to speak louder. Despite these significant differences, the sentences are identical except for their punctuation and the use of a capitalized *Are* in the second version.

This section covers the fundamentals of punctuation and mechanics. It discusses the following items:

apostrophes   question marks
commas   exclamation points
semicolons   quotation marks
colons   hyphens
dashes   capitals
parentheses   abbreviations
brackets   numbers
periods   italics

A good grasp of the uses of these items is essential to communicating your thoughts in writing.

UNIT 22

Apostrophes

Apostrophes (') are used to show possession; to mark contractions (the omission of letters or numbers in a word or date); and to form plurals of letters, figures, symbols, and words used in a special sense.

Possession

Ordinarily, possessive apostrophes show ownership (*John's book*). Sometimes, however, they are used to identify (*Shakespeare's plays*) or to indicate an extent of time or space (*one day's time, one mile's distance*).

Possessive apostrophes are used with nouns as well as with pronouns like *anyone, no one, everyone, someone, each other,* and *one another.* The way possession is shown depends upon how the word ends. If the noun is singular or if it is plural and does not end in an *s*, add an apostrophe followed by an *s*.

My *friend's* car was stolen. (possessive of the singular noun *friend*)

The *children's* toys were stolen. (possessive of the plural noun *children*)

Anyone's guess is as good as mine. (possessive of the singular pronoun *anyone*)

Mr. James's safety helmet saved him from a severe head injury. (possessive of the singular noun *Mr. James*)

The *boss's* orders must be obeyed. (possessive of the singular noun *boss*)

Although you will often see such forms as *James'* and *boss'* used as singular possessives, this usage is no longer considered correct. When you form the possessive of a singular noun, add an apostrophe followed by an *s*. If the word is plural and ends in an *s*, add only an apostrophe.

> All the *ladies'* shoes were covered with mud. (possessive of the plural noun *ladies*)
>
> The *Joneses'* new Cadillac is blue. (possessive of the plural noun *Joneses*)

At times you may wish to let your reader know that two or more people own something jointly. To do so, use the possessive apostrophe with the last-named person only. At other times, you may want to indicate individual ownership. In this case, use an apostrophe with each name.

> *Ben and Martin's* sailboat will be in the race next Saturday. (The single sailboat is owned by both Ben and Martin.)
>
> *Madeline's and Mary's* notebooks are on the kitchen table. (Each person owns a notebook.)

Possessive apostrophes provide a handy way of indicating very real differences in meaning. Consider these two sentences.

> The mayor listened to the *voter's* objections to the new tax.
>
> The mayor listened to the *voters'* objections to the new tax.

Except for the position of the possessive apostrophe, these two sentences are identical. However, the first sentence refers to the objections of just one voter, whereas the second probably refers to the objections of a great many voters.

Occasionally, you may have trouble telling whether a noun ending in *s* is showing possession or just naming more than one item. If you do, a simple trick will help you decide. When a noun is showing possession, it will almost always be positioned next to, or almost next to, another noun, and the two can be transformed into a phrase that includes the words *of* or *belonging to*. Suppose you have written these two sentences but are uncertain about *students* and *loudspeakers*.

> The *students* excuse for missing the test was unacceptable to the instructor.
>
> My *loudspeakers* are too large for my amplifier.

The word *students* is positioned next to the noun *excuse*, and the two can be rewritten so that the sentence reads

> The *excuse of the student* for missing the test was unacceptable to the instructor.

Students is therefore serving as a possessive, and your sentence should be as follows:

The student's excuse for missing the test was unacceptable to the instructor.

Loudspeakers, on the other hand, is positioned next to a verb and is a simple plural. The second sentence should be left as originally written, without any apostrophe.

Some businesses and other organizations with names that show possession write the names without the apostrophe.

The Veterans Administration

Allens TV Repair Shop

Citizens Bank and Trust Company

Do not, however, do this in your own writing. Use an apostrophe whenever the name of a company or organization calls for one.

Although the pronouns *his, hers, whose, its, ours, yours,* and *theirs* show possession, a possessive apostrophe is never used with them.

This car is *hers;* the other car is *theirs.* (No apostrophe is needed.)

EXERCISE

Supply apostrophes or apostrophes plus s's *where necessary to correct the following sentences.*

1. The child's mother arrived too late to see her daughter perform in

   the pageant.

2. Somebody's gloves were left in the classroom.

3. Roses' thorns can prick a person's fingers painfully.

4. The policemen's ball will be held on Friday evening.

5. That carrier pigeon's job requires more intelligence than we usu-

   ally associate with birdbrains.

6. Charles Dickens's novels are still favorites with people of all ages.

7. Both meetings will be held at Jake and Charlotte's house.

8. After years of wandering in the wilderness, Moses's followers en-

   tered the Land of Promise.

9. Grandpa made a point of visiting Cousin Donna's office while he was here.

10. Have you heard that Calvin's and Christine's jobs were abolished?

Contractions

Contractions of words or numbers are formed by omitting one or more letters or numerals. The omission is shown by placing an apostrophe exactly where the deletion is made.

Isn't our report longer than theirs? (contraction of *is not*)

I *don't* think *you're* qualified for the job. (contractions of *do not* and *you are*)

I'm a University of Delaware graduate, class of *'76*. (contraction of *I am* and *1976*)

The contraction *it's,* meaning *it is* or *it has,* presents a special problem, as it can be confused with the possessive pronoun *its,* which has no apostrophe. However, there's an easy way to tell whether you should use an apostrophe with an *its* you've written. Just expand the *its* to *it is* or, if necessary, to *it has,* and see whether the sentence still makes sense. If it does, the *its* is a contraction and needs the apostrophe. If the sentence becomes nonsense, the *its* is a possessive pronoun, and no apostrophe should be used. Let's try this trick with these three sentences.

Its raining outside.

Its been a tough day.

The dog is in *its* house.

The first of these sentences makes the same sense when the *its* is expanded to *it is*.

It is raining outside.

The second makes the same sense when the *its* is expanded to *it has*.

It has been a tough day.

Both of these sentences therefore require apostrophes. The last sentence becomes nonsense whether the *its* is expanded to *it is* or *it has*.

The dog is in *it is* house.

The dog is in *it has* house.

The *its* in the last example sentence is, therefore, a possessive pronoun and should not be written with an apostrophe.

EXERCISE

Supply apostrophes where necessary to correct the following sentences.

1. Arent you glad that weve been invited to the party?

2. Its not at all certain that hell sign this contract.

3. David doesnt realize that they arent his friends.

4. Surely you dont believe the rumors theyve been spreading.

5. My 69 Chevy is on its last legs—or should I say wheels?

6. If you consider the facts carefully, youll see that youre completely wrong.

7. Hazels had a difficult year, and its nice to know things are now improving for her.

8. The Pickles n Jam Maternity Shop is holding its semiannual clearance sale.

9. Its not what you do; its the way that you do it.

10. Well take a cup o kindness yet for auld lang syne.

Plurals

For the sake of clarity, the plurals of letters, numbers, symbols, and words used in a special sense—that is, singled out for particular attention rather than used for their meaning—are formed by adding an apostrophe and an *s*. In addition, an apostrophe is often used to form the plurals of abbreviations.

Your *i*'s look like *e*'s and your *a*'s look like *o*'s. (plurals of letters)
Your 2's and 3's should be spelled out. (plurals of numbers)
Your *&*'s should be written as *and*'s. (plural of symbol and word referred to as word)
The furnace has a capacity of 250,000 *Btu*'s. (plural of abbreviation)

When there is no danger of confusion, however, an *s* alone is sufficient.

> This turbine was installed in the *1960s*.
> The president gave a reception for the *VIPs*.

EXERCISE

Supply apostrophes wherever they are necessary or might properly be used.

1. When transcribing what you hear, you must be careful to distinguish the *ors* from the *oars*.

2. The *20s* and *30s* were decades of drastic changes in American social and economic life.

3. Gary's objections were sprinkled with *ifs*, *ands*, and *buts*.

4. The algebraic equation included two πs and three Δs.

5. Because Muriel did not dot her *is*, they were sometimes hard to tell from her *es*.

6. Ten members of the business club are CPAs.

UNIT SELF-TEST

Most of these sentences contain one or more items that require an apostrophe. Write the item or items, with the apostrophe correctly positioned, in the blank(s) to the left. If the sentence has no apostrophe error, write a "C" in the left-hand blank.

Pete's ___ *haven't* ___ For Petes sake, havent you finished the dishes yet?

___ *C* ___ ___ 1. There are four AWOLs on his service record.

___ *won't* ___ ___ *it's* ___ 2. Our cat wont come in at night until its good and ready.

brother's   _customers'_   3. My brothers job, carrying bags of groceries to customers cars, leaves him exhausted at the end of the day.

_i's_   _____   4. How many *is* are in Mississippi?

everybody's _nobody's_   5. When everybodys special, nobodys special.

The answers are on page 447.

UNIT REVIEW EXERCISE 22B
Apostrophes

Using the method shown in the example, supply apostrophes where necessary to correct each sentence; then write a similar, correct sentence.

For pity's sake, haven't you heard that expression before?

My gosh, don't you ever read the newspaper?

1. Williams father plans to attend the policemens ball next week.

2. All persons viewpoints will be aired at tonights meeting.

3. Lets see whether we can borrow Mikes motorcycle for a couple of days.

4. Boriss idea makes as much sense as anyones.

_____

_____

_____

5. It isnt the outcome but the principle thats important.

_____

_____

_____

6. Foxes tails make good decorations.

_____

_____

_____

7. There are two _ss_ and two _is_ in _Missouri_.

_____

_____

_____

8. Dave and Marvins plans met a cold reception from their wives.

_____

_____

_____

9. The class of 59 will hold its reunion next month, but its unlikely Pearl will attend.

_____

10. The countesss elaborate costume outshone all her companions costumes.

UNIT 23

Commas—to Separate

Commas (,) are used more often than any other mark of punctuation, and it's important that you learn to use them correctly. Doing so will make a real difference in your writing. Your sentence structure will be clear, and your reader will not have to pause and back up to grasp your meaning.

One important way commas clarify is by separating one sentence element from another. The elements that a comma can separate from the rest of a sentence include main clauses, items in a series, coordinate adjectives, and introductory words and word groups.

Main Clauses

You will recall that the coordinating conjunctions are *and, but, or, nor, for, yet,* and *so.* They join sentence elements of coordinate or equal rank, such as nouns or independent clauses. When two independent clauses are connected by one of the coordinating conjunctions, the conjunction should be preceded by a comma.

The clouds dispersed, *and* the sun shone once again.
Armand likes to watch TV, *but* his wife likes to read.
The meeting was canceled, *so* we went bowling instead.

Professional writers sometimes omit commas between short independent clauses, but it is safer to avoid this practice because you may temporarily confuse your readers.

No one spoke *but* the instructor appeared surprised. (*No one spoke but the instructor* . . . can cause confusion.)
No one spoke, but the instructor appeared surprised. (The confusion has been eliminated by the comma.)

265

They wished to go *for* the play was highly rated. (*They wished to go for the play* . . . can cause confusion.)

They wished to go, for the play was highly rated. (The confusion has been eliminated by the comma.)

Two or more independent clauses joined by a coordinating conjunction form a *compound* sentence. Do not mistake a simple sentence with a compound predicate—that is, a predicate with two or more separate verb parts but the same subject—for a compound sentence. Remember that a compound sentence must have two or more parts that can serve as separate sentences.

Harry washed the dishes and sliced the carrots. (simple sentence with compound predicate)

Harry washed the dishes, and Doreen sliced the carrots. (compound sentence)

If you are uncertain whether a comma is needed, read what follows the conjunction and see whether that part can stand alone. If it can, use a comma. If it can't, omit the comma. Note that in the first sentence the part following the *and* cannot stand alone.

EXERCISE

Add commas between independent clauses in the following sentences. If a sentence is correct, write a "C" in the blank to the left.

_____ 1. The car disappeared in the distance and John stood

glumly by the roadside.

_____ 2. Nick washed the car and mowed the lawn.

_____ 3. Hans ate the pie but Fritz was punished for the deed.

_____ 4. William could not drive for he had lost his glasses.

_____ 5. Loretta didn't want to read the book so she let Janice

borrow it.

_____ 6. Stuart didn't slow his pace or give any sign that he

had recognized me.

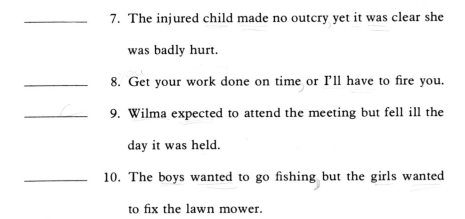

_____ 7. The injured child made no outcry yet it was clear she was badly hurt.

_____ 8. Get your work done on time or I'll have to fire you.

_____ 9. Wilma expected to attend the meeting but fell ill the day it was held.

_____ 10. The boys wanted to go fishing but the girls wanted to fix the lawn mower.

Items in a Series

A series consists of three or more words, phrases, or clauses grouped together. When words, phrases, or clauses are in a series, these items are separated by commas.

> *Alice, Silvano,* and *Keith* bought tickets to the concert. (words in series)
> He walked *through the door, down the hall,* and *into the kitchen.* (phrases in series)
> The employment director said *that his company had openings for chemists, that it was actively recruiting,* and *that a representative would visit the school soon.* (clauses in series)

Business writing often omits the comma after the next-to-last item, but it is best to avoid this practice because it can result in a confusing sentence.

> Yesterday I went swimming with the Bradleys, Elton and Jerry.

Without a comma after *Elton,* the reader might mistakenly think that the writer had gone swimming with two people—Elton Bradley and Jerry Bradley. To avoid such confusion, you should always use a comma before the last item.

> Yesterday I went swimming with the Bradleys, Elton, and Jerry.

When a coordinating conjunction comes between each successive pair of items, no commas are used.

> Feuding and fussing and fighting are our pastimes.

EXERCISE

Punctuate each series of items according to the guidelines indicated in the preceding material. If a sentence is correct, write a "C" in the blank to the left.

_____ 1. Tom, Jake, and William have been selected to represent the troop.

_____ 2. He walked into the motel, across the lobby, and up the stairs.

_____ 3. The newscaster said that the robbers had been recognized, that their license number had been taken, and that an arrest could be expected shortly.

_____ 4. Please bring beets, carrots, and broccoli from the farmers' market.

_____ 5. The rewards of hard work include financial security, peace of mind, and self-respect.

___C___ 6. Tomorrow and tomorrow and tomorrow creeps in this petty pace from day to day.

_____ 7. My least favorite foods are liver, onions, and rutabagas.

_____ 8. Paulette spent the day washing the car, painting the porch, and cleaning the basement.

___C___ 9. We waited and hoped and prayed for the war to end.

_____ 10. Congressmen Martin, Barton, and Fish all oppose this bill.

Coordinate Adjectives

Commas are used to separate coordinate adjectives—adjectives that modify the same noun or noun substitute and that can be reversed without changing the meaning of the sentence.

Sam was a sympathetic, intelligent listener.
Sam was an intelligent, sympathetic listener.

When the word order cannot be reversed, the adjectives are not coordinate, and no comma is used to separate them.

Many advanced models of computers were on display.

In this sentence, *many* and *advanced* cannot be reversed without making the sentence meaningless.

Advanced many models of computers were on display.

A second way of testing whether or not adjectives are coordinate is mentally to insert an *and* between them. If the meaning does not change when *and* is inserted, the adjectives are coordinate, and a comma is used to separate them.

EXERCISE

Add commas between the coordinate adjectives of the following sentences. If the sentence does not have coordinate adjectives, write a "C" in the blank to the left.

_____C_____ 1. Few short men ever become movie idols.

_____ 2. She is a shy quiet person.

_____ 3. That house has a grim forbidding look.

_____C_____ 4. Most expensive cars are bought partly as status

    symbols.

_____ 5. Give me a tall cool glass of lemonade.

_____C_____ 6. The portly laughing master of ceremonies helped

    make the banquet a big success.

_____ 7. The hot muggy weather sapped everyone's energy.

_____   8. Moe jumped violently when he heard the sharp high

scream.

_____   9. This house has several attractive features.

_____   10. Our small scrawny cat fancies himself a terrible

fighter.

Introductory Elements

Introductory elements separated from the rest of the sentence by commas include words, phrases, and clauses. When an introductory phrase is very short and there is no chance the sentence will be misread, the comma can be omitted.

> *After eating,* the children went outside to play. (short introductory phrase)
> *In all,* the task was a difficult one. (short introductory phrase)
> *By 1869* they had reached California. (short introductory phrase)

Without commas, the first two sentences might temporarily confuse the reader.

> After eating the children . . .
> In all the task . . .

Because there is no danger of mistaking the meaning of the last sentence, no comma is necessary, although it wouldn't be wrong to include one. Before omitting a comma after a short introductory phrase, be sure the sentence will be just as clear and easy to follow without the comma.

With introductory words, clauses, and longer phrases, commas are required.

> *Well,* the problem is not very serious. (interjection)
> *Below,* the river threaded its way through the valley. (adverb)
> *Whenever she felt depressed,* Pamela treated herself to a sundae. (introductory clause)
> *If you decide to apply,* Morris will hire you. (introductory clause)
> *To earn an A on the exam,* José studied six hours each night for a week. (introductory phrase)
> *After changing the oil and checking the tire pressure,* Angus started his journey. (introductory phrase)

EXERCISE

Add a comma after each introductory element that requires one in the following sentences. If the element does not require a comma, write a "C" in the blank to the left.

_____   1. After closing and bolting the door and securing the windows, he felt safer.

_____   2. Whenever she kissed, Mary would close her eyes.

_____   3. If you will come to the door of the theater, I'll give you two free passes.

_____   4. To win, Mae practiced her violin three hours each day.

_____   5. In April, we will move to Tennessee.

_____   6. If you change your mind, call me right away.

_____   7. Now, I don't know why you'd say that!

_____   8. In all, the directions were confusing and hard to understand.

_____   9. On Saturday, I'll buy Dad a birthday gift.

_____   10. When the roll is called up yonder, I'll be there.

UNIT SELF-TEST

Most of these sentences omit one or more necessary commas. Insert necessary commas where they have been omitted. If the sentence is correct, write a "C" in the blank to the left.

_____   Well, I suppose I can overlook this absence, but I won't overlook any more.

_____   1. After school, we went bowling and then to the movies.

_____ 2. Winter driving can be very hazardous in our town because of the winding ice-covered streets.

_____ 3. Jill and Mike are no longer engaged yet they continue to see each other regularly.

_____ 4. After waiting five weeks for her new desk lamp to arrive Sherry finally wrote the manufacturer.

_____ 5. Jeremy spent the afternoon raking the leaves mowing the lawn and washing the car.

The answers are on page 447.

UNIT REVIEW EXERCISE 23B
Commas—to Separate

Supply commas where necessary to correct each sentence; then write a similar, correctly punctuated sentence.

Despite being rated number one in the polls for most of the season,
Lincoln High School was eliminated in the regionals.

Even Though she studied until
2 A.M., Mildred made only a
73 on her midterm.

1. The smooth fast-talking pitchman told the television audience to
   hurry to the supermarket buy a box of the new cereal and start
   eating it right away.

   _____

   _____

   _____

2. To prepare for the annual music contest Carol practiced four hours
   a day and as a result she won first place in her division.

   _____

   _____

   _____

3. The loudspeaker crackled as the official opened the game balls were tossed to the server and a hush fell over the onlookers.

_____

_____

_____

4. As the last celebrity disappeared into the theater the noisy jostling crowd started to melt away.

_____

_____

_____

5. After considering the mediator's report the company accepted it but the employees narrowly rejected it.

_____

_____

_____

6. A wide variety of career programs low tuition and up-to-date shop and laboratory equipment are the most attractive features of Maple Valley Technical Institute.

_____

_____

_____

7. As we left for Lake Whitmore and a day's fishing the cold foggy

   mountain air made us shiver.

   _____

   _____

   _____

8. A harsh grating sound pierced the air as the worker moved the file

   cabinets yet none of the office personnel even glanced up.

   _____

   _____

   _____

9. Dr. Stillman does not require her students to attend her class but

   she holds them strictly accountable for the material she presents.

   _____

   _____

   _____

10. Brad worked very slowly but he nevertheless managed to develop

    and print all of the pictures by the end of the day.

    _____

    _____

    _____

UNIT 24

Commas—to Set Off

A second important way in which commas clarify is by setting off sentence elements. These elements include nonrestrictive expressions, geographical items, dates, and various kinds of parenthetical expressions.

Nonrestrictive Expressions

A nonrestrictive expression provides added information about the persons, places, and things that it modifies. This additional information, however, is *not essential* to the meaning of the sentence. A nonrestrictive expression is set off by commas from the rest of the sentence in which it appears. Here are three sentences that include nonrestrictive expressions.

The inspector, *engrossed in her work,* did not hear the fire alarm.

Mary, *who never went to college,* has written nine books.

Dr. Morden, *our new principal,* spoke at today's assembly.

Examination shows that the nonrestrictive expressions in the above sentences are not essential to the basic meanings of their sentences. For example, if we delete the phrase *engrossed in her work* from our first example, we still know that the instructor didn't hear the alarm. Similarly, removing the italicized portions of the other examples does not destroy their main ideas: that Mary has written nine books and that Dr. Morden spoke at the assembly.

Restrictive expressions—which are *not* set off with commas—single out the person, place, or thing that they modify from other persons, places, or things in the same category, thus *restricting,* or limiting, the noun modified. Unlike their nonrestrictive counterparts, they are almost always essential to the main idea of the sentence. When such an element is removed, the meaning often changes, and the resulting sentence sometimes makes no sense.

> Students *who intend to compete for the Nolan Scholarship* should see Mr. Szok within the next week.
>
> Anyone *running for governor in this state* must file a report on his campaign contributions within one month after the election.

Omitting the italicized material in these two sentences changes their meaning entirely. The first now says that all students, not just some, should see Mr. Szok. The second now makes the absurd statement that everyone, not just candidates for governor, must report campaign contributions. Applying the meaning test will tell you whether an expression needs to be set off with commas.

EXERCISE

In the following sentences set off each nonrestrictive expression with commas. If a sentence is correct, write a "C" in the blank to the left.

_____ 1. Myron's abstract painting rejected by the judges sold for ten thousand dollars.

_____ 2. His wife whom he first met on vacation works as an air traffic controller.

_____ 3. Jens Hansen our new classmate from Norway is an expert skier.

___C____ 4. Any mother who mistreats her children should lose custody of them.

_____ 5. Mary Jones wearing a pink ribbon in her hair burst into song.

_____ 6. Ann Worthington who attended Mazey High School with us has just graduated from Colby Junior College.

_____ 7. Jeremiah Cheever the character I play in my next

movie commanded a company of soldiers during the

Revolutionary War.

_____ 8. Customers who don't pay their bills within sixty days

are garnisheed.

Geographical Items and Dates

Geographical items include mailing addresses and locations. The sentences below show where commas are used.

I live at 2497 Jarrett Court, Westbury, New York 11590.
The Duponts will visit Pierre, France, this summer.
Skiing at Aspen, Colorado, is my idea of a perfect way to spend a winter vacation.

Note that although commas appear after the street designation and the city, state, and country, they are not used to set off zip codes.

Dates are punctuated by placing commas after the day of the week, the day of the month, and the year.

On Monday, June 9, 1975, I began working for the Bennett Corporation.

With dates that omit the day of the month, you have the option of using or not using commas.

In April, 1865, the Civil War ended.
In April 1865 the Civil War ended.

Although both of these examples are correct, the second is preferable.

EXERCISE

In the following sentences, supply commas between geographical items and dates where necessary. If a sentence is correct, write a "C" in the blank to the left.

_____ 1. Sherry Davis, 230 Archer Boulevard Morristown Oklahoma won the grand prize.

_____ 2. In September 1971 the school began offering a major in civil engineering.

_____ 3. On Sunday June 15 1975 Shirley received her degree in civil engineering.

_____ 4. You'll have to hold this bond until March 1990 if you want to keep it until it matures.

_____ 5. He returned from Ulm Germany just last week.

_____ 6. Pamela's home address is 219 Jermyn Street London England.

_____ 7. The package was delivered by mistake to 1811 Robin Road Anson Michigan 48642.

_____ 8. I have visited Omaha Nebraska Tulsa Oklahoma and St. Louis Missouri this summer.

Parenthetical Expressions

A parenthetical expression is a word or word group that is added to a sentence to link it to the preceding sentence, gain emphasis, or clarify the meaning in some way. Like a nonrestrictive expression, it can be omitted without affecting the basic meaning of the sentence, and it often interrupts the main flow of thought. Parenthetical expressions include:

incidental, interrupting, and clarifying phrases
names and titles of persons being addressed directly
terms of endearment and of respect or disrespect
degree titles and abbreviations of junior and senior following a person's name
echo questions
adjectives that follow, rather than precede, the words they modify

The following sentences illustrate the use of commas to set off such expressions.

Leo's whole life seems taken up with sports. Randy, *on the other hand,* is totally uninterested in athletics. (phrase linking a sentence to the one before it)

He knows, *of course,* that his decision to become a free-lance writer may cause him financial hardship. (phrase adding emphasis)

Cake, *not pie,* is my favorite dessert. (a *not* phrase)

You know, *Sally,* that your attitude is hurting your chances for promotion. (name of person being addressed directly)

Tell me, *Captain,* whether the battle is going well or badly. (title of person being addressed directly)

Come here, *honey,* and give me a kiss. (term of endearment for person being addressed directly)

All right, *slowpoke,* start working faster. (term of disrespect for person being addressed directly)

Martin Luther King, *Jr.,* was a noted civil rights leader. (personal abbreviation following name)

Marcia Mendel, *M.D.,* is tonight's lecturer. (degree title following name)

Tom realizes, *doesn't he,* that his research report is due this Friday? (echo question)

The kittens, *playful and energetic,* chased each other wildly through the house. (adjectives out of usual order)

EXERCISE

In the following sentences, set off parenthetical expressions with commas.

1. I suspect Harvey that heavy smoking is causing your cough.

2. The slacks not the sweaters are on sale.

3. Look Senator at these horrible figures on inflation.

4. The boss told you didn't he that you're being considered for promotion?

5. Dangerous Dan McGrew flushed and angry strode into the Last Chance Saloon.

6. Arthur plans to study hotel management. Denise on the other hand intends to study history.

7. This company it is clear intends never to install pollution-control equipment.

8. Let me know sweetheart whether you want to eat out tonight.

9. I don't believe dummy that you'll ever become a ventriloquist.

10. John Astorbilt Sr. made ten million dollars during his lifetime; John Astorbilt Jr. spent it all in two years.

UNIT SELF-TEST

Most of these sentences omit one or more necessary commas. Insert necessary commas where they have been omitted. If the sentence is correct, write a "C" in the blank to the left.

_____   Harry Hignite, an old friend of mine, has just graduated from medical school.

_____   1. He has lived in Galveston Texas for the last seven
years.

_____   2. On November 11 1918 World War I ended.

_____   3. You've never met my brother have you?

_____   4. Anyone who wishes to compete in the marathon must
have a complete physical examination first.

_____   5. I can't imagine Bill why you want to change your major.

The answers are on pages 447 and 448.

UNIT REVIEW EXERCISE 24A
Commas—to Set off

Most of these sentences omit one or more necessary commas. Insert necessary commas where they have been omitted. If the sentence is correct, write a "C" in the blank to the left.

_____ Highway 96, our state's newest freeway, will be opened on September 15, 1980.

_____ 1. My mother, speaking in a strained voice, told me that Father had lost his job.

_____ 2. We can all rest assured, thank God, that this murder suspect will be denied bail.

_____ 3. At present, we plan to hold our biennial conference in Miami, Florida, during November 1981.

_____ 4. They do realize, don't they, that January 23 is an unrealistic date for completing this project?

_____ 5. If you'll examine your personality closely, Sam, you may, perhaps, discover why you have such a hard time making friends.

_____ 6. Most researchers feel that high levels of cholesterol in the blood definitely cause heart attacks; Dr. Adam Willmette, however, feels that the evidence is not conclusive.

———————   7. When Terry awoke, her sister white-faced and trembling was standing by the bed.

———————   8. The washing machine, not the dryer, was making all those odd noises.

———————   9. Our faculty, you can be sure, will take every possible precaution to prevent cheating during final exam week.

———————   10. Until we married, darling, I never knew the meaning of true happiness.

———————   11. Virginia Duvall the valedictorian of our graduating class plans to become a career diplomat.

——— C ———   12. Any salesperson whose sales exceed one million dollars in October will be given a one-week vacation in Nome Alaska beginning January 15 1981.

———————   13. My father who owns a landscaping service in Wheatland hires several college students each summer.

———————   14. You are, make no mistake, the most stubborn person I've come across during my twenty-four years in business.

———————   15. The prosecuting attorney of Ingham County, Jacques LeBlanc, was born in Quebec, Canada.

UNIT REVIEW EXERCISE 24B
Commas—to Set off

Supply commas where necessary to correct each sentence; then write a similar, correctly punctuated sentence.

The living room, unlike the bedroom, had new drapes and carpeting.

Mark, unlike Tom, has no plans for the summer.

1. Pete Rose who pounded out his three thousandth hit during his sixteenth major league season did so on May 5 1978.

2. You must accept the fact Mrs. Battlemen that a 1981 Oldsmobile like all 1981 cars will cost more than your 1979 Olds did.

3. Sue Ann Krantz who grew up in my old East Side neighborhood has been elected president of the American Bar Association.

_____

_____

4. On July 21 1980 William Stark our regional sales manager flew to San Antonio Texas to attend the company's annual sales meeting.

_____

_____

_____

5. My former commanding officer whom I hadn't seen in thirty-five years attended the reunion of my old regiment last summer.

_____

_____

_____

6. Scott's sprained ankle swollen and painful kept him on the bench during the championship game.

_____

_____

_____

7. Kathy Bostock not Kathy Boatstock is the social butterfly of Oak Grove Tennessee.

_____

_____

_____

8. His home address which proved fictitious was listed as 123 Planter's Grove Allentown Pennsylvania.

_____

_____

_____

9. During the questioning, the senator never displayed the temper for which he is notorious. He was in fact a perfect gentleman.

_____

_____

_____

10. The defeated candidate for governor sporting a scraggly beard and looking emotionally drained was spotted in a Reno Nevada gambling casino.

_____

_____

_____

UNIT 25

Unneeded Commas

Properly placed commas contribute greatly to the clarity of your writing, but unnecessary commas create awkwardness and confusion. The preceding sections on the comma have pointed out where this mark of punctuation is needed. This section takes up the chief "do nots" of comma usage.

Commas After Subjects and Verbs

Unless an interrupting word or word group dictates otherwise, do *not* use a comma to separate a subject and a verb or a verb and its object or complement. Here are six sentences with unneeded commas.

> The end of this matter, is not yet in sight. (unneeded comma separating subject and verb)
> Working as a night watchman, proved too lonely for Wilbur. (unneeded comma separating subject and verb)
> Martin runs, his crew with a drill sergeant's gruffness. (unneeded comma separating verb and object)
> Kenneth has long believed, that meditation improves his powers of concentration. (unneeded comma separating verb and object)
> Florence is, tired of receiving inadequate recognition for her work. (unneeded comma separating verb and subject complement)
> Seth Gompers was, our mayor for six years. (unneeded comma separating verb and subject complement)

Sometimes a word or a word group follows a subject or a verb and must be set off by a pair of commas. The sentences shown below illustrate these situations and are correctly punctuated.

Dennis, my closest friend, is moving to Ohio next week. (The appositive *my closest friend* follows the subject; the commas are correct.)

You realize, don't you, that your behavior has been very bad? (The echo question *don't you?* follows the verb; the commas are correct.)

EXERCISE

Circle any unneeded comma in the following sentences. If a sentence is correct, write a "C" in the blank to the left.

_____ 1. The leader of the motorcycle gang, wore a brass-studded leather jacket.

_____ 2. I hope and trust, that this whole experience has taught you a lesson.

_____ 3. Wilma Myers, has been an asset to our community.

_____ 4. Fixing the dinner, gave Antonio a chance to display his culinary skills.

_____ 5. Mount St. Helens, America's only active volcano, could erupt again at any time.

_____ 6. Our landlady, took the hungry, shivering puppy into the house.

_____ 7. Commodore Benson has seen, many strange sights in his long, adventurous life.

_____ 8. Superman and Tarzan, are both courting Wonder Woman.

_____ 9. Our neighbors are planning, a trip to Spain, Portugal, and France.

_____   10. Father Illig, our parish priest, has a warm, humorous

personality.

Commas with Two Elements Joined by "And"

Do *not* use a comma to separate a compound subject, verb, object, or complement. Each of the following sentences contains an unneeded comma.

> Two horses, and three cows are grazing in the field. (An unneeded comma separates the compound subject.)
>
> Santa Claus whistled, and shouted to his reindeer. (An unneeded comma separates the compound verb.)
>
> Mildred bought steak, and asparagus for supper. (An unneeded comma separates the compound object.)
>
> Everyone realizes that Georgette has behaved very badly, and that she should be reprimanded. (An unneeded comma separates the compound object.)
>
> Montague is a true gentleman, and scholar. (An unneeded comma separates the compound subject complement.)

EXERCISE

Circle any unneeded comma in the following sentences. If a sentence is correct, write a "C" in the blank to the left.

_____   1. The boss can tell which workers are doing a good job,

and which are loafing.

_____   2. Sally watered the flowers, and her sister clipped the

hedge.

_____   3. Rip van Winkle awakened, and stretched lazily.

_____   4. Four larks, and a wren have made their nests in my

long, tangled beard.

_____   5. The victim of the attack cried, and pleaded, but the

attacker paid no heed.

——————— 6. Everyone thought that Professor Randall was a knowledgeable teacher, but a poor disciplinarian.

——————— 7. Before I go to bed, I must write a letter, and balance my checkbook.

——————— 8. Either Barbara or Otto, will bring the salad to the picnic.

——————— 9. Those nasty, thieving rabbits have eaten our carrots, and radishes.

——————— 10. Maggie was looking forward to her parents' visit, but Jiggs was dreading their arrival.

Commas with Items in a Series

Do *not* use a comma before the first item in a series or after the last item. In the following sentences, the unneeded commas have been enclosed in brackets ([,]).

> Farmer Al Falfa plans to grow[,] corn, wheat, and rye this season. (unneeded comma before the first item in a series)
> Farmer Al Falfa plans to grow corn, wheat, and rye[,] this season. (unneeded comma after the last item in series)

The unbracketed commas in these examples are correct.

EXERCISE

Circle any unneeded comma in the following sentences. If a sentence is correct, write a "C" in the blank to the left.

——————— 1. The furniture in our living room, dining room, and guest room, is completely worn out.

——————— 2. A touch of parsley, sage, rosemary, and thyme will enhance the flavor of this sauce greatly.

_____ 3. I like, scrambled eggs, bacon, and toast for breakfast.

_____ 4. According to the paper, local police have arrested, the
   butcher, the baker, and the candlestick maker for
   stealing a large tub.

_____ 5. We sang, danced, and played cards, at the party.

_____ 6. Vaulting the fence, he darted across the road, leaped
   the ditch, and vanished in the brush on its other side.

UNIT SELF-TEST

*Most of these sentences contain an unneeded comma. Circle any
unneeded commas. If the sentence is correct, write a "C" in the blank to
the left.*

_____ The man with the silver cane, asked for directions to

   Café Alfredo, but I couldn't help him.

_____ 1. Heavy, cold, wet, snow fell all night; but luckily school

   was closed the next day.

_____ 2. Mr. Charles Taylor, a tax consultant, will speak to our

   government class.

_____ 3. We need, more security officers in this building, but

   providing them will cost a great deal.

_____ 4. Molly vacuumed the kitchen, and living room before

   the party.

_____ 5. Running in the Boston Marathon was, exciting for me,

   and my parents were also thrilled.

The answers are on page 448.

UNIT REVIEW EXERCISE 25A
Unneeded Commas

Most of these sentences contain an unneeded comma. Circle any unneeded commas. If the sentence is correct, write a "C" in the blank to the left.

——————— Mr. Grimsell, our next-door neighbor, repairs⊗ and reconditions pianos.

——————— 1. Just as we sat down to our picnic lunch, a sudden downpour drenched us, and we ran for cover.

——————— 2. Mr. Ellery has long been a good friend, and trusted adviser.

——————— 3. Clarence, a straight *A* student, applied for a scholarship.

——————— 4. We sell, by mail, by phone, and by home demonstration.

——————— 5. Although Melissa started ten minutes late, her score on the math test was higher than anyone else's.

——————— 6. Always serve a balanced meal consisting of, meat, milk, a vegetable, and a fruit.

——————— 7. Whatever is decided by the committee, will be acceptable to our organization.

——————— 8. My friend Julia has two purebred dogs, and two Siamese cats.

_____ 9. Can we count on our friends for love, sympathy, and understanding?

_____ 10. The senator from Ohio, and the senator from Michigan were appointed to the Armed Services Committee.

_____ 11. My brother George, an actor, will be visiting, us this spring.

_____ 12. Your suggestion for increasing our sales is, the best one we've received so far.

_____ 13. If this nation is to conserve energy, we must all cut down our use of gasoline, electricity, and heating oil.

_____ 14. The painters scraped, primed, and repainted the siding, in two days.

_____ 15. The tired, sunburned hikers finally found, the camping spot their friends had told them about.

UNIT REVIEW EXERCISE 25B
Unneeded Commas

Circle any unneeded comma in the following sentences; then write a similar sentence with correct punctuation.

In years to come, I shall continue⊗to look to you for guidance and

reassurance.

Unless you work faster, you can't hope to finish the job by nightfall.

---

1. William was bored with the beach, and eager to return to town, but his friends refused to leave.

---

2. More openings are available in drafting, accounting, and survey-ing, this year than ever before.

---

3. After testing several water samples, the health department con-cluded that the lake was contaminated, and that swimming there should be prohibited.

299

_____

_____

4. Whoever wishes to go to the retreat, must see Father Ryan, obtain parental permission, and sign up by Friday.

_____

_____

_____

5. Every Tom, Dick, and Harry, wanted to date the pretty cheerleader.

_____

_____

_____

6. Following a cool shower, our visiting friends, Bob and Ray, wanted to head for town, and see a movie.

_____

_____

_____

7. Caught breaking into the candy machine, the small boys wept, and said they were sorry.

_____

_____

_____

8. The man I marry, must be good-humored, considerate, and willing, to share the housework.

   _____

   _____

   _____

9. If you'll look outside, Wesley, you'll see the weather is fine, and
   fair.

   _____

   _____

   _____

10. The quiet, grave-faced, somberly dressed, legislators rose, and stood
    silently when the president appeared.

    _____

    _____

    _____

UNIT 26

Semicolons

The semicolon (;) is used to mark especially pronounced pauses in the flow of sentences. We have already discussed the most common use of semicolons—to separate main clauses. These clauses may have no connecting word, or they may be connected with a conjunctive adverb (for example, *accordingly, furthermore, in addition, on the contrary, therefore*). In addition, semicolons are used to separate (1) two or more series of items, (2) items containing commas in a single series, and (3) main clauses that contain commas and are separated by a coordinating conjunction.

Main Clauses

The following sentences illustrate the use of semicolons to separate main clauses.

John apologized for being late; he said he had been caught in rush hour traffic. (No conjunctive adverb is used.)

Maxwell went shopping for a new suit; *however,* none of the colors or patterns pleased him. (A semicolon precedes the conjunctive adverb.)

June didn't feel very hungry; *therefore,* she ate only a salad for dinner. (A semicolon precedes the conjunctive adverb.)

Stuart was late for work nearly every day; *as a result,* he was fired after just one month. (A semicolon precedes the conjunctive adverb.)

Notice that in each instance a comma follows the conjunctive adverb. Use of a comma is common practice with every conjunctive adverb except *then.* Ordinarily, conjunctive adverbs are used between clauses whose ideas have some clear relationship, such as likeness, contrast, or cause and effect. When the ideas are less closely related, the clauses are separated with a semicolon alone.

Conjunctive adverbs can occur within, as well as between, main clauses. In such cases, they are set off with commas.

Barney's favorite winter recreation is skiing; his brother, *on the other hand,* likes skating best.

To determine whether or not you should use a pair of commas, read what comes on each side of the conjunctive adverb. Unless both sets of words make sense by themselves, use commas.

EXERCISE

In the following sentences supply semicolons where necessary to separate main clauses.

1. Living in San Francisco is wonderful, however, I'm often lonely for my home town of Peoria.

2. Tell me what my bill comes to I can't figure it in my head.

3. Susan soon found herself chatting and laughing with the guests Mary, on the other hand, hardly said a word all evening.

4. Jerome jogs three miles each day, thus, he never becomes overweight.

5. Sean cares nothing for clothes, all of his socks, in fact, have holes in the toes.

6. Some listeners tried to heckle the speaker, most, however, listened politely.

7. Seymour is no sportsman, on the contrary, he detests all forms of physical activity.

8. Miriam is due to arrive in thirty minutes, meanwhile, I'll read this magazine.

9. Hans liked to listen to Beethoven symphonies Irena preferred Chopin études.

10. I'm afraid of dogs, in fact, I'll cross the street to avoid one.

Two or More Series of Items

With sentences that contain two or more series of items, semicolons are often used to mark the end of each series and thus reduce the chances of misreading.

The table was cluttered with pens and pencils; newspapers, magazines, and books; and plates, cups, and saucers.

Because of the semicolon, this sentence is clearer and easier to read than it would be if only commas were used.

EXERCISE

Supply semicolons to separate the different series in the following sentences.

1. The wardrobe held a jumbled collection of women's slacks, slippers, and blouses, men's suits, sportcoats, and trousers, and children's snowsuits, boots, and mittens.

2. At the farmers' market we bought strawberries, raspberries, and blueberries, cherries, grapes, and apples, and carrots, peas, and radishes.

3. When I was a child, my favorite comedians were Curly, Larry, and Moe of the Three Stooges, Spanky, Alfalfa, and Buckwheat of Our Gang, and the three Marx Brothers, Groucho, Chico, and Harpo.

4. For recreation the Smiths golf, hike, and play tennis, the Browns swim, water ski, and fish, and the Greens attend plays, movies, and concerts.

Comma-Containing Items Within a Series

When one or more of the items within a series contain commas, the items are preferably separated by semicolons rather than commas.

The judges of the Homecoming floats included Jerome Kirk, Dean of Men; Elwood Barnes, the basketball coach; and Elsie La Londe, the president of the student council.

Again, using the semicolon improves clarity and reduces the chance that the sentence will be misread.

EXERCISE

Supply semicolons to separate the members of the series in the following sentences.

1. The candidates are Nancy, currently class treasurer, Steve, formerly class secretary, and Warren, always class clown.

2. During our visit to Ruritania we met with Vladimar Kissoff, Minister of War, Alexander Stakhanov, Minister of Labor, and Boris Tutirsky, Minister of Propaganda.

3. Topping the pile of trash were a set of bedsprings, rusted and misshapen, an old kitchen range, chipped and doorless, and a shop coat, grease-stained and ragged.

4. The buildings included a stone mansion, ivy-covered and copper-roofed, a guest house, shingled and thatch-topped, and a gazebo, open-sided and bearing an ornate cupola on its roof.

Independent Clauses with Commas and a Coordinating Conjunction

Ordinarily, a comma is used to separate independent clauses joined by a coordinating conjunction. However, when one or both of the clauses contain commas, a semicolon will provide clearer separation.

> The heavily painted, outlandishly dressed clown reached for the little boy; but the boy, squealing in fear, buried his face in his father's chest.

Using the semicolon in a sentence like the one above makes it easier to see the two main divisions.

EXERCISE

Supply semicolons to separate the independent clauses in the following sentences.

1. The long, sleek, powerful motorboat sat tied to the dock, and Marvin, eyes sparkling, gazed at it fondly.

2. An earsplitting, terrified scream rang out behind them, and Sam, Edward, and Marie whirled in alarm.

3. Our star runner, winner at last year's state meet, was ruled ineligible to participate this year, but the coach, upon appealing to the athletic board, got the decision reversed.

4. He wanted employees who were completely loyal, totally dedicated, and outstandingly brilliant, and so, after trying many humans, he turned to computerized robots.

UNIT SELF-TEST

Most of these sentences need, or would benefit from, one or two semicolons. Insert those semicolons. If the sentence is correct, write a "C" in the blank to the left.

_____ From the winners' locker room came the sounds of players shouting, laughing, and whistling; lockers rattling and clanging; and water splashing, hissing, and gurgling.

_____ 1. Everyone on the committee must help plan for the centennial those not wishing to do their part should resign now.

_____ 2. We must start searching for alternate sources of energy right away, otherwise, future generations will face great hardships.

_____ 3. For years Ms. Shanklin devoted her life to the company; her supervisors, however, never properly recognized her efforts.

_____ 4. The red-faced, gesturing orator shouted his message to his audience, but his listeners, mostly from other countries, seemed little interested in his attack on Parliament.

_____ 5. The investigating team included Mary Phillips, the secretary, John Holmes, the research analyst, and Barry Woods, the editor.

The answers are on pages 448 and 449.

UNIT REVIEW EXERCISE 26B
Semicolons

Supply semicolons where necessary or desirable in each of the following sentences; then write a similar sentence with correct punctuation.

The house looks small from the outside; nevertheless, it has seven

sizeable rooms.

My car is old and battered;
however, it gets me where
I want to go.

1. We have differing views on politics, children, and women's liberation, in addition, each of us prefers a different part of the country.

_____

_____

_____

2. Curiosity urged me to explore the abandoned house fear held me back.

_____

_____

_____

3. Faced with the difficult exam, Magda felt very confident, Dirk, however, was nervous and uncertain.

_____

4. The closet contained carpenters' saws and hammers, draftsmen's T squares, drawing boards, and triangles and machinists' calipers and micrometers.

5. Larry's restaurant is more attractive and has a more varied menu than Vic's, in addition, it is much less expensive.

6. The meal included steak, which was cooked to perfection, spinach, my favorite vegetable, and baked potatoes.

7. The partying children danced an hour, sang a dozen songs, and played a few games, then it was time to go home.

8. The short, serious student wanted to explain the experiment, but the visitor, nervous and impatient, refused to listen.

9. Most people enjoy tasty, well-prepared food, a few, however, don't care what they eat.

10. I've tried diets, exercise, and acupuncture, but nothing seems to stop me from gaining weight.

UNIT 27

Colons, Dashes, Parentheses, and Brackets

Like commas and semicolons, the marks of punctuation that we will discuss in this section are used to separate and enclose: they clarify the relationships among the various parts of the sentences in which they appear.

Colons

One important use of the colon (:) is to introduce appositives, formal lists, and formal explanations when they are preceded by material that could serve as complete sentences.

> All her efforts were directed toward one goal: becoming a successful songwriter. (appositive)
>
> Four occupations were represented by those in attendance: electrician, carpenter, plumber, and sheet-metal worker. (formal list)
>
> To determine if the product is suitable, do as follows: (1) select random samples of six-inch angle irons, (2) mount each sample in the testing machine, and (3) test for deformation tensile strength. (formal explanation)

Unless the introductory material can stand alone, *don't* use a colon. The following sentence is incorrect because of the colon.

> My courses for next semester include: algebra, economics, English, and history.

Here's how the sentence should look.

> My courses for next semester include algebra, economics, English, and history.

A colon is often used instead of a comma to introduce a long, formal quotation, particularly if the quotation consists of more than one sentence.

> The candidate arose, faced his audience, and said: "Ladies and gentlemen, we are living in troubled times. Millions of Americans are out of work, food prices are soaring, and we face critical fuel shortages. The present administration is doing nothing to solve these problems. We need new leadership."

With long quotations, the material preceding the colon may be a complete sentence or just part of one, as in our example. If a quotation is more than five lines long, it is indented and positioned below the introductory sentence or phrase. In this case a colon must be used.

Colons are also used to separate hours from minutes, titles of publications from subtitles, salutations of business letters from the body of the letters, the chapter from the verse in Biblical references, and numbers indicating ratios.

> The second show begins at 9:15 P.M. (The colon separates the hour from the minutes.)
>
> Our textbook for this course is entitled *The Short Story: Fiction in Transition*. (The colon separates the title from the subtitle.)
>
> The Ten Commandments are found in Exodus 20:1–17. (The colon separates chapter and verse in this Biblical reference.)
>
> To make French dressing, start by combining salad oil and wine vinegar in a 4:1 ratio. (The colon separates numbers indicating a ratio.)

EXERCISE

Supply colons where necessary to correct the following sentences.

1. The living room had three original paintings an Andrew Wyeth portrait, a Robert Motherwell abstraction, and a Peter Max supergraphic.

2. My bus leaves for Chicago at 850 A.M. and arrives there at 320 P.M.

3. Jeremy is reading Peter Fryer's *Mrs. Grundy Studies in English Prudery* for his course in sociology.

4. Mrs. Grimsby seems to have just one goal in life criticizing everyone and everything.

5. Our school has a 4 2 1 ratio of technical, business, and liberal arts
   students.

6. There is a simple explanation for our company's poor sales we do
   not advertise our products properly.

7. The Sermon on the Mount may be found in Luke 6 20–49

8. Mary writes novels for two reasons to make money and to win literary fame.

Dashes

Like colons, dashes (—) are used to set off appositives, lists, and
explanations, but they are employed in less formal writing.

> Only one person could be guilty of such an oversight—William! (ap-
> positive)
> The living room was very sparsely furnished—a couch, two end tables,
> and a single chair. (list)
> I know why your book has disappeared—it was stolen. (explanation)

A sudden break in thought is generally set off by two dashes—
one preceding the interrupting material and the other following it.

> Her TV set—she bought it just last month, didn't she?—is at the repair
> shop.

Dashes also set off parenthetical expressions that contain commas.

> The speaker—poised, articulate, and well informed—made a pleasing
> impression on her audience.

Finally, dashes are used to set off comments following a list.

> A can of tomato soup and a package of paper napkins—these were his
> only purchases.

In typing, a dash consists of two hyphens, one after the other with
no space between them and the words that come before and after. The
dash emphasizes the material it sets off.

EXERCISE

Supply dashes where necessary to correct the following sentences.

1. The new sports car long, low, and gleaming with chromium presented a very attractive appearance.

2. He ate just four things the whole week hot dogs, hamburgers, peanut butter sandwiches, and chocolate cake.

3. I have just one comment to make about your suggestion phooey!

4. Mary, Lisa, and Gretchen these are my best friends in the dorm.

5. For tomorrow your assignment will be Bob, pay attention to read the chapter on narration.

6. I know one cause of your financial difficulties that gas hog you're driving.

7. Certain members of this department I won't mention any names are going to be fired if they don't start shaping up right away.

8. Boots, shirts, trousers, and coats all were scattered about the floor.

Parentheses

Parentheses—( )—are used to enclose numbers or letters that accompany formal listings in sentences and to set off examples and other supplementary information or comments that would interrupt the main sequence of ideas.

> Each paper should contain (1) an introduction, (2) a number of paragraphs developing the thesis sentence, and (3) a conclusion.
>
> Some plays (for instance, *Annie*) are sold out for months ahead.
>
> John's first promotion came as a surprise. (He had been with the company only three months.) But his second promotion left all of us astounded.
>
> Julia Ward Howe (1819–1910) wrote "The Battle Hymn of the Republic."

Parentheses de-emphasize rather than emphasize the material they enclose. If the material in parentheses appears within a given sentence, it is not necessary to use an initial capital letter or a period even if the parenthetical material is itself a complete sentence.

Some animals (dogs, for instance) make very good household pets.

The development of nuclear energy (one cannot foresee where it will lead) is a controversial issue today.

If, however, the material in parentheses takes the form of a separate sentence, punctuate it as you would a sentence. In such sentences, the closing parenthesis—)—follows the final punctuation.

John's first promotion came as a surprise. (He had been with the company only three months.)

If the material in parentheses appears at the end of a sentence, the closing parenthesis precedes the final punctuation.

The development of nuclear energy is a controversial issue today (one cannot foresee where it will lead).

EXERCISE

Supply parentheses where necessary to correct the following sentences.

1. The procedure for taking a blood sample requires 1 a sterile syringe, 2 a sterile cotton ball, 3 alcohol, and 4 a tourniquet.

2. This study the Cuthbert study of 1979 offers a reasonable approach to the problem of welfare fraud.

3. Adlai Stevenson 1900–1969 ran unsuccessfully for president in 1952 and 1956.

4. If you haven't made your hotel reservations yet, remember that you were told to do so two weeks ago you may find that no more rooms are available.

5. Representative Guy Emmet Democrat, Texas announced yesterday that he would not seek reelection.

6. Self-contained breathing devices may be used where the atmosphere is 1 low in oxygen, 2 of unknown composition, and 3 heavily contaminated with substances having few or no warning properties.

7. In 1946, Michigan State College later, the name was changed to Michigan State University became a member of the Big Ten Conference.

8. Our own findings see Table 3 clearly support the state's conclusion that Lake Pilchard is contaminated with a variety of toxic chemicals.

Brackets

Brackets—[ ]—are used within quoted material to enclose words or phrases that have been added or changed for clarity. They are also used with the word *sic* (Latin for "thus") to identify errors in the material being quoted.

"The founder of the school [Woodbridge Ferris] also served as governor of Michigan." (The bracketed name is added to the original.)

"[Margaret Mead's] years of study have made her one of the foremost experts on culturally determined behavior." (The bracketed name replaces "her" in the original.)

"The accused man dennied [*sic*] all charges." (The word "denied" is misspelled in the original.)

As the third sentence illustrates, when a writer notices an error in material being quoted, he or she inserts the word *sic*, in brackets, directly after the error. The reader who sees this knows that the error was not made by the writer but is being accurately reproduced from the original.

EXERCISE

Supply brackets as necessary to correct the following sentences.

1. "His Evelyn Waugh's first novel established him as one of England's greatest satirists," said the review.

2. A young boy had written on the blackboard, "Our teecher *sic* is an old meany."

3. "This particular company Legree Products, Inc. is notorious for its low wages and poor working conditions," the union leader charged.

4. The report concluded with this sentence: "These statistics clearly show that drunk driving is the principle *sic* cause of traffic accidents."

UNIT SELF-TEST

Supply colons, dashes, parentheses, and brackets where necessary to correct the following sentences. A sentence may have more than one omission, and in some cases the omission can be corrected in more than one way.

To help the push for fewer restrictions on business, our company is sending a legislative consultant we dislike the term "lobbyist" to Washington.

OR

To help the push for fewer restrictions on business, our company is sending a legislative consultant(we dislike the term "lobbyist")to Washington.

1. In a quavering voice, the amateur actor started to deliver Marc Antony's famous funeral oration "Friends, Romans, countrymen . . ."

2. Representative Joseph P. Stark Republican, Florida is the most vocal opponent of the new defense appropriation bill.

3. All our graduates are expected to Heavens, what was that crash?

4. The student wrote, "Ernest Hemingway 1899–1961 committed suiside *sic* shortly after a stay at the Mayo Clinic."

5. The experiment calls for a 3 2 2 ratio of methyl alcohol, water, and glycerine.

The answers are on page 449.

Unit Review Exercise 27A
Colons, Dashes, Parentheses, and Brackets

Rewrite the following sentences, supplying colons, dashes, parentheses, and brackets where necessary. A sentence may have more than one omission, and in some cases the omission can be corrected in more than one way.

He Jimmy Brown has often been called the greatest fullback who ever played the game.

He (Jimmy Brown) has often been called the greatest fullback who ever played the game.

OR

He — Jimmy Brown — has often been called the greatest fullback who ever played the game.

Note that "Jimmy Brown" could also be set off with commas.

1. At 7:45 P.M. Gabrielle went to the university library and checked out *Documents in American History A Student Source Book,* which was part of her required reading.

   _____

   _____

   _____

2. The small child underweight, dirty, and wearing patched rags was found outside the delicatessen.

   _____

3. Ratbane County population 3,500 is notorious for three things bad roads, illicit liquor, and the most suspicious people in the state.

4. The advertisement contained the following statement "Our coffee is noted for it's *sic* rich taste and low price."

5. Intelligence, wit, a sincere interest in her students these are but three of the qualities for which Ms. Nowicki will long be remembered.

6. In tennis doubles, proper placement of the return of the serve see Figures 2 and 3 is one of the main keys to winning.

7. At next Sunday's service it begins at 10 30 A.M. the bishop will preach a sermon based on Deuteronomy 32 35.

8. George Orwell pseudonym of Eric Blair is the only notable writer of the World War II era who took a strong stand against both Stalinist communism and Nazism.

9. Whitman's outburst I never dreamed he was capable of such anger stunned everyone in the office.

10. In *Till We Decide to Part A Look at Why People Divorce,* the author points out that as the final break nears, "Both husband and wive *sic* are likely to develop feelings of guilt."

11. The convicted murderer gesturing wildly, shouting, and struggling with his guards was led from the courtroom.

12. Processing exposed X-ray film involves five steps 1 developing, 2 rinsing, 3 fixing, 4 rerinsing, and 5 drying the film.

_____

_____

13. The letter from the department head clearly details her Monique Levy's qualifications for promotion.

_____

_____

_____

14. I want just one thing out of life a million dollars!

_____

_____

_____

15. Icy roads, subzero temperatures, and a severe fuel shortage all of these prompted the governor to declare a state of emergency.

_____

_____

_____

UNIT REVIEW EXERCISE 27B
Colons, Dashes, Parentheses, and Brackets

Write three sentences for each of these marks of punctuation.

Colons

1. _____

_____

2. _____

_____

3. _____

_____

Dashes

1. _____

_____

2. _____

_____

3. _____

_____

Parentheses

1. _____

_____

2. _____

_____

3. _____

_____

Brackets

1. _____

_____

2. _____

_____

3. _____

_____

UNIT 28

Periods, Question Marks, and Exclamation Points

Periods, question marks, and exclamation points serve primarily to mark the ends of sentences, and thus they are sometimes called *end marks*. In addition, periods may indicate abbreviations and omissions and are used in certain numerical designations, whereas question marks are used to indicate uncertainty.

Periods

Periods (.) are used to end sentences that state real or supposed facts, make requests, give instructions, or ask indirect questions (that is, questions that have been restated without repeating the original wording).

Monty works for the Merrian County Sheriff's Department. (The sentence states a fact.)

Governor Quackenbush is incompetent. (The sentence states a supposed fact.)

Please lend me your scarf. (The sentence makes a request.)

Do your assignment before you leave. (The sentence gives instructions.)

She asked whether I had seen that television program before. (The sentence asks an indirect question; the original question was probably, "Have you seen that TV program before?")

Periods also follow common abbreviations as well as a person's initials.

Mr.	B.C.	Ave.
Mrs.	A.D.	Inc.
Ms.	A.M.	etc.
Dr.	P.M.	i.e.
Jr.	c.o.d.	vs.

Harvey H. Borden will address the Rotary Club this evening.

Today, periods are often omitted after abbreviations for the names of organizations or governmental agencies. Some abbreviations commonly written without periods are these:

AFL-CIO	TVA	FHA
ROTC	IBM	PTA
FDIC	CBS	NAACP
VA	FBI	CIA

If you don't know whether a particular abbreviation should be written with periods, check an up-to-date collegiate dictionary.

Periods are used to precede decimal fractions and to separate numeral designations for dollars and cents.

0.39 percent	4.39 percent	$6.29	$0.76

EXERCISE

Supply periods where necessary to correct the following sentences.

1. The normal temperature of the human body is 986° F.

2. The visitor to the antique shop asked how much the lamp in the window cost

3. Edwin Schuster, Jr, president of the local PTA, missed the last meeting because of illness.

4. Please don't dangle your arm out the car window

5. This box of detergent costs $ 198 on sale.

6. When you see Felice, give her my regards

7. The program begins at 9 PM and lasts about an hour.

8. It's been years since I last read this book

Question Marks

A question mark (?) is used after a whole sentence or a part of a sentence that asks a direct question (one that repeats the exact words of the person who asked it).

> Will you show me how to work this algebra problem? (The whole sentence asks a question.)
>
> Have you checked the oil? cleaned the windshield? replenished the battery water? (The series of parts asks questions. Note that only the first item in the series is capitalized.)
>
> Mrs. Kendall—wasn't she your teacher once?—has retired after thirty-five years of service. (The interrupting element between dashes asks the question. Note that the interrupting element is not capitalized.)
>
> The inspector asked, "Why is the guard missing from this gear box?" (The quotation asks the question.)

Question marks in parentheses are used to indicate that a writer is not certain of some piece of information. The question mark immediately follows the material in doubt.

> He reached America in 1768 (?) and settled in Boston.

EXERCISE

Supply question marks where necessary to correct the following sentences. If no question mark is needed, write a "C" in the blank to the left.

_____ 1. When do you plan to begin your vacation.

_____ 2. My parents keep wanting to know when I'm going to choose a major.

_____ 3. Mrs. Butwick asked, "Did you ever hear a more ridiculous statement in your life."

_____ 4. If you keep driving so fast, you'll probably get a ticket.

_____ 5. Stepanski's Grocery Shoppe—didn't it begin as a meat market—is moving to its new location next week.

_____ 6. The stranger asked whether the downtown stores stayed open on Monday evening.

———————— 7. While you were in New York, did you see the Statue

of Liberty visit Radio City Music Hall take a carriage

ride through Central Park.

———————— 8. In what ways does Doris think she's better than her

classmates.

Exclamation Points

Exclamation points (!) are used after words, phrases, or clauses to denote a high degree of fear, anger, joy, or other emotion or to express an emphatic command.

William! It's been years since I've seen you!
Walter! Get back to work immediately!
Ouch! That hurts!

Don't overuse the exclamation point. If you do, it will soon fail to produce the intended effect.

EXERCISE

Supply exclamation points where necessary to correct the following sentences. If no exclamation point is needed, write a "C" in the blank to the left.

———————— 1. Gosh, it's a lovely day.

———————— 2. Help. There's a shark coming toward us.

———————— 3. When I tell you to be quiet, you'd better be quiet if

you know what's good for you.

———————— 4. What a wonderful way to spend the weekend.

———————— 5. Now, let's talk about tomorrow's meeting.

———————— 6. For the love of Pete, watch what you're doing there.

UNIT SELF-TEST

Supply periods, question marks, and exclamation points where necessary to correct the following sentences. Some corrections will involve changing a mark. A sentence may require more than one correction.

Look out! That crazy fool is coming straight at us!

1. Paul de Vere, Jr, earned his BS degree at Wisconsin State University and then spent the next ten years working for the CIA

2. I asked my roommate where he would spend the weekend

3. What happened to the piece of cake I was saving for a snack

4. Great Heavens Who'd have thought that Dr Sawyer would be found guilty of malpractice

5. Nancy asked Ms Wilcox whether Chapter Four of the text would be covered on the next test

The answers are on page 449.

UNIT REVIEW EXERCISE 28A
Periods, Question Marks, and Exclamation Points

Supply periods, question marks, and exclamation points where necessary to correct the following sentences. Some corrections will involve adding a mark where there is none, whereas others will involve changing a mark. A sentence may require more than one correction.

What prompted Mr. Smith to rush from the room so excitedly ?

1. The reception committee consisted of Mrs Charles R Hilton, Dr Richard M Miles, Percival Worthington, Esq, and Mr Peter McCoy.

2. Did you hear the siren follow the fire truck watch the store burn down.

3. The report stated that the new steel alloy costs $150 per pound more than the old alloy but provides about 20 percent—197 percent, to be exact—more strength.

4. Hank Greenberg—or was it Hank Greenley—was a star player for the Detroit Tigers in the 1930s and 1940s.

5. Wow that was some shot.

6. With all the grade inflation that is going on, does a degree with honors mean anything today.

7. Our new neighbor from North Carolina, Dr Jerome Beardsley, Sr, has been elected president of the local PTA.

8. John asked his wife how she would like to celebrate their tenth wedding anniversary

9. You wipe that smirk off your face this instant

10. Julius Caesar—it wasn't Caesar Augustus, was it—was murdered by a band of conspirators that included his supposed friend Brutus

11. The president asked her assistant which of the district sales managers was most qualified for the position of sales director

12. Klingwell's, Inc, does not accept cod orders.

13. This year the profits of the IBM Corporation rose just 123 percent—scarcely any gain at all.

14. Was Pompeii destroyed in 79 AD, or did the catastrophe occur before then.

15. Dr Winkler asked, "What do you plan to do after you graduate."

UNIT REVIEW EXERCISE 28B
Periods, Question Marks, and Exclamation Points

Write three sentences for each of these marks of punctuation (periods, question marks, and exclamation points) and three additional sentences, each with at least two different kinds of the above marks.

Periods

1. _____

   _____

2. _____

   _____

3. _____

   _____

Question Marks

1. _____

   _____

2. _____

   _____

3. _____

   _____

Exclamation Points

1. _____

   _____

2. _____

   _____

3. _____

   _____

Two or More of the Above Marks

1. _____

   _____

2. _____

   _____

3. _____

   _____

UNIT 29

Quotation Marks

Quotation marks (" ") are used to set off direct quotations, titles of shorter works and subdivisions of books, and to identify expressions used in a special sense.

Direct Quotations

A direct quotation repeats a person's written or spoken comments in his or her own words.

> The placement director announced, "The Aeolian Heating and Air Conditioning Corporation's recruiter will be on campus this Thursday." (spoken comments)
>
> The first sentence of the newspaper story said, "Coffee prices are expected to increase by ten cents a pound in the next three months." (written comments)
>
> "Please hand me my notebook," Willis asked his roommate.
>
> Sally described her date as "a total bust."

As these examples show, the commas that come before direct quotations are positioned outside the quotation marks. Commas and periods that come at the end of direct quotations are positioned inside the marks. Quotations that are sentence fragments are not preceded by commas.

Quotation marks are used in dialogues to set off the exact words of each speaker. Each exchange, no matter how short, is treated as a separate paragraph.

> "Sit down," the instructor said. "Let me talk to you for a minute."
>
> "All right," Ann replied, settling herself in the chair beside his desk.
>
> "I wonder," the instructor asked, "whether you would consider enrolling in my advanced composition course next term."

When a speaker's words are separated by "he said" or a similar expression, and the two parts consist of just one sentence, the expression is set off with a pair of commas. When each part of the quotation is a complete sentence, a period follows the expression, and the first word of the second quoted sentence is capitalized. The preceding examples illustrate these rules.

EXERCISE

Supply properly positioned quotation marks where necessary to correct the following sentences.

1. Don't forget to write your name on your test before you hand it in, the instructor reminded the class.

2. Writing about Babe Ruth, Leo Durocher said, Babe Ruth was the greatest instinctive baseball player who ever lived.

3. Tell me, said the sales clerk, when you'd like us to deliver your new lamps.

4. The boss told John, This project should take about two weeks.

5. I like Woody Allen's movies, Owen declared. In fact, I've seen every one of them several times.

6. Elwood called William Styron's latest novel a real literary bombshell.

Titles of Shorter Works and Subdivisions of Books

Besides setting off written and spoken quotations, quotation marks also are used to denote titles of

magazine articles	chapters and sections of books
essays	short poems
short stories	songs
other short pieces of prose	television and radio programs

The article was titled "Results of Testing Willow Creek for Coliform Organisms." (article)

Did you see "Charlie's Angels" last night? (TV program)

Next week we will discuss Chapter 8, "Letters and Memorandums." (chapter of a book)

This week I plan to read Stephen Crane's "The Open Boat," "The Blue Hotel," and "The Bride Comes to Yellow Sky." (short stories)

With titles, as with direct quotations, commas and periods that directly follow the quoted material are positioned inside the quotation marks. Commas that precede the quoted material are outside the quotation marks.

EXERCISE

Supply properly positioned quotation marks where necessary to correct the following sentences.

1. Gunsmoke was a popular TV program for about two decades.

2. Irwin Shaw's short story The Dry Rock is about the death of principle in modern society.

3. Tomorrow we'll discuss the article Introduction to Sportsworld.

4. Many John Denver fans consider Take Me Home, Country Roads to be his greatest song.

5. Although I don't care much for Poe, I do like his poems The Bells, The Raven, and Annabel Lee.

6. The title of Chapter Seven is Solar America.

Expressions Used in a Special Sense

Words, letters, numerals, and symbols used in a special sense—that is, singled out for particular attention rather than used for their meaning—are sometimes set off by quotation marks. Unusual terms and peculiar or slang expressions used deliberately fall within this category.

"Bonnets," "valves," and "lifts" are British terms for car hoods, radio tubes, and elevators.

It's hard to tell whether this letter is a "G" or a "C."

When arrested, the suspect was carrying a "Saturday night special."

Often, however, such expressions are printed in italics (see page 394).

Note that the commas and periods in our examples again come inside the quotation marks.

EXERCISE

Supply properly positioned quotation marks where necessary to correct the following sentences.

1. In the Eastern part of the United States, a carbonated soft drink is called a soda.

2. The symbol π has a value of 3.1416.

3. The personal pronoun I should always be capitalized.

4. The 7 in my house number isn't lined up with the other numbers.

5. Irony is a term often used in discussions of literature.

6. In this typeface, the bottom loop of the g is not completely closed.

Quotation Marks Within Quotation Marks

Occasionally, a direct quotation or the title of a shorter work will occur within a direct quotation. In such cases the inner quotation or title is set off with single quotation marks (' ').

The witness told the court, "I heard the defendant say, 'Let's rob Peterson's Party Store.'"

"For tomorrow's class meeting read William Faulkner's 'A Rose for Emily,'" the instructor said.

Notice that the period and the comma at the end of these double quotations come ahead of both the single mark and the double mark.

EXERCISE

Supply properly positioned quotation marks where necessary to correct the following sentences.

1. I consider Alexander's Ragtime Band a very mediocre song, the music critic sneered.

2. If you say I told you so one more time, I'll scream, Penny snapped angrily.

3. Henry said, Each morning to keep abreast of the news, I watch the PBS news program, Good Morning, America, or The Today Show.

4. When I shower, I always sing Singing in the Rain, my roommate confessed rather sheepishly.

Quotation Marks That Accompany Semicolons, Colons, Exclamation Points, and Question Marks

Unlike periods and commas, semicolons and colons that come at the end of quoted material are always placed outside the quotation marks.

He said, "I want to study drafting"; however, his placement test indicated a low aptitude for that field.

I have two good reasons for reading "The Fall of the House of Usher": I like Poe's short stories, and my English instructor has assigned it for next week.

A question mark or exclamation point may be placed either inside or outside the quotation marks, depending upon what it applies to. If, for example, only the quoted part of a sentence asks a question, the question mark goes inside the quotation marks. If the entire sentence, but not the quoted material, asks a question, the question mark goes outside the quotation marks. If the entire sentence asks one question and the quoted material asks another, then the question mark goes inside the quotation marks.

He asked, "When will your new apartment be ready?" (The quoted material, not the whole sentence, asks the question.)

Why did Irma suddenly announce, "I've quit my job"? (The whole sentence, not the quoted material, asks the question.)

Where did he get the nerve to ask, "How much money did you earn last year?" (The whole sentence and the quoted material ask separate questions.)

William's mother shouted, "Come into the house immediately!" (The quoted material, not the whole sentence, expresses strong emotion.)

EXERCISE

Supply properly positioned quotation marks where necessary to correct the following sentences.

1. She called the following my favorite English authors: John Keats, Jane Austen, and Charles Dickens.

2. Sidney told everyone, I spend two hours every night on this course; nevertheless, he could never answer his instructor's questions.

3. The interviewer asked the applicant, Why do you want to work for this company?

4. The man screamed, Run for your lives; the dam has broken!

5. Who said, A little inaccuracy sometimes saves tons of explanation?

6. What made my father ask me, Don't you think you're acting awfully foolish?

UNIT SELF-TEST

Supply properly positioned quotation marks where necessary to correct the following sentences.

"Well, Brian," the boss said, "how do you propose to correct your mistakes?"

1. You, your, and yours are second person pronouns.

2. The student asked, May I take the test early?

3. Why did Clayton insult his hostess by saying, This party is awfully dull?

4. The coach shouted, Let's play ball!

5. Tomorrow we'll discuss the essay, Why a Liberal Education, Anyway?

The answers are on pages 449–450.

UNIT REVIEW EXERCISE 29A
Quotation Marks

Supply properly positioned quotation marks where necessary to correct the following sentences.

"I like your suggestion," he said. "It should solve our problem very nicely."

1. Check to be sure you've dotted your i's and crossed your t's; then turn in your spelling test, the teacher told the class.

2. The author chose an unfortunate title, The Gay Caballero, for his short story.

3. Todd! his mother screamed furiously, you get out of that cookie jar right now!

4. She said, Mr. Kincaid is the person whose advice I value most.

5. These three tips will help make any vegetable garden a success, according to the article Green Thumb Gardening: Fertilize properly, weed regularly, and water every few days.

6. The instructor asked, Did I hear someone call, Help! when I passed out the test?

7. Don't be so nervous, Mr. Ackroyd, the detective said. No one has accused you of anything—least of all, murder.

8. The class voted Hemingway's short story Hills Like White Elephants and Eliot's poem The Love Song of J. Alfred Prufrock the most interesting works read during the term.

349

9. Is Frank Dubonning the one who asked, When do you suppose this company will provide its employees with dental insurance?

10. My handwriting is hard to read because each r looks like an s.

11. Becky said, The prices at this supermarket are ridiculously high; because of its convenient location, however, she continued to shop there.

12. What do you suppose prompted Billy to say, I wish I had never been born?

13. Marie asked, Do you plan to discuss the story Revelation in your paper on Flannery O'Connor?

14. There are four characters in Stephen Crane's The Open Boat: a captain, a cook, a correspondent, and an oiler.

15. Each day she asked herself silently, Why do I put up with all the drudgery and abuse of this job?

UNIT REVIEW EXERCISE 29B
Quotation Marks

Write three sentences for each indicated use of quotation marks and three additional sentences that involve quotation marks within quotation marks.

Direct Quotations

1. _____

_____

2. _____

_____

3. _____

_____

Titles of Shorter Works and Subdivisions of Books

1. _____

_____

2. _____

_____

3. _____

_____

Expressions Used in a Special Sense

1. _____

_____

2. _____

_____

3. _____

_____

Quotation Marks Within Quotation Marks

1. _____

_____

2. _____

_____

3. _____

_____

UNIT 30

Hyphens

Hyphens (-) are used to separate compound adjectives and nouns, two-word numbers and fractions, numerals followed by units of measurement, and certain prefixes and suffixes from the words with which they appear. In addition, they are employed to prevent misreadings and awkward combinations of letters or syllables.

Compound Adjectives and Nouns

Perhaps the most common use of the hyphen is to link two or more words that precede a noun, thereby allowing them to function as a single adjective. Such combinations, called compound adjectives, occur frequently in writing, allowing a wide range of ideas to be expressed. Here are two examples.

> The *deep-blue* sea was beautiful.
> Elroy's *holier-than-thou* attitude has made him a great many enemies.

Note that the meaning of the first sentence would change if the hyphen were replaced with a comma or simply omitted. With the hyphen, we are referring to a sea that is deep blue in color. If the hyphen were replaced with a comma, we would be referring to a sea that is deep and blue. With neither a hyphen nor a comma, there would be no way to tell which is deep, the color blue or the sea itself.

When the first word of the compound is an adverb ending in *-ly* or when the compound adjective comes after the noun it modifies, the hyphen is omitted.

> The deeply embarrassed man apologized for his comment.
> The sea was deep blue.

In a series of two or more compound adjectives that all have the same term following the hyphen, the term following the hyphen need not be repeated throughout the series. It is often briefer and smoother to use the term only at the end of the series. However, the hyphens preceding omitted parts are retained. These hyphens are called *suspension hyphens*.

> The *third-, fourth-,* and *fifth-floor* rooms are being repainted.

Hyphenated nouns include such expressions as the following:

editor-in-chief	jack-of-all-trades
father-in-law	lady-in-waiting
go-between	man-about-town

Here are two sentences with hyphenated nouns.

> My *sister-in-law* is visiting us next week.
> Denton is *editor-in-chief* of the largest newspaper in this state.

EXERCISE

Supply hyphens where necessary to correct the following sentences.

1. I like the pea green blouse better than the one that's navy blue.

2. Wouldn't it be nice to have a six or seven figure income?

3. Morton's damn the public approach to his customers soon caused his business to fail.

4. My mother in law is both friendly and helpful.

5. I'm afraid you're living in a make believe world.

6. The grease coated stove looked as if it had never been cleaned.

7. As a former movie star, I'm an expert on fair weather friends.

8. Maxwell is a Johnny come lately in this industry.

Two-Word Numbers, Fractions, and Numerals with Units of Measurement

Hyphens are used in two-word numbers from twenty-one to ninety-nine and in fractions when these are written out.

> Alan McGee has served *twenty-three* years as a United States Representative.
>
> *Two-thirds* of the class will receive Cs.

Similarly, hyphens are used to separate numerals followed by units of measurement.

> The *40-hour* workweek was the exception, not the rule, fifty years ago.

EXERCISE

Supply hyphens where necessary to correct the following sentences.

1. Professor Hill's marching band has seventy six trombones.

2. Have you heard the latest 30 day weather forecast?

3. About one third of our work force will lose their jobs if this recession continues.

4. Within the next thirty days, we will start offering 90 day guarantees on our Fasklik line of cameras.

5. At the age of twenty three, Sidney was graduated from MIT with a doctorate in physics.

6. We'd better stop for gasoline; our tank is three fourths empty.

7. This 60 watt bulb is too dim to read by.

8. Jethro was horrified when fifty eight uninvited relatives descended on his new lakeshore cottage last weekend.

Prefixes and Suffixes

Prefixes and suffixes are words or a group of letters attached to words to expand or change their meaning. A prefix is attached at the beginning of the word; a suffix is attached at the end of the word. Although most prefixes are not hyphenated, the prefixes *self-* and *all-* and the suffix *-elect* are set off with hyphens, as is the prefix *ex-* when it precedes a noun.

The founder of this magazine is a *self-made* woman.

The timing of this announcement is *all-important.*

Norbert is *president-elect* of our club.

The *ex-governor* gave a speech.

How can I *ex*press my gratitude for your help? (Because *ex-* does not precede a noun, it is not hyphenated.)

A prefix used before a term that begins with a capital letter is always hyphenated.

The senator was accused of being *un-American.*

The *anti-CIA* speaker received little applause.

EXERCISE

Supply hyphens where necessary to correct the following sentences. Draw a caret (∧) at any point where a hyphen ought to be and put the hyphen above it.

1. The transCanadian pipeline brings Alaskan oil to the United States.

2. Let Kandu, the all knowing soothsayer, have a look into your future.

3. Those preColumbian statues of yours belong in a museum.

4. What is a self fulfilling prophecy, anyhow?

5. Mr. Gonzales, our chairman elect, has had twelve years' experience as a member of the board.

6. The post World War II period has witnessed many far-reaching social changes.

7. Our new neighbor, an excolonel in the army, feels that this country's military budget is inadequate.

8. Ever since her visit to Dublin, Sandra has been proIrish.

Preventing Misreadings and Awkward Combinations of Letters and Syllables

Hyphens are also used to prevent misreadings of certain words that would look like other words if they were not hyphenated, as well as to prevent awkward combinations of letters or syllables between some prefixes and suffixes and their core words.

> The *un-ionized* salt precipitates from the solution. (Without the hyphen, the word, meaning *not ionized*, might be misread as *unionized*.)
>
> The worker *re-covered* the exposed pipe. (Without the hyphen, the word might be misread as *recovered*.)
>
> The committee is determined to *de-emphasize* sports at Franklin Pierce High School. (The hyphen prevents the awkward repetition of letter *e* in *de-emphasize*.)

EXERCISE

Supply hyphens where necessary to correct the following sentences. Draw a caret (∧) at any point where a hyphen ought to be and put the hyphen above it.

1. This drawing is a recreation of the scene of the accident.

2. The President's antiinflationary policies seem woefully inadequate to me.

3. The reentry point for the space capsule is over the Indian Ocean.

4. Two student coops will open next semester.

5. Such ultraambitious fellows make me feel very tired.

6. The villain tried to whisper sweet nothings into the shelllike ear of the pure young maiden.

7. Twice in the last six weeks, my favorite TV program has been preempted by a sports special

8. The recount showed that Rakovitch, not Manders, had been elected sheriff.

UNIT SELF-TEST

Supply hyphens where necessary to correct the following sentences.

Please resort the three, four, and five-inch bolts; someone has mixed them up again.

1. The company's twenty eighth year brought a 41 percent increase over the previous year's sales.

2. Florian's devil may care behavior will land him in trouble one of these days.

3. Several four, six, and eight cylinder engines were overhauled yesterday.

4. The farmers' coop will hold a business meeting next Friday.

5. He's an ultraargumentative fellow, that's for certain!

The answers are on page 450.

UNIT REVIEW EXERCISE 30A
Hyphens

Supply hyphens where necessary to correct the following sentences.

This get-rich-quick scheme is bound to fail.

1. The new elevator operator already knows every tenant in the high rise apartment building on a first name basis.

2. Two 4 foot posters at the entrance to the arena announced in blood red letters that Killer McGurk was fighting the Canvasback Kid.

3. Lisa Marie asked her exboyfriend whether the antiUnited Nations rally would be held next Wednesday.

4. The icecovered roads kept two thirds of the students from attending school.

5. In late afternoon on the twenty seventh of August, the sky turned an eerie blood red because of a volcanic eruption hundreds of miles away.

6. Mr. Faber's four, five, and six chapter reading assignments are very unfair.

7. Elroy's superior, know it all attitude irritates his father in law, who labels him a dyed in the wool swelled head.

8. The doctor retreated the rash, but the insurance company refused to pay the bill, claiming that the problem was the result of a preexisting condition.

9. The proSoviet speaker received a cool reception from the American Legion, an antiRussian audience.

10. "Unless it rains within a week, at least three fourths of my crop will be ruined," the farmer moaned.

11. The coroner ruled that John Symonds, the vicepresident of Bacon, Little, Inc., had died of a selfinflicted gunshot wound.

12. Gary Hensley was an allAmerican football star thirty two years ago.

13. My son in law is an exmarine.

14. The two and one half mile walk across the windswept fields left the lightly dressed man shivering and half frozen.

15. Their house is a three story, twenty one room, four and a half bath Victorian mansion.

UNIT REVIEW EXERCISE 30B
Hyphens

Write three sentences for each indicated use of the hyphen.

To Separate Compound Adjectives and Nouns

1. _____

_____

2. _____

_____

3. _____

_____

To Separate Two-Word Numbers and Fractions, Numerals with Units of Measurement

1. _____

_____

2. _____

_____

3. _____

_____

To Separate Prefixes and Suffixes from the Words with Which They Appear

1. _____

_____

2. _____

_____

3. _____

_____

To Prevent Misreadings and Awkward Combinations of Letters and Syllables

1. _____

_____

2. _____

_____

3. _____

_____

UNIT 31

Capitalization

The first letter of any sentence, including any sentence that appears as a quotation within another sentence, is always capitalized, as is the pronoun *I*, both by itself and in contractions.

There are eight rooms in my new house.

He said, "When *I* finish this job, *I*'ll watch television with you."

In addition, capitals are used with *proper nouns* (nouns that name someone or something specific), adjectives derived from such proper nouns, certain abbreviations, personal titles preceding names, and titles of literary and artistic works.

Proper Nouns

Proper nouns refer to one particular person, group of persons, place, or thing, and they are always capitalized. They include names of the following:

persons
organizations and institutions
racial, national, political, and religious groups (but not *black* and *white*)
countries, states, cities, streets, and buildings
geographical locations and geographical features
days, holidays, and months (but not seasons)
trademarked products (and slogans that are trademarked)
languages
ships, trains, and airplanes
historical events, documents, and eras
God, the Bible and its parts, and other sacred writings

The following sentences illustrate the capitalization of proper nouns.

> He attends *Ferris State College,* a school that has pioneered in offering health-related programs. (The sentence names an institution.)
>
> *Lolita Martinez,* our class valedictorian, was born in *Matamoras, Mexico.* (The sentence names a person, a city, and a country.)
>
> Next *Sunday, June* 5, I begin work as a supervisor. (The sentence names a day and a month.)
>
> Many historians feel that the *Battle of Gettysburg* marked the turning point of the *American Civil War.* (The sentence names historical events.)
>
> Last spring we moved to 154 *Trinity Street, Omaha, Nebraska.* (The sentence names a street, a city, and a state.)
>
> My mother's father is a staunch *Roman Catholic* and a *Republican;* my other grandfather is a *Presbyterian* and a *Democrat.* (The sentence names religious denominations and political parties.)
>
> While visiting *Yellowstone National Park,* the Millards saw *Old Faithful,* a geyser that erupts every forty-seven minutes. (The sentence names a geographical location and a geographical feature.)
>
> My college program includes two years of *French.* (The sentence names a language.)
>
> Of all the books in the *Bible,* my favorite is *Ecclesiastes.* (The sentence names the Bible and a book in the Bible.)
>
> My belief in *God* has never been stronger; *He* has helped me through many troubled times. (The sentence names God and uses a pronoun meaning "God.")
>
> Although I'm no champion of any kind, I do eat a bowl of *Wheaties* every morning. (The sentence names a trademarked product.)
>
> The *Middle Ages* were a period of greater cultural achievement than is generally realized. (The sentence names a historical epoch.)
>
> Thomas Jefferson, our third president, is the author of the *Declaration of Independence.* (The sentence names an historical document.)
>
> Anthropologists divide humans into three major racial groups: *Caucasian, Mongolian,* and *Negroid.* (The sentence names racial groups.)

Terms such as "building," "street," "company," and the like are not capitalized unless they form part of a proper name. Thus, in the following sentence, "building" is not capitalized when it is written by itself.

> The Empire State Building was once the tallest building in the world.

Similarly, the names of nonlanguage courses are not capitalized unless they are followed by a course designation or begin a sentence.

> This term, Geology 101 is my worst course, but algebra is causing me no difficulty at all.

EXERCISE

Circle the first letter of each proper noun in the following sentences to show that it ought to be capitalized. Some sentences may have more than one proper noun.

1. Have you seen the new TV advertisement for scotchgard adhesive tape?

2. The walla walla cannonball, the only train line in the southern part of washington, has been in operation since before the civil war.

3. Paul gleason, one of the most prominent blacks in this city, holds a graduate degree from the wharton school of finance.

4. The artist erte, a native of russia, will issue a new portfolio of pictures, named vamps, this fall.

5. The book of genesis tells us that our lord created the earth in seven days.

6. Dewey cheetum, an officer in the people's party for purity in politics, lives at 811 web street.

7. Rumor has it that the big rock candy company will have bought out a small bubble gum company by labor day.

8. Pierre beaudin, a prominent french political leader, addressed the san francisco chapter of the league of women voters last tuesday evening.

9. During the renaissance, scholars wrote almost exclusively in latin.

10. The jesuit order will hold an important conference in the black hills sometime this spring, probably in may.

Proper Adjectives

Adjectives created from proper nouns are called proper adjectives. Like the nouns themselves, they should be capitalized.

Lolita Martinez, our class valedictorian, is of Mexican ancestry. (*Mexican* is derived from the proper noun *Mexico*.)

The most interesting English course I've taken at Bullock State College is English 251, Victorian literature. *(English* is derived from the proper noun *England* and *Victorian* from the proper noun *Victoria.)*

Certain usages of proper nouns and words derived from them have become so well established that the expressions are regarded as ordinary or general nouns—known as *common nouns*—and are written without capitals. Here are a few examples:

brussels sprouts	morocco leather
chinaware	plaster of paris
frankfurters	roman candle
french fried potatoes	swiss cheese
hamburger	turkish towel
india ink	volt
italics	watt

The smell of *brussels sprouts* and *frankfurters* wafted through the kitchen door and into the living room, warning the people there that another terrible meal was about ready.

EXERCISE

Circle the first letter of each proper adjective in the following sentences to show that it ought to be capitalized.

1. Cleo's house is an example of egyptian architecture at its finest.

2. The wrestling promoters, eager to fill the arena, have labeled Friday's main event as a texan death match.

3. The play we saw last week had two biblical characters.

4. In our part of the country, it's not wise to manifest marxist beliefs.

5. Professor Bacon is one of this country's most prominent shakespearean scholars.

Abbreviations

Abbreviations are capitalized if the first letters of the words they stand for would be capitalized; otherwise, they are not.

Stanley Kolinski is an *FBI* agent. *(FBI* is capitalized because "Federal Bureau of Investigation" would be.)

The shaft revolves 1,500 *rpm*. (The abbreviation *rpm* is not capitalized because "revolutions per minute" would not be.)

EXERCISE

Circle abbreviations that ought to be capitalized in the following sentences. If the sentence is correct, write a "C" in the blank to the left.

_____   1. Negotiations for a new contract between the auto makers and the uaw will begin sometime next month.

_____   2. Ralph says that each cigarette of the brand he's now smoking contains 9.5 mg of tar.

_____   3. Do you think that the 55 mph speed limit should be more strictly enforced?

_____   4. Yesterday, nbc announced that it had purchased the right to televise next year's Super Bowl.

_____   5. Congress voted less money for the cia this year than it did last year.

Personal Titles

Capitalize the first letter of a personal title that immediately precedes a name. A personal title not followed by a name is ordinarily left uncapitalized unless it is used in place of the name.

> The graduating seniors heard an address by *Dean* Arthur Swanson. (The title is capitalized because it precedes the name.)
>
> Tell me, *Dean,* will this year's enrollment exceed last year's? (The title is capitalized because it is used in place of the name.)
>
> The *dean* of our Special Education Division is Dr. Helen McConnell. (The title *dean* is not capitalized because it does not precede the name and is not used in place of the name.)

With persons of high rank, titles used in place of names are often capitalized as a mark of respect.

> I plan to watch the President on TV tonight.
>
> I plan to watch the president on TV tonight.

Either of these usages is acceptable, although the second is preferred.

EXERCISE

Circle the first letters of personal titles in the following sentences if they ought to be capitalized. If the sentence is correct, write a "C" in the blank to the left.

_____   1. Few queens have been as influential in shaping British policy as was queen Elizabeth I.

_____   2. We are fortunate to have as our speaker mayor Coleman Young.

_____   3. Do you believe that the popular image of politicians has improved, senator?

_____   4. Mr. Trevine was governor of this state for two terms during the fifties.

_____   5. Whether Walter is competent to stand trial will be determined in the courtroom of judge Mabel Mitty.

Titles of Literary and Artistic Works

Literary and artistic works include books, magazines, newspapers, articles, short stories, poems, reports, films, television programs, musical compositions, pictures, sculptures, and the like.

When you write such titles, capitalize the first and last words as well as all other words except *a, an, the,* coordinating conjunctions, and prepositions with fewer than five letters.

> My favorite play is Tennessee Williams's *The Glass Menagerie,* and my favorite painting is Salvador Dali's *The Last Supper.* (All the words in the titles are capitalized.)
>
> Our course textbook will be *The Basics of Industrial Hygiene.* (The short preposition *of* is not capitalized.)
>
> He used a study guide, *Solving Problems in Chemistry and Physics,* when he did his homework. (The short preposition *in* and the coordinating conjunction *and* are not capitalized.)
>
> Ambrose boarded a bus and sat next to a woman reading a book entitled *All About Psychic Phenomena.* (The five-letter preposition *About* is capitalized.)

Note that the titles of major literary and artistic works are italicized (see pp. 391–392).

EXERCISE

Circle the first letters of literary and artistic works where capitalization is necessary.

1. Shelley is in her room listening to Kenny Rogers' album *ten years of gold;* Paula is watching a special program, "justice delayed is justice denied."

2. *sports illustrated* and the sports section of the *los angeles times* keep me posted on my favorite athletes.

3. For Monday, our assignment is to read Robert Frost's poem "stopping by woods on a snowy evening" and Sherwood Anderson's short story "death in the woods" in our anthology *modern literature.*

4. I've decided to purchase Pegnor's painting *just above the clouds.*

5. Shall we watch "charlie's angels" on TV or go to the movies and see *the empire strikes back?*

6. This article, "after the me generation," offers a fine analysis of modern social trends.

UNIT SELF-TEST

Correct the following sentences by supplying and deleting capitals as necessary. Add capitals by circling the lowercase letters that ought to be capitalized. Draw a slash (/) through capitals that ought to be lowercase.

Merilee has just been graduated with an M.a. in History.

1. While visiting san francisco last Summer, janet stayed at the Mark Hopkins hotel.

2. After the attack on pearl harbor, many innocent people of japanese ancestry were sent to concentration camps.

3. Each account at people's savings bank is insured by the Federal Deposit Insurance Corporation (fdic).

4. After aunt Hannah's accident last Winter, everyone was very careful when crossing Harbor street.

5. Last night, i watched the widely acclaimed television documentary "africa: its land and people."

The answers are on page 450.

UNIT REVIEW EXERCISE 31A
Capitalization

Correct the following sentences by supplying and deleting capitals as necessary. Add capitals by circling the lowercase letters that ought to be capitalized. Draw a slash (/) through capitals that ought to be lowercase.

Ellen is a native Ⓜichigander, and every S̸ummer she returns to that state for a visit.

1. the industrial revolution came to america after it had come to europe.

2. three-fourths of father's estate was left to my mother; the rest was divided between my brother and me.

3. starting next week, we will begin an extensive study of the bible; our first assignment will be to read the book of genesis.

4. the members of the zonta club will hold their annual new year's eve party in bryan hall.

5. arapoosh's essay, "crow indian country," will be reprinted in the december issue of *the ethnic review*.

6. tom's family Doctor referred him to dr. Leland F. Hilton, who specializes in eye Surgery.

7. the announcer said, "tonight we will interview the republican candidate for governor, who, if elected, will be the first mormon to hold our state's highest office."

8. the trademark "breakfast of champions," registered by general mills, appears on every box of wheaties.

9. after receiving a low grade on his government 101 midterm, Bill moaned, "how will i ever pass this course?"

10. edward wallenberg, who speaks and writes chinese fluently, has accepted a government job as an Interpreter.

11. the naacp has filed charges of racial discrimination against Amboy technical college, a College with a national reputation for its automotive programs.

12. lucy bought reproductions of Mary Cassatt's *the bath* and paul gauguin's *by the sea* for her living room.

13. paul j. brock, a stockbroker for over twenty-five years, will speak at our july meeting.

14. several different magazines, including *scribner's, the woman's home companion, the literary digest,* and *flair* are in my Doctor's waiting room.

15. the irish and english soccer teams have traditionally been bitter rivals.

UNIT REVIEW EXERCISE 31B
Capitalization

Write two sentences for each use of capitals.

Proper Nouns

1. _____

_____

_____

2. _____

_____

_____

Adjectives Derived from Proper Nouns

1. _____

_____

_____

2. _____

_____

_____

Abbreviations

1. _____

_____

_____

2. _____

_____

_____

Personal Titles

1. _____

_____

_____

2. _____

_____

_____

Titles of Short Stories, Short Poems, and Articles

1. _____

_____

_____

2. _____

_____

_____

UNIT 32

Abbreviations and Numbers

At one time or another, most of us have come across sentences like this one:

I'll take my Geo. 101 test on Jn. 3, leave old M. St. for a vacation in Cal., and return on Jn. 17.

Such sentences are undesirable on at least two counts. For one thing, the reader often can't tell what an abbreviation means. Here, for example, "Geo." could mean "Geology," "Geography," or "Geometry," and "M." could stand for any one of several states. In addition, unwarranted abbreviations like "Jn. 3 . . . Jn. 17" are likely to irritate the reader and slow the pace of reading.

Knowing the rules that govern the use of abbreviations and the writing of numbers will allow you to avoid this sort of confusion and irritation.

Abbreviations

Abbreviations are used for certain personal titles, names of organizations and agencies, Latin terms, and for scientific and technical terms. Names of persons, streets, geographical locations, days, months, and school and college courses should be spelled out.

Personal Titles

Mister, doctor, and similar titles of address are always abbreviated when they immediately precede a name.

Mr. John Williams and *Mrs.* Sandra Barkon operate a small medical testing laboratory.
He spoke to *Dr.* Mandell about his standing in the class.

Junior, Senior, Esquire, and degree titles are abbreviated when they immediately follow proper names.

The company was founded by Anthony Cappucine, *Jr.*
The sign on the office identified its occupant as Elizabeth Williams, *M.D.*

EXERCISE

Substitute proper abbreviations where necessary in the following sentences by crossing out full forms and writing the abbreviations above them.

1. Gail Birnhausen, Master of Arts, has joined the faculty at Costa

   Blanca Community College.

2. Tell me more about these noises you've been hearing, Mister Usher.

3. Thomas S. Arnold, Esquire, has been asked to chair the conference

   on medieval architecture.

4. After deliberating for six hours, the jury returned a verdict of guilty

   against Arthur Lidlicker, Doctor of Dental Surgery.

5. If that pain in your chest doesn't go away, make an appointment

   with Doctor Abraham Goldberg, Senior.

Names of Organizations and Agencies

Some organizations or agencies are commonly referred to by their initials. Here are some typical abbreviations of this kind:

FBI	AMA	NASA	CIA
GOP	UN	HUD	ACLU

EXERCISE

In the following sentences, substitute proper abbreviations according to customary usage by crossing out full forms and writing the abbreviations above them.

1. The National Football League Monday night football game is pro-

   duced by American Broadcasting Company sports.

2. It's about time that the Environmental Protection Agency established and enforced strict rules for toxic waste disposal.

3. Ten years ago I sold all my stock in International Business Machines, and now I couldn't be sorrier.

4. Practically every month the Food and Drug Administration says something is hazardous to our health.

5. The Interstate Commerce Commission is investigating the Central States Trucking Company.

Latin Terms and Abbreviations with Dates

Certain Latin terms are always abbreviated; and other terms, mostly Latin, are abbreviated when they occur with dates or numerals.

e.g. (*exempli gratia*: for example)
etc. (*et cetera*: and [the] others)
i.e. (*id est*: that is)
vs. (*versus*: against)
B.C. (before Christ)
A.D. (*anno Domini*: In the year of our Lord)
A.M. (a.m.) (*ante meridiem*: before noon)
P.M. (p.m.) (*post meridiem*: after noon)

The last two terms (A.M. and P.M.) should be written with capitals; often, however, they are written with lowercase letters.

The Greek philosopher Aristotle died in 322 B.C.
I'll pick you up around 7 P.M.
Certain diseases—e.g. measles and polio—are no longer serious childhood threats.

EXERCISE

Write the abbreviation for the Latin term in each of the following sentences in the blank to the left.

_____ 1. It looks as if it will be the Dodgers *versus* the Yankees in this year's World Series.

_____ 2. Applications received after 5:00 *post meridiem* next Friday won't be considered.

_____ 3. The Roman Emperor Nero was born in 37 *anno Domini.*

_____ 4. The expression *et cetera* should be used very sparingly in one's writing.

_____ 5. I think 5:00 *ante meridiem* is too early in the morning to begin our trip.

Scientific and Technical Terms

Science and technology make use of many terms of measurement. When these terms occur repeatedly in a single article or report, they are generally abbreviated. Whenever the meaning of the abbreviation might not be known to every reader, the term is written out the first time it is used and its abbreviation, in parentheses, put immediately after it.

The heater was a 250,000 British thermal unit (Btu) model.

Ordinarily, such an abbreviation is written without periods. However, if it has the same spelling as another word, a period is generally used after the last letter to distinguish the abbreviation from the word. Thus, *inch* is abbreviated *in.* to distinguish it from *in,* and *fig.* rather than *fig* is used for *figure.*

EXERCISE

Write the abbreviation for the scientific term in each of the following sentences in the blank to the left.

_____ 1. I prefer to watch ultra high frequency television stations.

_____ 2. Will you hand me that thirty cubic centimeter syringe, please?

_____ 3. The analysis showed that the air contained 20 parts per million of sulfuric acid.

_____ 4. This engine is now operating at 3,500 revolutions per minute.

_____ 5. Terence didn't know that 212° Fahrenheit is the same as 100° Centigrade.

Numbers

Figures are usually used for numbers higher than one hundred. Numbers smaller than one hundred are usually written as words. This is not a hard-and-fast rule, however, and some writers prefer to spell out numbers through nine and use figures for all others. No matter which general practice your instructor prefers, there are several specific exceptions. These are discussed below.

Numbers in a Series

Numbers in a series should be written in the same way, regardless of their size.

We have 150 salesmen, 52 research engineers, and 7 laboratory technicians.

Harley owns three cars, two motorboats, and two snowmobiles.

EXERCISE

Correct any miswriting of numbers in the following sentences by crossing out errors and writing the proper forms above them.

1. The line totals for the Cubs were 6 runs, fourteen hits, and 2 errors.

2. Jay has twenty-four suits, eighty-seven shirts, and 114 ties.

3. This year we planted only 4 rows of radishes, 3 rows of onions, and

   2 rows of cucumbers.

4. Sandy has 7 bluegrass, sixteen hard rock, and 139 classical albums

   in her record collection.

5. During the last two years, Jerry has worked 7 months in a grocery

   store, 3 months in a car wash, and four months as a carpenter.

Dates

In dates that include the year, figures are always used.

January 3, 1975 (not January 3rd, 1975)

When the year is not given, the number may be spelled out or figures may be used.

August 5
August fifth
the fifth of August

All of the above examples are correct.

EXERCISE

Correct any miswriting of dates in the following sentences by crossing out errors and writing the proper forms above them. If a sentence is correct, write a "C" in the blank to the left.

_____ 1. The last time the Cleveland Indians won the American League pennant was back in nineteen fifty-four.

_____ 2. My parents' wedding anniversary is June eighth.

_____ 3. They were married June eighth, 1957, in Houston, Texas.

_____ 4. October twenty 9, 1929, the day the stock market crashed, is sometimes known as "Black Monday."

_____ 5. Billy must appear in court on the ninth of January.

Addresses and Page Numbers

Figures are also used for numbers in street addresses and for page numbers of publications.

Her photographic studio is located at *139* Powell Street.
The diagram is on page *223* of the text.

EXERCISE

Correct any miswriting of addresses and page numbers in the following sentences by crossing out errors and writing the proper forms above them. If a sentence is correct, write a "C" in the blank to the left.

_____ 1. The corporate headquarters of the W. E. Slaughter

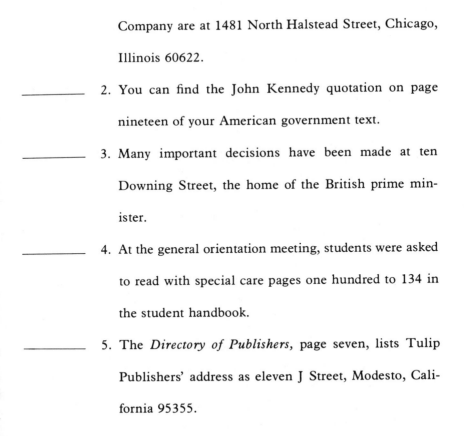

Company are at 1481 North Halstead Street, Chicago,

Illinois 60622.

_____ 2. You can find the John Kennedy quotation on page

nineteen of your American government text.

_____ 3. Many important decisions have been made at ten

Downing Street, the home of the British prime min-

ister.

_____ 4. At the general orientation meeting, students were asked

to read with special care pages one hundred to 134 in

the student handbook.

_____ 5. The *Directory of Publishers,* page seven, lists Tulip

Publishers' address as eleven J Street, Modesto, Cali-

fornia 95355.

Numbers Beginning Sentences

Any number beginning a sentence should be spelled out. If this would require too many words, the sentence should be rewritten so that the number occurs within the sentence.

Forty thousand voters went to the polls.
A crowd of *115,394* people attended the game. (If this number began the sentence, eight words, an excessive number, would be needed to write it out.)

EXERCISE

Correct any miswriting of numbers in the following sentences by crossing out errors and writing the proper forms above them. If a sentence is correct, write a "C" in the blank to the left.

_____ 1. A total of two hundred eighty-six thousand four

hundred signatures is needed before the Goetsch proposal can be placed on the November ballot.

———————— 2. 309 people are now confirmed dead in Thursday's air
disaster.

———————— 3. 8 to ten students usually earn *A*'s in Dr. Tallman's
psychology class.

———————— 4. 1 more remark out of you, young man, and you're
grounded this weekend.

———————— 5. Thirteen has long been considered an unlucky number.

Decimals, Percentages, Expressions of Time

Figures are used for decimals, percentages, and expressions of
time with A.M. or P.M.

The metal is *0.125* inch thick. (decimal)
The project has been *35* percent completed. (percentage)
My father's workday starts at *9* A.M. and ends at *4:30* P.M. (expression
of time)

EXERCISE

*Correct any miswriting of numbers in the following sentences by
crossing out errors and writing the proper forms above them. If a sentence
is correct, write a "C" in the blank to the left.*

———————— 1. Paula isn't thrilled about her fourteen and a half percent mortgage, but at the time she got it, no better rate
was available.

———————— 2. The auction will start promptly at ten A.M. next
Thursday.

_____ 3. If the racquet club is to make a profit, its courts must

be filled at least forty-five percent of the time.

_____ 4. There must be a clearance of 0.025 inch between the

two parts.

_____ 5. By five P.M. Friday, less than thirty percent of the

questionnaires had been returned.

UNIT SELF-TEST

Correct any misuse of abbreviations or miswriting of numbers in the following sentences by crossing out errors and writing the proper forms above them.

For ~~6~~ six consecutive ~~yrs.~~ years the ~~Int. Rev.~~ Internal Revenue Service has audited my income

tax returns.

1. Doctor Albert Hamilton received his degree in Aug., 1971.

2. The television special is being shown at seven P.M.

3. About seventy-five percent of the project will have been completed

by August, Nineteen Eighty-One.

4. The freighter carried a cargo of 250 tons of coal, five hundred bar-

rels of palm oil, and 350 gasoline pumps.

5. 14 teams have already signed up to play in the tennis doubles tour-

nament at E. Hills Racquet Club.

The answers are on page 451.

UNIT REVIEW EXERCISE 32A
Abbreviations and Numbers

Correct any misuse of abbreviations or miswriting of numbers in the following sentences by crossing out errors and writing the proper forms above them.

Our department chairman, ~~Doctor~~ *Dr.* Thomas Nagy, has been named ~~vice-pres~~. *vice-president* for Academic Affairs.

1. Ormond Cathedral is 500 feet long, three hundred feet wide, and 250 feet high at its tallest point.

2. Fred's family doctor referred him to Doctor Mary Anne James, an eye specialist who had graduated from the U. of Miss.

3. Bertha will be 8 yrs. old next June ninth, and to celebrate we're planning a party that will be held at her home, 241 Lombard St.

4. The Federal Bureau of Investigation was voted a twenty-five percent budget increase by Congress, but the National Aeronautics and Space Administration had its budget cut by 7 percent.

5. On Fri., Sept. 9th, John will have one of his wisdom teeth extracted.

6. Alfred Michaels, my old college roommate, now lives at four five six Desert Dr., Scottsdale, Mont.

7. My dr. bought 6 flowering crab trees for his backyard.

8. According to the latest government figures, housing costs have risen forty-two percent in the last 4 years.

9. 5 candidates will be invited to the Dodge Company's main office, at eighty-nine Lancaster Ave., to interview for a new engineering position.

10. In one hundred forty-six before Christ, Carthage was destroyed by the Romans.

11. Pres. John Kennedy was assassinated in Nov., Nineteen hundred and sixty-three.

12. Doctor Charles Ruth, Junior, will be the chief speaker at the monthly meeting of our health forum.

13. Page two hundred ninety-one of our govt. book has 3 typographical errors.

14. 144 sq. ft. of floor space will be needed for the new press.

15. The club selected Mister Harold Barkowitz, Joyce Atkins, Doctor of Philosophy, and Stanley Winkelman, Esquire, to take part in a panel discussion on ecology.

UNIT REVIEW EXERCISE 32B
Abbreviations and Numbers

Write one sentence for each use of abbreviations and numbers indicated below.

Abbreviations

Personal Titles

_____

_____

_____

Names of Organizations and Agencies

_____

_____

_____

Latin Terms

_____

_____

_____

Scientific and Technical Terms

_____

_____

_____

Numbers

Numbers in a Series

_____

_____

_____

Dates

_____

_____

_____

Addresses

_____

_____

_____

Page Numbers

_____

_____

_____

Numbers Beginning Sentences

_____

_____

_____

Decimals

_____

_____

_____

Percentages

_____

_____

_____

Expressions of Time

_____

_____

_____

UNIT 33

Italics

Italics are used for the titles of longer publications and of artistic works, the proper names of vehicles and vessels, foreign words and phrases, and expressions used in a special sense—that is, called to the reader's attention rather than used for their meaning. In handwritten and typed papers, underlining indicates italics.

Titles of Longer Publications and of Artistic Works

Italics are used to designate the titles of the following:

books	full-length movies
magazines	long musical works and poems
newspapers	plays
journals	sculptures
bulletins	paintings

Titles of articles, newspaper columns, short stories, short poems, one-act plays, and the like are set off with quotation marks.

Ann's favorite novel is Tolstoy's *War and Peace,* yet she never misses an issue of *True Romances.* (book, magazine)

His paper included quotations from *The New York Times,* the *Journal of Business Education,* and a U.S. Office of Education bulletin entitled *Business School Enrollments, 1965–1975.* (newspaper, journal, bulletin)

Have you ever seen Picasso's *Guernica*? (painting)

West Side Story, which had great success both as a Broadway musical and as a film, was based on Shakespeare's *Romeo and Juliet.* (musical and movie, play)

John Milton's sonnet "On His Blindness" is one of the greatest short poems in English, but his masterpiece is surely *Paradise Lost.* (short poem in quotes; long poem in italics)

An exception to this rule occurs with references to the Bible and the parts of the Bible, which are written without italics.

My favorite part of the Bible is the Book of Psalms, which is found in the Old Testament.

EXERCISE

Supply italics by underlining where necessary to correct the following sentences. If a sentence is correct, write a "C" in the blank to the left.

_____   1. "My turn," a column by Felix Farnsworth, appears five days a week in the Columbus Post Gazette.

_____   2. One whole wall of our basement is lined with my father's back copies of the quarterly bulletin Business Barometer.

_____   3. A copy of van Gogh's picture Sunflowers hangs in Mr. Lintner's living room.

_____   4. I never tire of reading the Sermon on the Mount, which appears in the book of Matthew.

_____   5. Gone with the Wind, starring Clark Gable and Vivien Leigh, is my all-time favorite movie.

_____   6. Rosalita Lopez subscribes to Ms., Working Woman, and New Dawn.

_____   7. Did you read Martin Kane's article on professional boxing in the latest issue of Sports Illustrated?

_____   8. The Best-Loved Fiction of Edgar Allan Poe begins with a story entitled "The Purloined Letter."

_____   9. Dale Pemerantz has had an article accepted for publication in the winter issue of the New England Law Journal.

_____   10. Stephen Crane's novel Maggie: A Girl of the Streets sold almost no copies when first published.

Names of Vehicles and Vessels

Proper names of individual airplanes, ships, trains, and spacecraft are italicized (but not their model designations, such as DC-7 or Boeing 747, or abbreviations preceding them, such as S.S.).

He flew to Oslo on the *Star of the North*. He sailed back on *Queen Elizabeth II*. (plane, ship)

EXERCISE

Supply italics by underlining where necessary to correct the following sentences. If a sentence is correct, write a "C" in the blank to the left.

_____ 1. The luxury liner S.S. Princess Victoria sailed from Bristol the fourteenth of last month.

_____ 2. Because of several recent crashes, the FAA has grounded all DC-10's until further notice.

_____ 3. Voyager II is the second in a series of unmanned spacecraft that this country will launch.

_____ 4. The only streamlined passenger train that passes through this town is the Peoria Pearl.

_____ 5. William P. Whittenden, chairman of the board of Conway, Inc., flew to the annual stockholders' meeting in Zodiac Zephyr, the company's private jet.

Foreign Words and Phrases

Many foreign words and phrases have made their way into English over the centuries. At any one time there are many that have not been completely absorbed, and these are italicized.

He committed a terrible *faux pas* (social blunder).

I have a strange feeling of *déjà vu* (a sensation that something has been experienced before).

When a foreign word is completely absorbed into the English language, the italics are dropped. For example, the word *employee,* originally a French word, used to be italicized but no longer is. Collegiate dictionaries use a special symbol such as an asterisk (*) or a dagger (†) to mark words or phrases that should be italicized. Check the introductory part of your dictionary to see what symbol it uses, and italicize any items marked with the symbol.

EXERCISE

Supply italics by underlining where necessary to correct the following sentences.

1. I often hear the French expression c'est la vie, which means "that's life."

2. Detective Holmes tried to piece together a modus operandi for the series of robberies in Pinehurst subdivision.

3. The two young boys went swimming au naturel, that is, in the nude.

4. Maria excused herself with a pleasant hasta mañana.

5. The sudden coup de main took the enemy completely by surprise.

Expressions Used in a Special Sense

Expressions used in a special sense—that is, singled out for special attention, rather than used for their meaning—include words, letters, numerals, and symbols.

> The English word *thou* is related to the German word *du*.
> My handwriting is hard to read because each *r* looks like an *s*, and each *4* looks like a *9*.
> The symbol *&* is called an ampersand.

As we noted on page 343, quotation marks are sometimes used instead of italics for words, letters, numerals, and symbols.

EXERCISE

Supply italics by underlining where necessary to correct the following sentences.

1. The second person pronoun you is often used in informal writing.

2. Is the last number of your locker combination a 6 or an 8?

3. Mark is a noun in the first sentence and a verb in the second.

4. I mistook that M for an N; that's why I marked the word as mis-spelled.

5. The familiar symbol @ means at.

UNIT SELF-TEST

Supply italics by underlining where necessary to correct the following sentences.

Yesterday, John left for Nova Scotia on the U.S.S. <u>Catatonia</u>.

1. The Chicago Tribune has a long article on Rembrandt's picture The Night Watch.

2. The m's and 3's in the typewritten copy were very faint.

3. He said auf Wiedersehen to his friends, then departed for Great Britain on the liner Queen Elizabeth II.

4. This week's Time magazine reviewed the Chicago Civic Theater's production of Hamlet.

5. "In this sentence, for is a preposition," said the instructor.

The answers are on page 451.

UNIT REVIEW EXERCISE 33A
Italics

Supply italics by underlining where necessary to correct the following sentences.

The movie critic John Westborn praised <u>Bonnie and Clyde</u> as one of the greatest movies ever made.

1. While sailing to the Far East on the Empress of China, Ruth read the novel Gone with the Wind and saw the movie Superman.

2. An article on the revival of the playwright Arthur Miller's The Crucible appeared in this morning's Christian Science Monitor.

3. The German term Weltanschauung, which literally means "world view," refers basically to one's philosophy of life.

4. The agent at the Acme Travel Bureau told me that a new Amtrak train, the Rock Island Rocket, would soon begin running to San Francisco.

5. "Mind your p's and q's" is a well-known warning—and also an overworked expression.

6. Patty graduated summa cum laude—that is, with highest honors—from Westgate College.

7. The May, 1980, issue of Today's Backpacker contains an article on avoiding blisters.

8. Emory booked a flight on a Boeing 727 named Sky Nomad.

9. The word educate is derived from the Latin ducere, meaning "to lead or draw"; the word duke also stems from the same source.

10. While in Washington, D.C., we visited the National Gallery and saw Salvador Dali's painting The Last Supper.

11. My American history text, America in the Twentieth Century, has a photo of Grant Wood's painting American Gothic on page 432.

12. The G and A keys on this typewriter were broken, so I took it to the Monarch Office Supply Company for repairs.

13. There were many delicious hors d'oeuvres at the Bradens' party, but I ate more smoked oysters than anything else.

14. The name Isabella is the Spanish equivalent of Elizabeth.

15. Their new oceanfront home, the Breakers, is featured in this month's House and Garden magazine.

UNIT REVIEW EXERCISE 33B
Italics

Write two sentences for each use of italics indicated below.

Titles of Longer Publications and of Artistic Works

1. _____

_____

_____

2. _____

_____

_____

Names of Vehicles and Vessels

1. _____

_____

_____

2. _____

_____

_____

Foreign Words and Phrases

1. _____

_____

_____

2. _____

_____

_____

Expressions Used in a Special Sense

1. _____

_____

_____

2. _____

_____

_____

Becoming a Proficient Speller

The professor who fails otherwise excellent papers because they contain one or two spelling errors is the subject of many campus tales. Such professors—if they actually exist—certainly overemphasize the importance of correct spelling, but not by as much as you might think. Spelling errors mar your writing and lead your readers to regard you as careless. Accurate spelling, on the other hand, stamps you as conscientious and helps indicate your attitude toward your work.

This section will help you to sharpen your language skills. Along with the usual exercises, it includes a set of spelling rules and tips to help you memorize spellings, a list of frequently misspelled words, and a list of commonly confused words. Learning this material will be another step toward effective writing.

UNIT **34**

Spelling Rules

When you attempt to improve your spelling, you soon come to realize that it's no easy job. Unlike some other languages, English often uses the same combination of letters for several sounds, as the differing pronunciations of the *ough* in *though, through, tough,* and *bough* demonstrate. Conversely, the same sound is often written in a number of ways (gr*ea*se, f*ee*l, p*eo*ple, mach*i*nery, desirabilit*y*).

Despite its many inconsistencies, however, English spelling is not entirely lacking in rules. This section discusses four rules that should prove helpful to you. Before taking them up, though, we should mention the meaning of five terms: *vowel, consonant, prefix, suffix,* and *syllable.* For our purposes,

> *Vowels* are *a, e, i, o,* and *u,* and *consonants* are all other letters in the alphabet.
>
> A prefix is a group of letters that comes at the beginning of a word and alters its meaning (*ante* + room = anteroom; *extra* + ordinary = extraordinary; *para* + medic = paramedic, and so on).
>
> A suffix is a group of letters that comes at the end of a word and alters its meaning (polite + *ness* = politeness, see + *ing* = seeing, afford + *able* = affordable, and so on).
>
> A syllable is a single, unbroken sounding of the voice (*dash* has one syllable, *fix-ing* has two syllables, and *em-ploy-ee* has three).

Now let's take a look at the rules.

Rule 1: Words with "ie" and "ei"

With words in which the double vowel has a long *e* sound (as in *he*), the *i* comes before the *e* except after *c*.

ie	*ei* (after *c*)
achieve	ceiling
believe	conceit
chief	conceive
grieve	receive
piece	receipt

If the vowel combination has a long *a* sound (as in *say*), the *e* also precedes the *i*.

ei (*a* **sound**)

eight
freight
neighbor
reign
weight

Among the chief exceptions to this rule are the following: *either, financier, leisure, neither, seize, species,* and *weird*. This rule does not apply to words in which an *ei* or an *ie* has neither a long *e* nor a long *a* sound.

Rule 2: Words Ending in "y"

When a word ends in a *y* preceded by a consonant, change the *y* to an *i* before every suffix except *ing*.

"y" Changed	"y" Not Changed
duty + ful = dutiful	carry + ing = carrying
pretty + ness = prettiness	bury + ing = burying
vary + es = varies	delay + ing = delaying
study + ous = studious	imply + ing = implying

When the *y* is preceded by a vowel, keep the *y*.

annoy + ed = annoyed
enjoy + able = enjoyable
valley + s = valleys

Rule 3: Silent "e" at the End of a Word

Drop the silent *e* before adding a suffix beginning with a vowel.

advise + ing = advising
dense + ity = density
fame + ous = famous
love + able = lovable

An exception occurs with words in which the *e* is preceded by a soft *c* or *g* sound. (A soft *c* is pronounced like the letter *s*, and a soft *g* is pronounced like the letter *j*). In such cases, the *e* is retained before suffixes beginning with *a* or *o*.

courage + ous = courageous
notice + able = noticeable
service + able = serviceable

Retain the final *e* when adding a suffix beginning with a consonant.

hate + ful = hateful
move + ment = movement
safe + ly = safely
white + ness = whiteness

With a few words that end in *ue*, however, the *e* is dropped before the addition of the suffix.

true + ly = truly
due + ly = duly
argue + ment = argument

Rule 4: Words Ending in a Single Consonant Preceded by a Single Vowel

With a one-syllable word ending in a single consonant preceded by a single vowel, double the consonant before adding a suffix starting with a vowel. Do the same for words of two or more syllables if the final syllable is *accented*.

admit + ed = admitted
drum + er = drummer
fit + ing = fitting
refer + ed = referred

If the last syllable is unaccented, don't double the final consonant.

audit + ing = auditing
exhibit + ed = exhibited

Even though the above rules will help you become an accurate speller, you'll need to rely mainly on memorization. The following tips will help.

1. Examine the word closely, noting such features as prefixes (*audi*ble, *audi*tion, *audi*ence), suffixes (tempor*ary*, caution*ary*, prelimin*ary*), and double consonants within the word (di*ss*atisfy, permi*ss*ion, di*ss*ipate).

2. Sound the word out carefully, syllable by syllable. Words such as *February, candidate, environment,* and *government* are often misspelled merely because they are mispronounced.

3. Make a list of the words that give you the most problems, and study it frequently. In reviewing a word, note particularly each individual syllable and any unusual features (contin*uou*s, flu*o*rescent).

4. Use any tricks that will help you remember how a particular word is spelled. *Supersede* is the only *sede* word in English; there is *gain* in a *bargain;* to *breakfast* is to *break* a *fast;* a *disease* causes *dis-ease).*

These tips will not guarantee that you will become a perfect speller. Most people experience difficulty now and then in spelling words they have always known. If you are unsure of a spelling, check it in your dictionary before using the word in a paper.

UNIT SELF-TEST

Supply the proper combination of e *and* i *for the items illustrating Rule 1, and combine the word-suffix pairs properly for the other rules.*

Rule 1

pr_____st

f_____ld

Rule 2

deploy + ed = _____

perky + ness = _____

Rule 3

use + ful = _____

combine + ation = _____

Rule 4

brim + ing = _____

meander + ed = _____

The answers are on page 451.

UNIT REVIEW EXERCISE 34
Spelling Rules

Rule 1: Words with "ie" and "ei"

　　Supply the proper combination of e *and* i *in each of the following words.*

perc_____ve   br_____f

w_____gh   sl_____gh

n_____gh   dec_____ve

p_____rce   th_____f

Rule 2: Words Ending in "y"

　　Combine each word-suffix pair properly.

Vary + ous = _____

marry + ing = _____

tragedy + es = _____

mercy + ful = _____

employ + ed = _____

lady + es = _____

carry + ed = _____

fly + ing = _____

betray + er = _____

Rule 3: Silent "e" at the End of a Word

　　Combine each word-suffix pair properly.

Prepare + ing = _____

inspire + ed = _____

lose + ing = _____

venge + ful = _____

enforce + able = _____

bride + al = _____

large + est = _____

peace + ful = _____

like + ness = _____

Rule 4: Words Ending in a Single Consonant Preceded by a Singular Vowel

Combine each word-suffix pair properly.

equip + ing = _____

control + er = _____

credit + able = _____

rig + ed = _____

inhibit + ing = _____

cramp + ing = _____

limit + ing = _____

occur + ence = _____

infer + ed = _____

UNIT 35

Basic Word List

The following list includes 400 words that are frequently mis-spelled. The listing is divided into eight 50-word sets, so that learning the proper spellings can be accomplished in easy stages. Mastering these spellings will help you to produce more acceptable papers and also reduce the time you will spend looking up words as you write.

First Fifty-Word Set

absence	aggravate	apparatus
absorption	aisle	apparent
accept	all right	appearance
accommodate	altogether	appetite
accumulate	amateur	appropriate
accustomed	amount	argument
achievement	analysis	arrangements
acknowledge	analyze	article
acquaintance	anecdote	ascend
acquire	anguish	assignment
across	angular	assistant
address	anniversary	association
adequate	answer	assurance
adolescent	anxiety	athletics
advantageous	anxious	attendance
advertisement	apologizing	awkward
against	apology	

Second Fifty-Word Set

becoming
beginning
benefited
bicycle
brilliant
Britain
boundaries
buoyant
bureau
business
calendar
candidate
carburetor
carrying
ceiling
cemetery
certain

changeable
characteristic
choose
chosen
clothes
colloquial
column
combustion
commission
commit
committee
comparative
compel
compelled
compensate
compulsory
conceivable

condemn
confident
conqueror
conscientious
conscious
consensus
consistent
continuous
controversial
convenience
convenient
coolly
courteous
courtesy
criticism
curiosity

Third Fifty-Word Set

cylinder
dealt
definite
definitive
demonstration
demonstrator
dependent
descend
describe
description
desirability
desire
despair
desperate
detergent
development
dictionary

dining
disappoint
disastrous
discipline
discussion
dissatisfied
disease
distribute
efficiency
eighth
eligible
eliminate
embarrass
emphasize
enthusiastic
entrance
equipped

equivalent
especially
exaggerated
excellent
exercise
exhaust
existence
experiment
explanation
extension
extraordinary
extremely
familiar
fascinate
February
fictitious

Fourth Fifty-Word Set

fiery	grievance	independent
finally	guarantee	indispensable
financial	harass	inevitable
foreign	having	infinite
forfeit	height	influential
fortunately	hindrance	ingredients
forth	hoping	innocence
forty	humorous	intellectual
fourth	hygiene	intelligence
fraternity	hypocrisy	interested
friend	imaginary	interesting
fundamental	imitation	interpreted
generally	immediately	interrupt
genius	immense	irresistible
government	imminent	irrelevant
grammar	incidentally	judgment
grateful	independence	

Fifth Fifty-Word Set

juvenile	manufacture	nowadays
knowledge	marriage	nucleus
laboratory	meant	obedience
led	medicine	obstacle
legitimate	merely	occurrence
leisure	miniature	off
length	mischievous	omission
library	mortgage	omitted
license	mysterious	operate
likelihood	necessary	opinion
literature	nevertheless	opportunity
livelihood	niece	organization
loneliness	ninety	original
magazine	ninth	outrageous
maintain	noticeable	overrun
maintenance	notoriety	paid
maneuver	notorious	

Sixth Fifty-Word Set

paragraph
parallel
paralyzed
parliament
particularly
passed
pastime
perform
permanent
permissible
perseverance
persistent
personal
personnel
persuade
physically
picnicking

piece
plausible
pleasant
politician
politics
possession
possible
practically
preference
preferred
prejudice
prejudiced
preparation
prevalent
primitive
privilege
procedure

proceed
professor
prominent
pronunciation
propaganda
propagate
prophecy
psychology
pursue
quantity
questionnaire
quiet
quite
really
receipt
receive

Seventh Fifty-Word Set

recommend
reference
regulate
reign
relevant
relieve
religious
reminisce
repetition
representative
resistance
restaurant
rhetoric
rhythm
ridiculous
sacrifice
satisfactorily

satisfactory
schedule
scissors
secretary
seize
sense
sensible
sentence
separate
shining
siege
significant
similar
sincerely
sophomore
source
specimen

spectator
speech
staring
stature
statutes
stopped
stopping
straight
strength
stretch
stretched
strenuous
successful
sufficient
suggestion
suicide

Eighth Fifty-Word Set

studying	transferred	vegetable
superintendent	tremendous	vengeance
surprise	truly	vicinity
syllable	Tuesday	view
symmetry	twelfth	vigorous
technical	tyranny	vitamin
temperament	unanimous	village
temperature	undoubtedly	volume
temporary	unnecessary	weather
tendency	universally	Wednesday
themselves	until	weird
theory	unusual	whether
therefore	using	wholly
thorough	usually	whose
thought	valuable	woman
tournament	varieties	women
tragedy	various	

UNIT 36

Homonyms and Other Commonly Confused Words

Homonyms are words that are pronounced exactly the same but are spelled differently and have different meanings. The English language includes a considerable number of homonyms as well as numerous other words with only slight pronunciation differences. Further, there are words that resemble each other in appearance but are different in pronunciation, spelling, and meaning—however slightly. Often these words are related, contributing still more to confusion between or among them. Not surprisingly, such words often trouble writers. This unit provides basic definitions and examples illustrating the use of the most troublesome commonly confused words. Mastering this material will improve both the precision and the authority of your writing.

First Sixteen Sets of Words

accept	*To receive willingly or favorably; to approve*
	Jim will *accept* the award.
except	*To take out, exclude, or omit; other than.*
	Don't think I will *except* you from any of the course requirements.
	We are all here *except* Joan.
access	*Means or right to enter, approach, or use.*
	I have *access* to a cottage for the summer.
excess	*Too much; more than needed; lack of moderation.*
	The airline booked an *excess* number of passengers on that flight.

advice   *Opinion as to how to deal with a situation or problem.*

My *advice* is to stop smoking.

advise   *To recommend or warn.*

I *advise* you to stop smoking.

affect   *To influence the outcome of, cause a change in, arouse the emotions of.*

This administration's new policy will undoubtedly *affect* next week's vote.

effect   *To bring about or achieve; the result or outcome of.*

The *effect* of the announcement was felt immediately.

The doctor was soon able to *effect* a cure.

angle   *Shape made by two straight lines that come together at some point; to move or bend sharply.*

A mile north of here, the road *angles* to the left.

angel   *Winged messenger of God; beautiful or innocent person.*

She was an *angel* in the Christmas play.

all together   *In unison; simultaneously.*

All together men; heave ho!

altogether   *Completely; entirely.*

Sally's assessment of the situation proved *altogether* mistaken.

allusion   *Indirect reference.*

The teacher made an *allusion* to my bad study habits when I failed.

illusion   *Something false that seems real.*

The magician created an *illusion* of sawing a lady in half.

aural   *Received by way of the ear.*

Those who cannot see rely on *aural* messages.

oral   *Spoken; pertaining to the mouth.*

Terence gave an *oral* report to his biology class.

belief	*Idea or opinion held to be true.*
	It is my *belief* you can win.
believe	*To think or hold true; to trust.*
	I *believe* you can win.
breath	*Air drawn into the lungs and then released; whiff or puff; life or spirit.*
	Step outside and take a deep *breath* of that wonderful spring air.
breathe	*To draw air into the lungs and then release it.*
	The room is so stifling I can hardly *breathe*.
berry	*Small, fleshy fruit such as a blueberry or strawberry.*
	The *berry* wasn't as sweet as I thought it would be.
bury	*To cover up, usually with earth.*
	They will *bury* the dog under the maple tree.
berth	*Place where a ship lies at anchor; built-in bed.*
	The S.S. *Algonquin* lies in its *berth* in New York's harbor.
birth	*Act of bringing forth young; one's national origin or background.*
	She gave *birth* to twins.
	Yvette is a Frenchwoman by *birth*.
capital	*City that serves as a seat of government; goods or money owned by a business.*
	Lansing is the *capital* of Michigan.
	He invested all his *capital* in a grocery store.
capitol	*Building in which a state legislature meets.*
	The *capitol* in Lansing is popular with visitors.
choose	*To select.*
	We will *choose* a new president for our company.
chose	*Past tense of* choose.
	Yesterday, we *chose* a new president for our company.
cite	*To refer to as an authority.*
	When I questioned his position, he proceeded to *cite* two reports that backed it.

site	*Place or location.*
	We selected a shady *site* for our picnic.
sight	*The act of seeing; something that is viewed.*
	Many people wear glasses to improve their *sight.*
	There's a pretty *sight* for you!
clothes	*Wearing apparel, usually made of fabric.*
	In the fall, we will buy new *clothes.*
cloths	*Pieces of woven or knitted fabric.*
	He used clean *cloths* to polish his car.

UNIT REVIEW EXERCISE 36A
Homonyms and Other Commonly Confused Words

Choose the correct word from the words in parentheses for each of these sentences, and write it in the blank to the left.

effect —— The medicine didn't have the desired (affect, effect).

—————— 1. Please (accept, except) my congratulations on your raise.

—————— 2. That (access, excess) road to the expressway is closed.

—————— 3. I asked my professor for (advise, advice) about my next term's program.

—————— 4. This mistake will seriously (affect, effect) your chances for promotion.

—————— 5. There are four right (angels, angles) in a square.

—————— 6. I (all together, altogether) agree with your proposal.

—————— 7. The perspective in this picture creates an (allusion, illusion) of great depth.

—————— 8. Ear specialists diagnose and treat (aural, oral) problems.

—————— 9. Mrs. Edwards will (belief, believe) you if you tell her why you were absent.

—————— 10. Once the damaged aircraft had touched the runway, all the passengers began to (breath, breathe) easily.

—————— 11. We discovered an unfamiliar (berry, bury) on a bush in the woods.

421

_____ 12. In his Gettysburg Address, Abraham Lincoln expressed the hope that our country would experience a new (berth, birth) of freedom.

_____ 13. Our class visited the (capitol, capital) building in Harrisburg.

_____ 14. The child (choose, chose) a milkshake for her lunch.

_____ 15. Doctors (cite, sight, site) numerous studies that show cigarette smoking is hazardous to one's health.

_____ 16. We covered the furniture with clean (clothes, cloths) to protect it from dust.

Second Sixteen Sets of Words

complement	*Something that completes or perfects; to bring to completion or perfection.* This fruit will *complement* the meal beautifully.
compliment	*Flattering or praising remark; to flatter or praise.* Mother *complimented* me for cleaning my room.
confidant (male) **confidante** (female)	*Someone with whom one can share personal matters.* My girl friend is my closest *confidante*.
confident	*Self-assured.* June is *confident* she will pass this course.
conscience	*Sense of right or wrong.* Ernie's *conscience* made him return the billfold he had found.
conscious	*Awake; able to perceive, think, and feel.* Two hours after his surgery, Bob was still not *conscious*.
continual	*Occurring again and again in rapid succession.* The phone kept up a *continual* ringing all morning.
continuous	*Occurring or extending without interruption.* The *continuous* wailing of the siren prevented Edith from studying.
council	*Group that meets for discussion, consultation, or the passage of ordinances.* The city *council* met to discuss zoning rules.
counsel	*Advice; lawyer or other consultant who provides advice.* As a result of the broker's *counsel*, I bought ten shares of Exxon stock. The company lawyer acted as *counsel* in this case.
coarse	*Common, inferior, rough in texture, crude.* Jeffrey is a *coarse* fellow. The covering on my couch has a *coarse* weave.

course	*Direction, unit of instruction, series of studies, path or track, stage of a meal.*
	My father is on the golf *course* this morning.
	Pete is afraid he's failing this *course.*
decent	*Honorable, good, fair, fitting, kind.*
	You can count on *decent* treatment from this teacher.
descent	*Act of proceeding to a lower level.*
	The *descent* from the mountain peak proved more dangerous than we had anticipated.
desert	*Dry, barren, sandy region; to abandon, forsake, or leave without permission.*
	Each spring the Arizona *desert* blossoms for a brief time.
	Howard would never *desert* his post in the face of the enemy.
dessert	*Sweet food served as the last course of a meal.*
	The *dessert* was the best part of that meal.
device	*Mechancial contrivance, gadget, or tool.*
	This new *device* gives us better gas mileage.
devise	*To plan or invent.*
	We must *devise* a new approach to our problem.
die	*To cease living.*
	The mass murderer was sentenced to *die* in the electric chair.
dye	*Coloring agent; to tint or color fabric, hair, and the like.*
	I want to *dye* my hair red.
discussed	*Talked or written about.*
	Our vacation plans were *discussed* with a travel agent
disgust	*Distaste, dislike, loathing.*
	The filthiness of the room filled him with *disgust.*
elicit	*To draw forth.*
	The prosecutor tried to *elicit* a confession from the defendant.
illicit	*Unlawful; improper.*
	Mr. Beatty used *illicit* deductions to reduce his income tax.

eminent

Prominent, distinguished.

Senator Soapwell is the most *eminent* graduate of my high school.

imminent

About to take place.

Those clouds and that thunder mean a storm is *imminent.*

envelop

To enfold.

Soon darkness will *envelop* the sky.

envelope

A wrapper.

She put the St. Patrick's Day greeting card in a green *envelope.*

ere

Soon, before long, lest.

Slow down, *ere* you stumble.

err

To make a mistake, do wrong.

To *err* is human; to forgive, divine.

extant

Still existing.

The dodo bird is no longer *extant.*

extent

Scope; size, range; limit.

From Michigan to Ohio is the *extent* of my travels.

UNIT REVIEW EXERCISE 36B
Homonyms and Other Commonly Confused Words

Choose the correct word from the pair in parentheses for each of these sentences, and write it in the blank to the left.

Course.   I received four phone calls during the (coarse, course) of the afternoon.

_____ 1. Marion received a (compliment, complement) about her new dress.

_____ 2. I feel (confident, confidant) that my knowledge of Japanese will win me a job in our Tokyo sales office.

_____ 3. Ted's (conscious, conscience) will not permit him to lie.

_____ 4. Disgusted by the (continual, continuous) complaints of the customers, Sandra quit her job as a waitress.

_____ 5. My father's lawyer acted as my (council, counsel) during my trial.

_____ 6. His (coarse, course) jokes have offended many people.

_____ 7. Brutus is a (descent, decent), honorable man; Marc Antony just said so.

_____ 8. The transportation for our (dessert, desert) safari was provided by Hertz Rent-A-Camel.

_____ 9. Perhaps we can (device, devise) a better way to do this job.

_____ 10. Some hair (dyes, dies) can irritate the scalp.

427

———————————   11. For more than two hours, the group angrily (discussed, disgust) the proposal.

———————————   12. The governor's stand on gun control will (elicit, illicit) much protest.

———————————   13. Dr. Spock is an (eminent, imminent) authority on babies.

———————————   14. Horror-struck, we watched the flames (envelop, envelope) the entire building.

———————————   15. The judge did not (ere, err) in giving him a stiff sentence.

———————————   16. Company officials do not yet know the (extant, extent) of the damage caused by the fire.

Third Sixteen Sets of Words

fiancé	*A man engaged to be married.*
	Bob is my *fiancé.*
fiancée	*A woman engaged to be married.*
	Carol is my *fiancée.*
formally	*According to established forms, conventions, and rules; ceremoniously.*
	The ambassador greeted his dinner guests *formally.*
formerly	*In the past.*
	Formerly, smallpox was one of our most serious diseases.
forth	*Forward; out into view.*
	The knight went *forth* to do battle.
fourth	*Next after third in a series or in importance.*
	Howard won *fourth* place in the pie-making contest.
foul	*Offensive, dirty, indecent, malodorous.*
	The garbage dump had a *foul* odor.
fowl	*A bird.*
	Chickens are our most common barnyard *fowl.*
hear	*To perceive through the ear.*
	I *hear* America singing.
here	*Present; in this place.*
	Everyone is *here* today.
heard	*Past tense of hear.*
	We *heard* the president's special address last evening.
herd	*Group of large animals.*
	A *herd* of cows grazed in the meadow.
holy	*Spiritual, dedicated to religious use; sinless, saintly; worthy of adoration.*
	Leviticus is a *holy* text.
wholly	*Entirely.*
	We were *wholly* wrong about him.

human	*Person; having qualities typical of people in general.*
	A *human* has greater reasoning power than an animal.
humane	*Kind; merciful; sympathetic; tender.*
	Let us treat our enemies in a *humane* manner.
ingenious	*Clever; inventive.*
	That was certainly an *ingenious* solution to the problem.
ingenuous	*Innocent; open; naïve.*
	She is as *ingenuous* as a child.
its	*Possessive form of* it.
	The dog is in *its* house.
it's	*Contraction of* it is *or* it has.
	It's too cold in here.
later	*Farther ahead in time.*
	I will do that *later* in the week.
latter	*The most recent or last named of two items or events.*
	Although Bill and Tom are twins, the *latter* weighs at least fifty pounds more.
lightening	*Making something less heavy or harsh.*
	By *lightening* his load, Morris was able to walk faster.
lightning	*Flashes of light in the sky during storms.*
	Never stand under a tree during a storm; you could be struck by *lightning*.
loose	*Unconfined; not firmly fastened; slack, irresponsible.*
	Tommy's baby tooth is *loose*.
	Loose talk can get you in trouble.
lose	*To mislay, be deprived of; fail to maintain or retain.*
	I will *lose* my driver's license if I get another ticket.
pair	*Two closely associated or similar persons or things; a single thing comprising two corresponding parts that function as a unit.*
	Sandra bought a *pair* of shoes that were on sale.

pare	*Peel.*
	Jeff will *pare* the potatoes.
peace	*State of harmony; freedom from war; mental calm.*
	During war, nations pray for *peace*.
piece	*Part of something; single specimen or example.*
	May I have a *piece* of cake?
	That's a lovely *piece* of music!
personal	*Private; involving human beings.*
	That is my *personal* property.
personnel	*People employed in an enterprise or establishment.*
	The *personnel* of the Dalton Company have a reputation for being honest.

UNIT REVIEW EXERCISE 36C

Homonyms and Other Commonly Confused Words

Choose the correct word from the pair in parentheses for each of these sentences, and write it in the blank to the left.

lose   Did our team (loose, lose) the game?

_____   1. George is Sandra's (fiancé, fiancée).

_____   2. Alice Wise's name was (formally, formerly) Alice Brown.

_____   3. The mountain labored and brought (forth, fourth) a mouse.

_____   4. The latest forecast calls for (foul, fowl) weather tomorrow.

_____   5. The children made such a racket that I was unable to (hear, here) the newscaster.

_____   6. Have you (herd, heard) about the robbery of our bank?

_____   7. I am (holy, wholly) in agreement with our minister's proposal to build a new church.

_____   8. The investigators concluded that the malfunction had occurred because of (human, humane) error.

_____   9. A clever person, Sally soon thought of an (ingenuous, ingenious) way to save money.

_____ 10. When (its, it's) evening, the fox that lives in our woods comes out of its den.

_____ 11. The inscription on the old sundial read, "It's (later, latter) than you think."

433

————————   12. Because (lightening, lightning) was flashing, we were afraid to use the telephone.

————————   13. The mechanic discovered a (loose, lose) wire to my car battery.

————————   14. Ask Ellen to (pair, pare) the potatoes.

————————   15. I'd like to give him a good (peace, piece) of my mind for that foul-up!

————————   16. A well-run company should not have a high turnover in (personnel, personal).

Fourth Sixteen Sets of Words

pore
: *A microscopic opening in the skin, the surface of a leaf, and so on.*
  Our skin breathes through its *pores.*

pour
: *To cause to flow from one container to another; to flow freely or in large quantities.*
  Please *pour* me some coffee.

poor
: *Needy, lacking in something.*
  Many *poor* tenant farmers have left for the city.

pray
: *To address God.*
  Let us *pray* for divine guidance.

prey
: *Intended victim or victims; to plunder, kill for food.*
  The cat regarded her intended *prey,* a fat robin.

presence
: *attendance or appearance at an event or place.*
  When Ben was sick, we missed his *presence* at our meeting.

presents
: *Gifts.*
  I like to give *presents* to my friends.

principal
: *Foremost in authority or importance; the head of a school.*
  His *principal* shortcoming is laziness.

principle
: *Basic truth, rule, law, or quality.*
  The *principle* behind today's experiment is discussed on page 231 of our text.

quiet
: *Silent, motionless, calm.*
  The class grew *quiet* when the teacher came through the doorway.

quite
: *Entirely; to a considerable extent or degree.*
  He is *quite* finished.

raise
: *To elevate to a higher level; to increase in value, degree, intensity, and so on; to put in an upright position.*
  Next week we will *raise* the price of our refrigerators.

raze
: *To tear down.*
  The city plans to *raze* the abandoned factory on Spring Street.

right
Correct; suitable; true.

Shirley gave the *right* answer when the instructor called on her.

write
To mark down a message; to fill in a check or printed form.

Did you *write* the letter?

stationery
Letter-writing paper and envelopes.

Beth wrote the letter on perfumed *stationery.*

stationary
Immobile; unchanging.

My wages have remained *stationary* for three years.

than
A word used to make comparisons.

He has more money *than* I do.

then
At that time; next; in that case.

First we will eat, and *then* we will discuss business.

their
Possessive form of they.

That yellow Ford is *their* car.

there
In or at that place; at that point.

Put your wraps *there.*

they're
Contraction of they are.

The Haskins tell me *they're* moving to Alaska in June.

thorough
Careful, complete; exact; painstaking.

Belinda did a *thorough* job of cleaning the car.

through
In one side and out the other; from end to end; from start to finish; over the whole extent of.

Wee Willie Winkie runs *through* the town.

to
Toward; as far as; until; onto.

He went *to* the movies.

too
Excessively; also.

I'm afraid I had *too* much to eat at last night's party.

Marvin wants to go, *too.*

two
One more than one.

Perry has *two* hunting dogs.

weather
Condition of the atmosphere as regards temperature, humidity, wind velocity, and so on.

Stormy *weather* is predicted for this weekend.

whether	*If it is the case or fact that.*
	I don't know *whether* he is home.
were	*Past form of verb* be, *used with* we, you, *and* they.
	I'm sorry to learn that you *were* ill yesterday.
where	*In, at, from, to a particular place or situation.*
	Ms. Morris will show you *where* to register.
who's	*Contraction of* who is *or* who has.
	Who's coming to see you tonight?
	Who's read this new best seller?
whose	*Possessive of* who.
	Whose book is this?
your	*Possessive form of* you.
	Where is *your* book?
you're	*Contraction of* you are.
	Tell me when *you're* ready.

UNIT REVIEW EXERCISE 36D
Homonyms and Other Commonly Confused Words

Choose the correct word from the words in parentheses for each of these sentences, and write it in the blank to the left.

_____than_____ It's better to have loved and lost (than, then) never to have loved at all.

_____ 1. Those black clouds mean it may (pour, pore, poor) rain any minute.

_____ 2. Deer hunters stalked their (pray, prey) in the early morning.

_____ 3. Edna's (presence, presents) of mind has averted a very serious accident.

_____ 4. Our principal has published an article on the (principals, principles) of American education.

_____ 5. You were (quiet, quite) right to object to the recommendations of the committee.

_____ 6. That building is an eyesore; let's (raise, raze) it and use the land for a parking lot.

_____ 7. That's not the (write, right) attitude to adopt toward college writing.

_____ 8. The letter was written on the prime minister's official (stationary, stationery).

_____ 9. A chain is no stronger (than, then) its weakest link.

_____ 10. Surely they're approaching (their, there, they're) destination by now.

_____ 11. We need to give the house a (thorough, through) cleaning.

439

———————— 12. This textbook is (to, too, two) easy for our freshman composition students.

———————— 13. I'm not sure (weather, whether) I'll be able to stand this climate for another year.

———————— 14. As we (were, where) taking our seats, someone shouted, "Fire!"

———————— 15. Can you tell me (who's, whose) decided to attend the state convention?

———————— 16. Please clear (your, you're) desks of books and papers before I hand out your tests.

Answers to Unit Self-Tests

Looking into the Sentence

Unit 1: Subjects and Verbs

tractor	sat	1. Behind the barn sat/a rusty tractor.
dog	jumped barked	2. The little dog/jumped and barked at the door.
you	are feeling	3. Are/you/feeling any better today?
they	waited	4. With great impatience, they/waited at the corner for the parade.
(You)	look	5./Look over there by that big tree!

Unit 2: Complements

1. SC

2. OC

3. DO

4. IO

5. IO

Unit 3: Nouns, Pronouns, and Verbs

1. P, N

2. V, N

3. V, P

4. N, V

5. N, P

Unit 4: Adjectives, Adverbs, Prepositions, Conjunctions, and Interjections

1. ADJ, ADV

2. ADV, P

3. ADJ, C

4. P, ADJ

5. ADV, C

6. I, P

Unit 5: Subordinate Clauses

1. N

2. ADJ

3. N

4. ADV

5. ADV

Unit 6: Noun, Adjective, and Adverb Phrases

1. ADV

2. ADJ

3. ADJ

4. ADV

5. N

Sharpening Your Usage Skills

Unit 7: Avoiding Sentence Fragments

1. F

2. S

3. F

4. F

5. F

Unit 8: Avoiding Comma Splices and Run-on Sentences

1. C

2. RO

3. C

4. RO

5. CS

Unit 9: Making Subjects and Verbs Agree

1. were (*chair* and *vase* are subjects)

2. was

3. are

4. seems

5. makes

Unit 10: Choosing the Right Verb Form

1. lie

2. burst

3. torn

4. ridden

5. supposed

Unit 11: Avoiding Errors in Showing Time

1. S

2. C

3. S

4. I

5. C

Unit 12: Avoiding Overuse of the Passive Voice

1. A

2. P

3. P

4. P

5. A

Unit 13: Making Pronouns and Antecedents Agree

1. its

2. their

3. his or her

4. he

5. themselves

Unit 14: Avoiding Faulty Pronoun Reference

1. F

2. F

3. F

4. C

5. F

Unit 15: Avoiding Unwarranted Shifts in Person

1. S

2. S

3. S

4. C

5. S

Unit 16: Choosing the Right Pronoun Case Form

1. us

2. her

3. who

4. me

5. she

Unit 17: Avoiding Errors with Adjectives and Adverbs

1. sweet

2. considerably

3. older

4. cross

5. really

Unit 18: Avoiding Misplaced Modifiers

1. MM

2. C

3. MM

4. MM

5. MM

Unit 19: *Avoiding Dangling Modifiers*

1. C

2. DM

3. DM

4. C

5. DM

Unit 20: *Avoiding Nonparallelism and Faulty Comparisons*

1. NP

2. C

3. NP

4. FC

5. FC

Unit 21: *Avoiding Wordiness*

1. W

2. W

3. W

4. C

5. C

Learning to Punctuate and Use Mechanics Properly

Unit 22: Apostrophes

1. Correct

2. won't, it's

3. brother's, customers'

4. *i*'s

5. everybody's, nobody's

Unit 23: Commas—to Separate

The commas required appear in parentheses.

    C   1. After school we went bowling and then to the movies.

              2. Winter driving can be very hazardous in our town because of the winding(,) ice-covered streets.

              3. Jill and Mike are no longer engaged(,) yet they continue to see each other regularly.

              4. After waiting five weeks for her new desk lamp to arrive(,) Sherry finally wrote the manufacturer.

              5. Jeremy spent the afternoon raking the leaves(,) mowing the lawn(,) and washing the car.

Unit 24: Commas—to Set Off

The commas required appear in parentheses.

              1. He has lived in Galveston(,) Texas(,) for the last seven years.

              2. On November 11(,) 1918(,) World War I ended.

              3. You've never met my brother(,) have you?

_____C_____ 4. Anyone who wishes to compete in the marathon must have a complete physical examination first.

_____ 5. I can't imagine(,) Bill(,) why you want to change your major.

Unit 25: Unneeded Commas

The unneeded commas appear in parentheses.

_____ 1. Heavy, cold, wet(,) snow fell all night; but luckily school was closed the next day.

_____C_____ 2. Mr. Charles Taylor, a tax consultant, will speak to our government class.

_____ 3. We need(,) more security officers in this building, but providing them will cost a great deal.

_____ 4. Molly vacuumed the kitchen(,) and living room before the party.

_____ 5. Running in the Boston Marathon was(,) exciting for me, and my parents were also thrilled.

Unit 26: Semicolons

The required or desirable semicolons appear in parentheses.

_____ 1. Everyone on the committee must help plan for the centennial(;) those not wishing to do their part should resign now.

_____ 2. We must start searching for alternate sources of energy right away(;) otherwise, future generations will face great hardships.

_____C_____ 3. For years Ms. Shanklin devoted her life to the company; her supervisors, however, never properly recognized her efforts.

_____ 4. The red-faced, gesturing orator shouted his message to his audience(;) but his listeners, mostly from other countries, seemed little interested in his attack on Parliament.

_____ 5. The investigating team included Mary Phillips, the secretary(;) John Holmes, the research analyst(;) and Barry Woods, the editor.

Unit 27: Colons, Dashes, Parentheses, and Brackets

The punctuation to have been added is underlined.

1. In a quavering voice, the amateur actor started to deliver Marc Antony's famous funeral oration: "Friends, Romans, countrymen . . ."

2. Representative Joseph P. Stark (Republican, Florida) is the most vocal opponent of the new defense appropriation bill.

3. Our graduates are expected to—Heavens, what was that crash?

4. The student wrote, "Ernest Hemingway (1899-1961) committed suiside [_sic_] shortly after a stay at the Mayo Clinic."

5. The experiment calls for a 3:2:2 ratio of methyl alcohol, water, and glycerine.

Unit 28: Periods, Question Marks, and Exclamation Points

The punctuation to have been added or changed appears in parentheses.

1. Paul de Vere, Jr(.), earned his B(.)S(.) degree at Wisconsin State University and then spent the next ten years working for the CIA(.)

2. I asked my roommate where he would spend the weekend(.)

3. What happened to the piece of cake I was saving for a snack(?)

4. Great Heavens(!) Who'd have thought that Dr(.) Sawyer would be found guilty of malpractice(?)

5. Nancy asked Ms(.) Wilcox whether Chapter Four of the text would be covered on the next test(.)

Unit 29: Quotation Marks

Quotation marks should appear as follows:

1. "You," "your," and "yours" are second person pronouns.

2. The student asked, "May I take the test early?"

3. Why did Clayton insult his hostess by saying, "This party is awfully dull"?

4. The coach shouted, "Let's play ball!"

5. Tomorrow we'll discuss the essay, "Why a Liberal Education, Anyway?"

Unit 30: Hyphens

Hyphens should appear as follows:

1. The company's twenty-eighth year brought a 41-percent increase over the previous year's sales.

2. Florian's devil-may-care behavior will land him in trouble one of these days.

3. Several four-, six-, and eight-cylinder engines were overhauled yesterday.

4. The farmers' co-op will hold a business meeting next Friday.

5. He's an ultra-argumentative fellow, that's for certain!

Unit 31: Capitalization

The sentences should be capitalized/lowercased as follows:

1. While visiting San Francisco last summer, Janet stayed at the Mark Hopkins Hotel.

2. After the attack on Pearl Harbor, many innocent people of Japanese ancestry were sent to concentration camps.

3. Each account at People's Savings Bank is insured by the Federal Deposit Insurance Corporation (FDIC).

4. After Aunt Hannah's accident last winter, everyone was very careful when crossing Harbor Street.

5. Last night, I watched the widely acclaimed television documentary "Africa: Its Land and People."

Unit 32: Abbreviations and Numbers

Abbreviations, full forms, and numbers should appear as follows:

1. Dr. Albert Hamilton received his degree in August, 1971.

2. The television special is being shown at 7 P.M.

3. About 75 percent of the project will have been completed by August, 1981.

4. The freighter carried a cargo of 250 tons of coal, 500 barrels of palm oil, and 350 gasoline pumps.

5. Fourteen teams have already signed up to play in the tennis doubles tournament at East Hills Racquet Club.

Unit 33: Italics

Your corrected sentences should appear as follows:

1. The *Chicago Tribune* has a long article on Rembrandt's picture *The Night Watch.*

2. The *m*'s and *3*'s in the typewritten copy were very faint.

3. He said *auf Wiedersehen* to his friends, then departed for Great Britain on the liner *Queen Elizabeth II.*

4. This week's *Time* magazine reviewed the Chicago Civic Theater's production of *Hamlet.*

5. "In this sentence, *for* is a preposition," said the instructor.

Becoming a Proficient Speller

Unit 34: Spelling Rules

priest, field (Rule 1)

deployed, perkiness (Rule 2)

useful, combination (Rule 3)

brimming, meandered (Rule 4)

Index